THE AMA HANDBOOK OF BUSINESS LETTERS

THE
AMA
HANDBOOK
OF
BUSINESS
LETTERS

Jeffrey L. Seglin

amacom

American Management Association

This book is available at a special
discount when ordered in bulk quantities.
For information, contact Special Sales Department,
AMACOM, a division of American Management Association,
135 West 50th Street, New York, NY 10020.

Library of Congress Cataloging-in-Publication Data

Seglin, Jeffrey L., 1956–
    The AMA handbook of business letters.

    Bibliography: p.
    1. Commercial correspondence.   2. Letter-writing.
I. Title.
HF5726.S42   1989   651.7'5   88-48034
ISBN 0-8144-5835-1

Printing number

10 9 8 7 6 5 4 3 2 1

To
Nancy

Contents

Preface

Several years ago, I was asked by a financial publisher to write a book on letter writing for bankers. I was puzzled about the need for such a book. Surely bankers who had risen to any level of responsibility knew how to write. Why did they need a book to show them the way?

I agreed to write the book. Dozens of generous bankers offered to open their files to me. I was shocked. Not only was there a fundamental lack of basic letter-writing skills, there also was a dearth of bankers who knew basic writing skills. The bankers who helped me with that book kept telling me how unskilled the writers were with whom they dealt. But I was surprised to find the volume of correspondence that was going out with grammatical mistakes, usage problems, unclear statements, and nonstandard letter formatting.

Several thousand copies and a second edition later, I am more convinced than ever that bankers are clamoring for a book that shows them how to write better letters. But I've also become convinced that the need doesn't stop with bankers.

Professionals in all walks of the business world are in need of a book that can help them hone their letter-writing skills. *The AMA Handbook of Business Letters* is designed to answer that need. It will arm professionals with both the skills needed to be good letter writers and more than 270 model letters on which to base their own correspondence. *The AMA Handbook of Business Letters* will not just show you how to write better letters; it will show you how to write better.

Sections on grammar, usage, and word processing in the first part of the book complement the sections on basic letter-writing skills. Part III features a host of appendixes that give you the tools you can use to build better writing skills. Sections giving tips on punctuation, frequently misused words, and abbreviations are featured. The Grammar Hotline Directory lists dozens of telephone hotlines around the country that will answer your grammar questions. These hotlines can be a saving grace to the professional trying to put the finishing touches on an important letter.

The second part of *The AMA Handbook of Business Letters* is the heart of the book. Here, more than 270 model letters have been collected. The vast majority of them are based on actual letters that were used in business. They were chosen to represent the broad spectrum of the type of letters professionals will most commonly have to write. The names of the people, companies, and products have all been disguised. If a name resembles an actual name, it is purely by coincidence.

The only way that a book like this could ever have been completed is through the cooperation of many professionals who were kind enough to open their files to me and let me pour through their correspondence. Among the professionals without whose help the book would never have reached completion are: Peggy R. Broekel, W. Loren Gary, Lisa T. Gary, Beall D. Gary, Jr., of Haskell Slaughter & Young, Dr. Lindsey Harlan, Martha Jewett, Joan Kenney, Jim Lewis, Sam Mickelberg (owner of Sam's Camera Shop) Howard Palay, Patti Palay, Louis J. Roffinoli, owner of Woodcraft, Matthew Rovner, Lester Seglin, Nancy Seglin, Mark Stoeckle, Bethany Coleman, and John Waggoner.

Donna Reiss Friedman, director of the Writing Center and Grammar Hotline at Tidewater Community College, was kind enough to grant me permission to reprint the Grammar Hotline Directory that her center compiles every year.

Adrienne Hickey, my editor at AMACOM, worked with me patiently to get the manuscript in the best possible shape for publication. Her suggestions for organization and letters were invaluable.

Evan Marshall, my agent, was once again a wonderful sounding board for the project. On many occasions he was able to get me out of a quagmire that resulted from hundreds of letters cluttering my office.

Robert Roen, publisher of the book division at Bank Administration Institute, has been a diehard supporter of this project. Bob is responsible for the original idea of a book on letter writing for bankers. It is as a result of his idea and his support on this and countless other projects that I was able to complete this book.

Jeffrey L. Seglin
Boston, Massachusetts

THE AMA HANDBOOK OF BUSINESS LETTERS

PART I
THE BASICS

All letters methinks, should be as free and easy as
one's discourse, not studied as an oration. . . .

Dorothy Osborne (Lady Temple)
Letter to Sir William Temple, October 1653

Successful professionals know the importance of effective letter writing. You can't
have a good business relationship with customers if they don't know what you're
trying to tell them in a letter. The services or products of a company cannot be
marketed if a prospective customer is baffled by the service or product described.
How can a salesperson expect to make a sale when, because of a muddled letter, the
prospect can't even understand what it is that's being sold?

Letter writing is crucial to the success of every professional. Without letter-
writing skills, the professional's effectiveness is stymied.

Approaching This Book

The objective of *The AMA Handbook of Business Letters* is to help you write effective
letters. Ineffective letters are a waste of time and money. This realization should be
enough to convince every professional of the need to be a good letter writer. Letters
may not seem like the crux of your business, but if you consider that effectively
written letters can increase the quality of working relationships and the quantity of
business you can attract, and decrease wasted hours and money, you can begin to
see the importance of learning to write letters well.

You should be prepared to approach this book with one chief goal in mind—to
learn how to write effective letters. Remember, too, that although letter writing is
not a simple skill, with practice you can become a good letter writer. Once you learn
the basics and put them into practice, your letters will get better and begin to flow
more easily.

Approach of This Book

Before you begin to write more effective letters, you must learn what makes up a
good letter. The first part of this book takes you step-by-step through the basics of
letter writing. You'll learn the importance of planning a letter and gathering all the

1

information you need. The plan is put into practice when you decide on the approach your letter will take and the components necessary to achieve the selected approach. The components of a letter are effective only if you know the proper mechanics involved in a letter's structure and appearance. Grammar, punctuation, spelling, and language usage are important if your letter is to be understood and well accepted by its reader. You needn't fear an extensive course in grammar. What you'll receive here are the fundamental "common-sense" rules of grammar that are easily learned and should become natural not only to your letter writing, but to all of your other writing as well.

There is also a chapter in Part I on word processing. While it won't answer all of the technical questions you might have about the uses of computers in an office environment, it will guide you toward effectively using both the information and letters in *The AMA Handbook of Business Letters* on your business' or your own word processing system.

The second part of this book consists of more than 270 sample letters, divided into categories reflecting various aspects of business. Each chapter also contains a brief analysis of the strong points of many of the sample letters. Most of the sample letters are based on those that were written and used by professionals. Names of people or corporations have been changed, but the content remains essentially unaltered. The letters chosen serve as models for those you may have to write in your everyday business life. You can adapt them to meet your needs or use them as a touchstone to aim toward in your letter writing.

The four appendixes to this book consist of helpful lists and rules to refer to in your letter writing. The annotated bibliography directs you to and gives you a brief synopsis of books and publications that may be of use to you in increasing the effectiveness of your letters.

As with all things, perfection can be reached only with practice. If you apply the basics learned in the first part of *The AMA Handbook of Business Letters,* and study the examples presented in the second, your letter-writing skills will become more effective. The end result will be making your readers think that what took much thought and planning on your part flowed as smoothly and effortlessly as discourse.

CHAPTER 1
Planning the Letter

Planning is a key factor in the accomplishment of any goal. Letter writing is no exception. To successfully construct a clear, effective letter, you need a good plan.

Some letters do not require as elaborate a plan as others. A letter to a customer detailing a proposal for a product purchase will obviously need a more elaborate plan than a thank-you note for a business lunch.

Common sense can usually dictate how elaborate your plan needs to be. If the information you need to present in a letter is limited enough for you to outline it in your head, there is no real need for an elaborate outline featuring Roman numeral headings and subpoints beneath subpoints. The elaborateness of your plan should suit the elaborateness of the letter to be written.

Of course, if you, as a letter writer, are more comfortable constructing detailed outlines for each of your letters, there is nothing wrong with following that procedure. With enough practice, however, the simpler letters should flow more easily, and the time you might have spent laboring over outline after outline can be directed more constructively to other areas of your business.

The following three steps will be essential in the planning of any letter:

1. Researching the facts
2. Analyzing the subject and reader
3. Knowing your objectives and how to accomplish them

If you follow these steps as you are planning to write any letter, you should find that your letters will be clear and well received, and will achieve your desired goal.

Researching the Facts

Before you write a letter, it makes sense to know what you plan to talk about. If you wing it and write whatever comes into your head, chances are you will end up with a confused, ineffective letter.

Get the facts together prior to composing anything resembling a first draft of a letter. For example, if you are corresponding with a customer, examine all previous correspondence with him or her. Depending upon the volume of this correspondence, and assuming the customer to be a fairly good letter writer, you can learn a good deal about the personality, interests, and values of the person to whom you are writing.

As you examine previous correspondence, jot down a note or two about some key traits you discover about this customer. For example, you have gone through your correspondence file for a customer named Sam Johnson. From what he has written you realize the following things about him. He:

- Is committed to existing business relationships
- Places importance on a personal relationship between the professional and the customer
- Often suggests ideas for improving business practices and professional/customer relationship
- Has a strong interest in reducing costs

After jotting down this information, try to visualize the person to whom you are writing. You know something about the customer's interests. To learn more, you might examine the file on business dealings with the customer. If you learn as much as possible about your reader, it will be easier to write a letter that is directed to that reader.

After you have collected some facts on your customer, you should direct your attention to the topic or topics to be covered in the letter. Once again, the simplest and ultimately most effective thing to do is to take a piece of paper and write down those topics you plan to cover. Under each topic you might write some examples or a few words recalling a discussion you might have had with your customer about it.

Let's stick with the example of customer Sam Johnson. You have had a business meeting with Mr. Johnson and you want to write a follow-up letter. You already know something about his personality from the earlier research you did. You decide you want to cover the following topics in your letter:

- Thanks for meeting
- His idea for a lock box
  —Speeds up collections
  —Cost-effectiveness
- Appreciate his views on business
  —Loyalty to existing business relationships
  —Personal relationship
- Arrange for another meeting

The order in which you write down ideas for topics is unimportant at this point in the planning stage. The main thing is to make sure the letter covers the topics that will let customer Johnson know you are writing to him about issues that are of concern to him.

Timeliness is extremely important in any letter, including the one we are using as an example. You want to get a letter to your customer while the topics being discussed are still fresh in both of your minds. As you are doing your research, determine how long discussion has been taking place about the topics to be included in your letter and what, if any, action has already been taken. A fundamental rule to remember in all of your correspondence is that timeliness is essential for effectiveness.

Analyzing the Subject and Reader

You've completed your research. You know something about the person to whom you are writing. You have a good idea what topics will be covered in the letter. The information you have gathered must now be analyzed so you can logically organize it for the best results.

An outline is a good method of organizing topics and visualizing the order in which you wish to discuss them in the letter. You can order the letter chronologically, by importance of the topics discussed, or in whatever order is most effective. Your choice is flexible, but it must be logical and you should not mix thoughts in sentences or drop them before they are completed.

Continuing with the example of the follow-up letter to Sam Johnson, you might decide to outline your letter as follows:

Paragraph 1. a. Thanks for meeting
              b. Appreciate view on business
                  (1) Loyalty to existing business relationships
                  (2) Importance of personal relationships
Paragraph 2. a. Idea for lock box
                  (1) Speed up collections
                  (2) Cost-effectiveness
Paragraph 3. a. Arrange for another meeting

You'll notice that the only difference between this rough outline and the list of topics jotted down earlier is the order. The ordering of topics is an important function of the outline.

With a letter as simple as this follow-up to Sam Johnson, it is perfectly acceptable to outline the topics in your head and go directly to the rough draft of your letter. The important thing in writing an effective letter is not writing a good outline, but rather being able to write a letter that is ordered logically and is structured well enough for you to know where it is going. If you can do this in your head, fine. You may have to work out some kinks in the rough draft, but if you can save yourself some time and still write an effective letter, more power to you. As your letters become more elaborate, you may find that working with a written outline helps to remind you of all the facts and the best order in which to present them.

When you analyze the subject matter to be covered in your letter, you should also keep in mind the research you did on your customer. Your research can serve as a brief analysis of your customer's personality, interests, and values. All of this information is important to remember as you organize the information to be included in your letter. What is important to you may not necessarily be as important to your reader. Your letter must be aimed toward your reader.

With outline in hand or in your head, you can now begin to write your letter. Keep in mind that, in order to be as clear as possible, you should write simple sentences, avoiding any unnecessary information. Don't try to combine ideas in sentences. In order to get your point across most clearly, write about one thing at a time. For example, when you write the first paragraph of your letter to customer Johnson, don't try to thank him for the meeting and express your appreciation for his views in the same sentence. Take one thought at a time.

> Thank you for an interesting meeting yesterday. I appreciate the time and information you shared with me.

Avoid any excess in the sentences of your letter. If you start rambling, you are bound to get off the track and lose your reader. Remember, to be effective in letter writing you must be able to grab your reader's attention and make that reader react positively to whatever it is you are writing about.

Another important thing to remember is that ideas placed at the beginning or end of a paragraph will often stand out most clearly to the reader. This placement of ideas is a good practice to use for emphasis in your letter writing.

Knowing Your Objectives and How to Accomplish Them

Set an objective for every letter you write. If you want a customer to accept credit terms you are offering, keep that goal in mind as you plan and write your letter. As you choose the order of each paragraph and the wording of each sentence, you should keep your goal clearly in mind.

The research you did before beginning to write to your customer can help you decide how best to write the letter that will be most effective in getting your reader to react the way you would like. Your research can help make you familiar with your reader and what might have moved that reader to act in the past.

The objectives of your follow-up letter to Sam Johnson are to thank him and to attract his business. You know the value he places on loyalty to existing business relationships and on a personal relationship between the professional and the customer, so you might express your understanding of these values. It also might be a good idea, knowing Mr. Johnson's ability to make good suggestions, to react to a suggestion he might have made at your original meeting. Since your goal is to attract his business, closing your letter by telling him you will call him to set up another meeting is a good approach. Such a closing lets Mr. Johnson know you are appreciative of his ideas and anxious to meet with him again to discuss the possibility of doing business with him. Consider the following example of the complete text of a letter to Johnson:

> Thank you for an interesting meeting yesterday. I appreciate the time and information you shared with me. I can understand your sense of loyalty to existing business relationships and the importance you place on knowing and being known by the people you do business with.
>
> During our conversation you suggested that a lock box arrangement might speed up the collection of cash available for investment. I would like to investigate this possibility and estimate the dollar benefit to your company.
>
> I will give you a call early next week to arrange lunch together as you suggested. Thanks again for your time. I look forward to doing business together.

Judging from the final letter to prospective customer Johnson, the research, analysis, and knowledge of objectives were handled well by the letter writer. The result of careful planning in the construction of a letter, such as in the example above, is the increased chance of a positive response from the letter's reader.

CHAPTER 2
Components of an Effective Letter

Planning by itself is not enough to assure you of a positive response from your reader. There are, however, essential components of any letter that *can* multiply the chances of its effectiveness.

Before you begin to worry about the basic mechanics of a letter (structure, appearance, and grammar), think seriously about the attitude you wish to convey. Your attitude is conveyed through your choice of language, tone, and focus of attention. Each of these individual components is as important as anything else that goes into making up a successful letter.

The attitude conveyed in your letter can make the difference between a letter that is tossed aside and one that is read, understood, and reacted to favorably. It is basically very simple to convey a reader-oriented attitude. Remember as you write your letters that you are addressing a specific reader. Your language, tone, and focus of attention must capture the reader's interest for your letter to be successful.

Language—Clarity vs. Ambiguity

Language is a means of communication. This may seem like a foolishly simple observation to make, but remember that for communication to be completed successfully a sender must convey his or her message so that the receiver not only receives, but also *understands*, the message. If language is not used clearly and accurately, the communication process cannot be successfully completed.

A simple rule to remember is that the English you use in your everyday business should be the same good English used by people in all walks of life. Granted, there may be terms intrinsic to your industry, but there is not a special type of "business English" to be learned and used when writing business letters. Good English is good English.

Be clear and straightforward in your letters. Write what you mean. Don't write in circles, making your reader guess what you mean.

Take the following example of a writer who wants to tell a customer about an important organization:

> My correspondence was initiated to inform you of the high calibre of programs and activities of an organization in which I have enjoyed being involved over the past few years. The County Business Association has served to keep me informed of, and actively involved in, the current political and economic issues

affecting small businesses through its monthly breakfast meetings with interesting and impressive speakers, its newsletter on legislative activities in Washington, and several other programs outlined in the attached letter.

There are many problems with this example. Let's start by examining the clarity and directness of the statement. Since the writer of the letter wants to inform the reader about an important organization, why didn't the writer come right out and do so by writing:

I am writing you about the high calibre programs and activities offered by the County Business Association, an organization in which I have been involved for the past few years.

In the writer's version of the letter, it is not until the second sentence of the paragraph that we even learn the name of the important organization. If you are writing about a particular subject, and that subject happens to be an organization, why not get its name right up front so the reader might enjoy learning about it throughout the rest of the letter instead of being left in suspense?

Instead of using many words ("My correspondence was initiated to inform you of . . ."), why not say simply, "I am writing to you about . . ."? If you come right out and say what you mean instead of beating around the bush, not only are you going to grab your reader's attention right away, but you also stand a stronger chance of convincing your reader that he or she should go on reading and find out more about what you have to say.

Be as direct as possible in your letter writing. If you can convey your message in five words instead of ten, do so.

You don't have a great deal of space in a letter to convey your thoughts. You are not writing a novel or a treatise on the economy. The idea is to get your message across clearly and directly.

Avoid the use of pompous or inflated language in your letters. It may sound lofty to write: "My correspondence was initiated to inform you of . . ." but you are not writing to see how you can turn a catchy phrase on the page. You are writing to communicate with your reader, and if you mean, "I am writing to you about," you should write what you mean.

Sometimes when you think you are communicating clearly in a letter, the reader receives a different message from the one you intended. If such ambiguity is present in your letters, you can never be sure that the reader will understand your message. Ambiguous language is another problem with the example paragraph above. The writer wrote:

The County Business Association has served to keep me informed of, and actively involved in, the current political and economic issues affecting small businesses through its monthly breakfast meetings with interesting and impressive speakers, its newsletter on legislative activities in Washington, and several other programs outlined in the attached letter.

The writer did not mean to suggest that the current political and economic issues were affecting small businesses as a result of the County Business Association's monthly breakfast meetings. Because of careless wording, however, the sentence could be read to mean exactly that. The writer may be defensive and quip, "Well, you knew what I meant," and in this case would be correct. But if we have to read something twice to make sure of its meaning, then the chances are that it was not written clearly in the first place. The writer could have written:

> As a result of monthly breakfast meetings with interesting speakers, a newsletter on legislative activities in Washington, and several other programs, the County Business Association has kept me informed of and involved in the current political and economic issues affecting smaller businesses.

This version leaves little doubt in the reader's mind about the writer's intended meaning.

The meaning of an ambiguous passage often cannot be as easily detected as it was in the above example. A classic example is the following:

> The loan officer approved the loan for David Marshall because he was obviously of superior moral fiber.

From what is written above we cannot tell who is of superior moral fiber, the loan officer or Mr. Marshall. The pronoun "he" can refer to either the loan officer *or* Mr. Marshall. To avoid ambiguity, the sentence could be written:

> Because David Marshall was obviously of superior moral fiber, the loan officer approved the loan.

or:

> Because the loan officer was of superior moral fiber, he approved the loan for David Marshall.

Be clear, direct, and unambiguous in your letter writing.

Tone—Personality

The tone or personality of a letter can help you get a positive reaction from a reader. The tone should be set at the very start of a letter and maintained throughout. The tone of any business letter should be courteous and friendly, and written as if you were talking with the reader. You don't want to get too technical in a letter. Write in language that the reader can understand.

The tone should help to show that someone with a personality—a human being—is writing the letter. If the reader believes that the writer is genuinely concerned about how the topic of the letter affects him or her, a positive response is likely.

Consider Sample Letter 2.1. The letter sets a tone emphasizing efficiency and personal response to the reader from the beginning by addressing both the writer's past involvement with the customer and the customer's needs. Credit manager Nilges comes directly to the point by announcing that his letter contains a credit proposal for his customer's company.

In the first paragraph, the writer establishes the tone of the letter:

> We are proud to have you as a customer.

In the second paragraph, Nilges addresses his customer by his first name, maintaining a personal, courteous tone. Not only does Nilges express positive feelings about his customer, he also suggests that the tone of the entire letter will remain one of positive feelings.

Sample Letter 2.1 is written with a positive tone directed toward its reader, which is maintained throughout the letter. If the reader is convinced that he is receiving a fair proposal from an official who is committed to helping the reader's company, then chances are the letter will be successful. A positive tone increases the likelihood of a positive response.

SAMPLE LETTER 2.1. Business letter with efficient and personal tone.

January 4, 19X8

Mr. Bertrand R. Levine
Levine's Lumber Land
P.O. Box 567
Richmond, South Dakota 34345

Dear Mr. Levine:

Welcome! Your account at Nilges Wood Supply has been approved. We are proud to have you as a customer.

Bert, as you probably know, Nilges Wood Supply is a 50-year-old company, with 85 stores in nine Midwestern states. We supply a complete line of building products to our customers, including millwork, plumbing, electrical, paint, kitchen supplies, bath supplies, hardware, and tools. As a leader in this industry, we strive to provide the best service possible to our customers. Our goal is to be your most valuable supplier. Customer satisfaction is our number-one priority.

Your approved credit line is $2,000, with billing terms of Net 10th. Monthly statements are mailed on the first or second working day each month. A service charge is added to past-due balances that are not paid by the twenty-fifth day of the billing month.

We at Nilges Wood Supply welcome the opportunity to serve you and look forward to a long and prosperous relationship.

Your branch manager is Sheila McGulicuty. Her telephone number is 890-765-8765.

Yours very truly,

Larry E. Nilges
Vice President—Credit Sales

len/jls

Focus of Attention—The "You Attitude"

An important concept in letter writing is something called the "you attitude." The "you attitude" insists that the focus of attention in your letters be directed toward the reader, the "you" to whom you are writing.

Directing a letter toward a reader may seem very simple, but a letter writer too often incorrectly assumes that his or her interests and knowledge are the same as the reader's. Some legwork needs to be done when you are deciding how to make a letter reader-oriented. This legwork may come at the planning stage of your letter, discussed in Chapter 1.

What you need to know are answers to basic questions, such as: What will motivate this reader to react favorably to my letter? What interests this reader? What is this reader's viewpoint on issues I am addressing in my letter?

Sometimes you will not know the answers to these questions. If you sit down, however, and think clearly about what it is that will convince your reader that what you are writing is beneficial to him or her, you have attempted to direct the focus of attention of your letter to the reader, the "you" who is receiving the message.

The reader of your letter must be convinced that what you are trying to get him or her to do or react to is of some personal value. If you are responding to someone about the lack of job openings at your bank, you don't want to scare off a potential employee by sending a cold form letter. Nothing overly elaborate is necessary, of course, but a cordial negative response to a potential employee now may pay off in the future when your bank does need someone with his or her expertise.

Sample Letter 2.2, acknowledging an employment application, is courteous to and considerate of the reader even though no jobs are available. Ms. Kenney has written a letter that reflects a sincere interest in Mr. Krauss. By writing, "We are complimented that you would consider the Bethany Bagel Company as a place of employment," she has flattered Mr. Krauss. This might cause him to react positively to Ms. Kenney's letter. If he does react positively now, and jobs should open up at a later date for which he is qualified, then Ms. Kenney's letter has served a good purpose by keeping a positive relationship with a prospective employee.

Ms. Kenney has not gotten caught up in the need to use only the personal pronoun "you" in her letter. That is certainly important in focusing attention on a reader, but part of the whole idea of creating a personality or tone in a letter is to let the reader know that a living person—an "I"—has indeed written the letter, as Ms. Kenney did when she wrote:

> I would appreciate it if you would notify me if you wish to cancel your application for any reason.

SAMPLE LETTER 2.2.   Form response letter reflecting use of the "you attitude."

December 26, 19X8

Mr. Michael Krauss
69 Camran Terrace
Norristown, Pennsylvania 02134

APPLICATION FOR EMPLOYMENT

Mr. Krauss, thank you for your recent employment application. We are complimented that you would consider the Bethany Bagel Company as a place of employment.

Your application will be retained in our open files. Should any appropriate opening occur you may be contacted for an interview.

I would appreciate it if you would notify me if you wish to cancel your application for any reason.

JANE KENNEY—VICE PRESIDENT
HUMAN RESOURCES

mn

    If Ms. Kenney had used a passive voice here and had written, "It would be appreciated," instead of "I would appreciate," she would have risked taking the personality out of her letter, almost as if she were reluctant to admit her involvement in the process.
    A writer must focus the attention of a letter on the reader. If you choose the language and tone for your letter to convey an attitude of commitment to and interest in your reader, you will find that your letters will be more successful in grasping your readers' attention and encouraging them to respond favorably.

CHAPTER 3
Structure: The Parts of a Letter

As you are reading this chapter, you will find it helpful to refer to Chapter 4, where various letter formats are discussed. Different formats require different placement of various parts of a letter. Although placement may vary, the content and function of these parts of a letter remain constant. You will easily be able to apply the principles learned here to the formats discussed in Chapter 4.

Dateline

Every letter should have a dateline. The date appears on a single line two to eight lines below the letterhead or the top margin of the page. With the exception of the simplified letter format, three lines down from the letterhead is the usual space allotted in most letter formats. Because a letter should be well framed on a page, the placement of the dateline is flexible.

The date typed on a letter should be the date on which the letter was dictated, no matter when it is to be typed or mailed, unless, of course, the letter is a standard form letter sent out time and time again. The months of the year should always be spelled out, and the day should always be indicated by a cardinal number (e.g., 1, 2, 3), never using "nd," "th," or "st" after the number as you would with ordinal numbers.

The order of the dateline is month, day followed by a comma, and year.

May 5, 19X8

Sometimes government and foreign correspondence will feature a reversal in the order of day and month, omitting the comma.

5 May 19X8

The most standard order, however, for the elements in the dateline is month, day followed by a comma, and year.

The placement of the dateline varies depending upon the letter format used. In the full-block format (see Sample Letter 4.1), the dateline is typed flush with the left margin, or sometimes centered, if centering the date blends well with the letterhead. In the simplified letter format (see Sample Letter 4.4), the dateline is typed flush with the left margin, six lines below the letterhead.

The dateline in the block (see Sample Letter 4.2), semiblock (see Sample Letter 4.3), official style (see Sample Letter 4.5), and hanging-indented (see Sample Letter 4.6) formats is usually flush with the right margin. The last figure of the year

13

should never overrun the right margin. However, in these formats the date can also be either centered under the letterhead, if this adds to the balanced look of the letter, or five spaces to the right of the center of the page.

Reference Line

The reference line is optional. It is a number or a series of numbers and letters referring to previous correspondence. It is usually included for the benefit of a person who must file all correspondence dealing with the same specific issues or topics.

The number is aligned with and typed directly below the dateline. It is usually typed one to four lines beneath the date unless your company policy stipulates that it should be placed elsewhere. (See Sample Letter 4.1 for an example of a reference line.)

If your letter is to be more than one page long, the reference number must be carried over to all continuation sheets. On these sheets, the location of the reference line should correspond to its location on the first sheet, or as indicated by bank policy.

Personal or Confidential Note

The inclusion of a personal or confidential note is optional. When such a notation is used, however, it should always be because the writer wants the letter to remain confidential between him or her and the reader. If such notations are used as come-on gimmicks to attract a reader to a letter, they will lose their effectiveness.

Except with the official-style format, the personal or confidential note should be located four lines above the inside address. It does not need to be underlined or typed in all capital letters. If a writer feels it necessary to underline or capitalize, he or she should choose one or the other (i.e., either all capital letters or underlining), but not both.

Personal
PERSONAL
Personal

The personal note is rarely used in the official-style format because this format is usually reserved for personal letters. Should you decide it is necessary to include a personal note in the official-style format, it should be typed four lines above the salutation.

Inside Address

The inside address must be included in all letters. With the exception of the official-style format, the inside address is typed two to twelve lines beneath the dateline (or reference line or confidential note, should there be such notations). The placement of the inside address is flexible, depending upon the length of the letter, but four lines is the most common.

In the simplified-letter format, the inside address is typed four lines below the dateline or the last previous notation. In the official-style letter, the inside address is typed two to five lines below the last line of the signature block.

The inside address is always typed flush with the left margin of the letter. It should be no longer than five lines. No line should cross over the center margin of the page. If a line is too long, it should be broken in half and continued on the next line, indented two spaces.

The inside address of a letter addressed to an individual should include that individual's courtesy title and full name, professional title, company name, and full address. If a woman's courtesy title is unknown, "Ms." should be used.

> Ms. Nancy Simons
> Production Supervisor
> Bethany Bagel Company
> 25 Francis Avenue
> Boston, Massachusetts 02222

Even if the courtesy title "Mrs." is used in a business letter, a woman's and not her husband's first name should be used.

If a person's name and professional title are short enough, they can be separated by a comma and placed together on the first line of the inside address.

> Mr. Robert Miles, Treasurer

If the professional title and company name are short enough, the title and the company name (separated by a comma) can be placed together on the second line of the inside address.

> Ms. Rebecca Gray
> Editor, The Tower

When a company is being addressed, the inside address should include the name of the company, the individual department desired, and the full address of the company.

> Pauly Industries, Inc.
> Distribution Department
> 79 Grand Forks Drive
> Winnipeg, Virginia 23444

You should always use the company's official name in the inside address, including any ampersands, abbreviations, or other items the company uses in its name when it is printed.

When the address is too long, the person's title is sometimes omitted. If you are addressing two or more people, you can either list the names alphabetically on separate lines or use the designation "Messrs." (Messieurs) for all men or "Mesdames," "Mmes.," or "Mses." for all women. When using Messrs. or Mesdames (or its abbreviations), you omit the addressees' first names.

> Mesdames Cole, Kenney, and Long

or

> Ms. Bethany Cole
> Ms. Jane Kenney
> Ms. Marie Long

Sometimes a company uses both a street address and a post office box in its letterhead. If such is the case, use the post office box number in the inside address of your letter and on the envelope. This will ensure that the post office sends your letter to the proper place.

The names of numbered streets should be spelled out for streets numbered one through twelve. Arabic numerals should be used for streets numbered 13 and above.

> 186 First Street
> 186 - 13th Avenue

Arabic numerals should be used for all house, building, or office numbers, with the exception of the number "one," which always should be spelled out.

> One Savin Hill Avenue
> 210 Savin Hill Avenue

When compass directions appear before numbered streets, cardinal numbers (e.g., 16, 17, 18) should be used. If compass directions don't appear before a numbered street, ordinal numbers (e.g., 16th, 17th, 18th) should be used.

> 226 West 78 Street
> 226 - 78th Street

When a compass direction appears before a street name, it should be spelled out. If the compass direction follows the street name, it should be abbreviated.

> 226 West 78 Street
> 3233 - 38th Street N.W.

If a building or house number appears immediately before a numbered street, separate the two with a spaced hyphen.

> 226 - 78th Street

A suite or apartment number following a street address should be placed on the same line as the street address, separated by a comma or two spaces.

> 25 Huntington Avenue, Suite 408
> 25 Huntington Avenue Suite 408

Although the inside address should match the address on the envelope, it generally looks more attractive to spell out the state name in the inside address. On the envelope, the two-letter state abbreviation should always be used. (See Appendix III for a list of two-letter state abbreviations.) The zip code should be included two spaces after the state in the inside address.

Attention Note

If you are addressing a letter to a company but wish to direct it to the attention of a specific person, you may include an attention note. The attention note is typed two lines below the last line of the inside address and two lines above the salutation.

In the full-block, block, or simplified formats, the attention note is typed either flush with the left margin or centered. The attention note is usually not included in the official-style format since this format is generally used for a personal letter and it would already be clear to whom the letter is addressed. The attention note can be included in a hanging-indented letter, but because the format is generally reserved for sales letters, the inclusion of an attention note would not be common.

The attention note can be written with or without a colon following the word "attention." The first letter of the main elements of the attention note should be capitalized.

> Attention: David Marshall
> Attention David Marshall
> Attention: Order Department
> Attention Order Department

Salutation

The salutation appears in all letters but those using the simplified-letter format. It is usually typed two to four lines below the inside address or the attention note (if there is one). Two spaces is most typical.

In the official-style format, the salutation is typed four to six lines below the dateline, since the inside address appears at the bottom of the letter in this format.

The word "Dear" before the person's courtesy title and name is standard. The phrase "My Dear" is no longer in style. The "D" in the word "Dear" should be capitalized. The word should be typed flush with the left margin. If the letter is informal, you address the person by his or her first name in the salutation.

Courtesy titles such as Ms., Miss, Mrs., and Mr. should be used where appropriate. If you are unsure about a woman's marital status or her courtesy title preference, it is best to use "Ms." before her name in the salutation.

Professional or academic titles (e.g., "Dr.") take precedence over courtesy titles for both men and women. A comma before the abbreviations "Jr." and "Sr." depends upon the preference of the individual being addressed.

The most conventional ways of addressing a group consisting of males and females are:

> Ladies and Gentlemen:

or

> Dear Sir or Madam:

The simplified-letter format contains no salutation. As a result, this format can be used if the letter writer wishes to avoid the problems of sexist language that sometime exist in choosing the appropriate salutation for a letter.

Subject Line

The subject line identifies the content of a letter and is an optional addition to all but the simplified-letter formats. The simplified letter always includes a subject line typed three lines below the last line of the inside address.

In the full-block, block, semiblock, or hanging-indented formats, the subject line is typed either two lines above or below the salutation. It is typed either flush with the left margin or centered, and consists of the word "subject" followed by a colon and the subject to be covered in a letter.

The subject line can be typed in all capital letters or with each important word capitalized. Sometimes when just the important words are capitalized, the whole subject line is underlined. When the subject line is typed in all capital letters, it is never underlined.

> Subject: Proposed Distribution Arrangement
> Subject: Proposed Distribution Arrangement
> SUBJECT: PROPOSED DISTRIBUTION ARRANGEMENT

The subject line is generally used when only one subject is covered in a letter.

Paragraphs

The body of a letter should begin two lines below the salutation or subject line in the full-block, block, semiblock, official-style, and hanging-indented formats. It should begin three lines below the subject line in the simplified-letter format.

The letter should be single-spaced within paragraphs and double-spaced between paragraphs. If the letter is very short, double-spacing can be used within the paragraphs, using the semiblock style of indentation to indicate new paragraphs.

Paragraphs should be indented five or ten spaces in the official or semiblock styles. Five-space indentations are usually standard. In the full-block, block, and simplified-letter formats, no indentation is used.

In the hanging-indented format, the first line of the paragraph is flush left and the rest of the paragraph is indented five spaces. Single-spacing within paragraphs and double-spacing between paragraphs are used in the hanging-indented format.

Numbered material within letters should be indented five spaces or centered. The numbers should be placed in parentheses or followed by a period. Double-spacing should be used between each item. Punctuation is used either after each item listed in the numbered material or after none of the items.

Long quotations should be blocked in the letter, setting the quotation off by indenting all of it five spaces and keeping it single-spaced.

Long paragraphs should be avoided in letters. Of course, the use of brief paragraphs should not be carried to a ridiculous extreme by writing a letter full of one-sentence paragraphs that cause it to sound like a machine gun because of the staccato rhythm. Be sensible about paragraph length. Say what you have to say and move on; avoid any padding or inconsequential information.

The first paragraph should introduce a letter's subject or refer to a previous correspondence or conversation to which you are responding. The following paragraphs of your letter should elaborate on the subject set up in the first paragraph. The closing paragraph should briefly summarize the topic and close on a positive note, encouraging a positive working relationship with the letter's reader.

Continuation Sheets

The printed letterhead is used only for the first page of a letter. The second and following pages are typed on plain sheets of paper matching the letterhead.

The heading on a continuation sheet is typed six lines below the top of the page and includes the addressee's name, the page number, and the date. At least two lines of text, preferably more, should be carried over for a continuation sheet to be used.

In the full-block format, the information in the continuation sheet heading should be typed flush with the left margin. It should include the page number on the first line, the addressee's courtesy title and full name on the second, and the date on the third.

> Page 2
> Mr. David Marshall
> May 5, 19X8

The block, semiblock, official-style, or hanging-indented formats can use either the flush left continuation sheet heading shown above, or a continuation typed on one line with the addressee's name typed flush left, the page number centered and set off by spaced hyphens, and the date flush with the right margin.

> Mr. David Marshall   - 2 -   May 5, 19X8

Complimentary Close

The complimentary close must be included in all but the simplified-letter format. It is typed two lines below the last line of the body of the letter.

In the full-block format, the complimentary close should be flush with the left margin. In the block, semiblock, official-style, and hanging-indented formats, the complimentary close should start at the center of the page, directly under the dateline, about five spaces to the right of center, or at a point that would put the end of the longest line at the right margin. However, note that it should never cross over the right margin. The simplified letter has no complimentary close.

The first letter of the first word of the complimentary close should be capitalized. The entire complimentary close should be followed by a comma.

The choice of the proper complimentary close depends upon the degree of formality of your letter. If the letter is formal, the choices for a proper complimentary close include:

> Very truly yours,
> Yours truly,
> Yours very truly,

If the letter is less formal, but still not friendly or informal, among the complimentary closes to choose from are:

> Yours sincerely,
> Very sincerely yours,
> Sincerely yours,
> Sincerely,
> Cordially,
> Most sincerely,
> Most cordially,
> Cordially yours,

A friendly or informal letter to a person with whom you are on a first-name basis can end with a complimentary close such as:

> As ever,
> Best regards,
> Kindest regards,
> Best wishes,
> Regards,

Signature Block

Directly under the complimentary close, the letter writer signs his or her name. Four lines below the complimentary close, and aligned with it in the full-block, block, semiblock, official-style, and hanging-indented formats, the writer's name is typed, usually the same way it is signed. In the simplified-letter format, the letter writer's name is typed in all capital letters five lines below the last line of the letter, flush with the left margin.

Single-spaced beneath the typed name, the letter writer's title is typed, unless it is short enough to fit on the same line as the name after a comma.

If the letterhead includes the letter writer's business title and the business name, these are not typed again in the signature block. If a letterhead is not used and your letter is a formal one requiring the business' name, type the business' name in all capital letters two lines below and aligned with the complimentary close, or, in the case of the simplified-letter format, two lines below the last line of the letter.

Directly below the typed business name should be the signature. Four lines below the typed business name, the letter writer's name should be typed. If the business' name is long it can be centered beneath the complimentary close in the block and semiblock format letters.

Yours truly,

BETHANY BAGEL COMPANY

Louis Leigh

Louis Leigh, President

If a woman wishes to use a courtesy title before her name, then Ms., Mrs., or Miss should be enclosed in parentheses before the typed name. These are the only titles that may precede the name in the signature block. Academic degrees (e.g., Ph.D., M.B.A.) or professional designations (e.g., C.L.U., C.P.A., C.F.P.) follow the typed name and are separated by a comma.

A person signing the letter for someone else should initial just below and to the right of the signature.

Yours truly,

Louis Leigh js

Louis Leigh, President

If a secretary signs a letter in his or her name for someone else, the secretary's name and title are typed below the signature.

Yours truly,

Edward Cole

Edward Cole
Assistant to Mr. Leigh

Identification Line

The identification line is an optional addition to any letter. It consists of the initials of either the typist or the writer *and* the typist, and is typed flush with the left margin two lines below the signature block.

The identification line can be typed in a variety of ways. The typist's lowercase initials may be typed alone.

js

The writer's initials may be typed uppercase followed by a colon or virgule followed by the typist's lowercase initials.

MN:js
MN/js

The writer's initials and the typist's initials can both be uppercase, or both lowercase.

MN:JS
MN/JS
mn:js
mn/js

Any version of the identification line above can be used as long as it serves the purpose of identifying the typist of the letter.

In the odd case that a letter should be dictated by one person, typed by another, and signed by a third, the identification line should include the signer's uppercase initials followed by a colon followed by the dictator's uppercase initials, followed by another colon, followed by the typist's lowercase initials.

MN:JS:ms

Enclosure Notations

If an enclosure is included with the letter, one of the following should be typed two lines below the identification line or the signature block if there is no identification line:

Enclosure
Enc.
Encl.
enc.
encl.

If there is more than one enclosure the plural of one of the above notations is used, with the number of enclosures indicated before the notation, or after it in parentheses.

Enclosures (2)
2 Enclosures
encs. (2)
2 encs.
Encs. (2)
2 Encs.

The enclosures should be placed behind the letter in order of importance. If a check is one of the enclosures it should be placed in front of the letter.

The enclosures can be numbered and listed next to the enclosure notation, one per line. If they are to be returned, indicate such in parentheses next to the item.

> encs. (2) 1. Credit analysis worksheet (please return)
>   2. International financing brochure

Distribution Notation

If you would like the recipient of the letter to know to whom you are sending copies of the letter, a distribution notation is used. Sometimes distribution notations appear only on copies of the letter.

The distribution notation consists of the words "Copy to" (or "Copies to") or the abbreviation and colon, "cc:" followed by the recipient's or recipients' names.

> Copy to Louis Leigh
> cc: Louis Leigh

Multiple recipients are listed alphabetically by full name or by initials, depending upon the letter writer's preference or company policy.

> Copies to: Louis Leigh
>   David Marshall

If other information about the recipient is useful (e.g., a company's name) it should be placed next to the person's name in parentheses.

> Copies to: Louis Leigh (Bethany Bagel Company)
>   David Marshall (The David Marshall Agency)
>
> cc: LL (Bethany Bagel Company)
>   DM (The David Marshall Agency)

If space is tight and a distribution notation is essential, it can be typed a single-space above either the enclosure notation or the identification line.

Postscript

A postscript is rarely used in a business letter unless it is in a sales letter to emphasize a point or to make a special offer. It is typed flush with the left margin two to four lines below the last notation in a letter. The writer should initial the postscript. The abbreviation "P.S." should not be used before a postscript.

CHAPTER 4
Appearance of the Letter

A friend of mine is the president of a public relations company he founded in Boston. His customers include small businesses, restaurants, and financial services companies throughout New England. He is a superb spokesman for his company and is quite adept at convincing companies and executives that his organization can serve them better than other public relations firms can.

One reason for my friend's success is the contacts he's built over the several years he's worked as a public relations professional. Another is the good press he has gotten his clients.

But another important reason for his success is his appearance. He is well groomed and dresses well—nothing ostentatious, but when he arrives for a business meeting, the customer can tell that he or she is dealing with a public relations professional who at least appears to be very professional.

In letter writing too, appearance is very important. The message you are sending is obviously the most important aspect of your letter. However, if the reader opens an envelope and finds a note scrawled across a piece of notebook paper, the most important of messages is not going to get through to the reader.

There are certain conventions used in letter writing that are fairly well established, yet they are flexible enough to allow you to communicate exactly what you want to your reader. If you take into consideration the appearance of your letter—the stationery, format, length, and envelope—your reader will be drawn to it. Once your reader gives your letter his or her attention, your message is sure to get through.

Stationery

Letterhead design varies from business to business, but it usually consists of at least the following items:

- Business logo
- Business' full, legal name
- Full street address and/or post office box number
- City, state, and zip code
- Telephone number

A business' letterhead also sometimes includes the business' cable or telex number.

There are important considerations to make when choosing a letterhead design. The information included should be uncluttered and readable. The design should be simple enough for the reader to find the information he or she needs without being distracted from reading the rest of the letter.

Business stationery is usually white or some other conservative color. The standard size of the stationery is 8.5 by 11 inches.

Margins on the typed letter should be consistent. The margins on the top and the bottom of the letter should be the same. The side margins should also be equal to one another. The size of the margins depends upon the length of the letter to be written. Long letters typically have smaller margins than short letters. Margins of one inch for long letters and two inches for short letters is a good rule of thumb to follow.

If a letter is very short, containing a few short sentences or a couple of short paragraphs, then a half-sheet of stationery can be used. The half-sheet measures 8.5 by 5.5 inches. It is usually printed as a miniature version of the letterhead, with the same letterhead design as the normal-size stationery.

The full-block, block, or semiblock letter formats discussed in this chapter can be used on the half-sheet. The techniques and rules governing letter writing apply to letters written on a half-sheet.

Some professionals will use an executive letterhead. In addition to the basic elements contained in a letterhead, the executive letterhead features the executive's printed name and title beneath the letterhead.

With all types of letters, the letterhead is always used only as the first sheet of a letter. If the typed letter is more than one page, a plain sheet of paper matching the letterhead should be used for subsequent pages. (See the section on continuation sheets in Chapter 3 for more information.)

Various Formats for Letter Writing

The format used for a letter is typically determined by the person writing the letter. Sometimes a company will have a house style for a format in which letters must be written, but typically the writer must choose the format.

The full-block, block, semiblock, and simplified-letter formats presented here can all be used effectively for writing any business letter. Some letter writers find that the simplified letter is not traditional enough for their taste; others find it a perfect solution to the problem of sexist language in letter salutations. Be that as it may, these four formats are the standard ones used for most business letters written today.

The hanging-indented and official-style formats discussed here are not used for everyday business letters. Their use indicates that a particular type of letter is being written. A discussion of the appropriate use of these formats is included in this chapter.

Chapter 3 discusses the placement and function of the parts of each of the letter formats discussed in this chapter. You might find it useful to look back at Chapter 3 for reference when you are studying the various letter formats in this chapter.

Full-Block

The full-block format, sometimes called "complete block" or simply "block," is shown in Sample Letter 4.1. In this format, all the lines of the letter, from the dateline to the last notation, are flush with the left margin.

Paragraphs are not indented but rather begin flush with the left margin. Single-spacing is used within the paragraphs, and double-spacing between.

The dateline is most often typed three lines below the letterhead. Depending upon the length of the letter, however, it may be typed anywhere from two to six lines below the letterhead. If there is a reference line, it should be typed directly below the dateline.

The inside address is most often typed four lines below the dateline (or reference line if there is one) but may be typed anywhere from two to twelve lines below the dateline depending upon the length of the letter. If there is an attention line it should be typed two lines below the address and two lines above the salutation.

SAMPLE LETTER 4.1.   Example of full-block format letter.

April 20, 19X7
A-354-29

Mr. Alexander Campbell
Bethany Bagel Company
14 Pendleton Road
Scots, Pennsylvania 00012

Dear Mr. Campbell:

The records you requested are enclosed. Due to the technical difficulties we have in processing microfilm, I am unable to provide better quality copies.

I am sorry for any inconvenience this may cause. If I can be of any further assistance, please call me or another customer service representative on our toll-free number.

Sincerely,

Ambrose Kemper
Customer Service Representative

jls

Enclosure

The salutation should be typed two lines below the inside address or attention line if there is one. If there is a subject line, it is typed two lines above or below the salutation. The body of the letter begins two lines below the salutation or subject line if there is one.

Two lines below the last line of the letter, the complimentary close is typed. The signature block is typed four lines below the complimentary close.

An identification line is typed two lines below the signature block. All other notations (e.g., enclosure, distribution) are typed two lines below the identification line.

Block

The block format, sometimes called "modified block," is shown in Sample Letter 4.2. This format differs from the full-block in the position of the dateline (and reference line if there is one) and the complimentary close and signature block.

The dateline is usually aligned with the right margin, although sometimes it is centered in relation to the printed letterhead if this presents a more balanced look. In the samples in this book, the dateline is flush with the right margin.

The complimentary close and signature block can correctly be placed in any of several locations (see Chapter 3). In the samples in this book, they appear just to the right of center, but you should realize that other positions may also be used.

Paragraphs are not indented. The spacing of various parts of the block-format letter is the same as for the full-block format.

SAMPLE LETTER 4.2.   Example of block format.

May 29, 19X6

Mr. Jacob L. Martin
Investigative Management
25 Huntington Avenue, Suite 408
Boonton, New Jersey 07005

Subject: Membership of Bill Senyl

Dear Mr. Martin:

As we feared, Mr. Senyl is no longer a member of the Investment Managers Society of America. He was a member for just one year from May 19X4 through May 19X5, at which point he allowed his membership to lapse.

In his application, he indicated licenses and registrations in accounting, life insurance, law, real estate, and securities. He also indicated he was a registered investment advisor with the Securities and Exchange Commission. He indicated his highest level of education was a Ph.D., not a Masters degree, as you mention he suggested to you. He also stated that he had memberships in the American Bar Association, American Society of Certified Life Underwriters, and the Million Dollar Round Table.

We certainly appreciate your interest and assistance. Your information will be lodged with the membership department of the Investment Managers Society of America.

Sincerely,

Lisa Antolini
General Counsel

la/js

The block format is widely used because of the balanced look it gives to a letter. Since everything is flush with the left margin in the full-block format, it almost appears as if the letter might tip over to the left. In the block format, since the date, complimentary close, and signature block are toward the right, the letter is balanced in place and not tipped to either side.

Semiblock

The semiblock format is shown in Sample Letter 4.3. The only difference between this and the block format is the fact that the paragraphs in the semiblock format are indented either five or ten spaces, usually five.

Simplified Letter

The simplified-letter format departs significantly from the formats described thus far; an example appears in Sample Letter 4.4.

SAMPLE LETTER 4.3.   Example of semiblock format letter.

March 3, 19X8

Mr. Roger Perkins
95 Belltoll Road
Ketchum, Idaho 00005

Dear Mr. Perkins:

Thank you for sending your work samples and discussing your views about the editor's position we have open. I've reviewed your work and reflected at length on our last conversation, particularly your hesitancy to take on an assignment to demonstrate your editorial approach to analytical topics. Since we talked I've interviewed several other candidates with substantial editorial credentials and have become convinced that proven analytical skills or technical knowledge of the investments area are important prerequisites for the job.

My conclusion is that your background is not appropriate for the position and, frankly, that you would not enjoy the job during a necessary period of training. If, however, you are interesting in establishing a free-lance relationship with our publication, I'd be happy to consider using you.

Thanks again, Roger, for your interest in the job.

Cordially,

Gloria Hoagland
Publisher

GH/ec

SAMPLE LETTER 4.4.   Example of simplified-letter format.

May 5, 19X8

Professor Alan Campbell
Lazarus College
43 Lorraine Terrace
Plattsburgh, New York 02134

OPINION LETTERS ON MARKETING TEXTBOOK

Enclosed is a group of opinion letters for your text, Marketing: A New Approach. We hope these letters will be of considerable interest to you and help you in making revisions to the second edition of the book.

As more of these letters come in, I will send groups of them along to you so that you may read the comments your colleagues have made about your book.

OTTO SCOTT—EDITOR

OS/js
Enclosures

The most obvious variation in the simplified-letter format is its lack of salutation and complimentary close. The lack of salutation is a good way to avoid the problem of knowing how to address a woman if you do not know which, if any, courtesy title she prefers. It is also a good way to address an unknown audience that may consist of both men and women or only one of these two groups.

In a simplified letter, all lines are flush with the left margin, including the dateline, reference line (if there is one), and the signature block. The dateline is typed six lines below the letterhead. The inside address is typed four lines below the dateline or reference line.

A subject line always is included in the simplified letter format. It is typed in all capital letters, three lines below the inside address and three lines above the body of the letter.

Paragraphs are not indented in the simplified letter format. Five lines below the body of the letter, the signature block is typed in all capital letters. The writer's signature is signed above the signature block. If there is an enclosure notation it is typed a single space below the identification line. Any other notations are typed two lines below the enclosure notation.

If a continuation page is needed, the heading should be the same as used with the full-block format. The addressee's name should appear six lines from the top of the plain sheet, flush with the left margin. The page number should be typed directly below the name, and the date directly below the page number.

Official Style

The official-style format is used mostly for personal correspondence, and is often written by executives on their personalized business stationery. This format is the same as the semiblock format with the exception of the placement of the inside address, which is typed two to five lines below the signature block. See Sample Letter 4.5 for an example of an official-style letter.

If there is an identification line in the official-style format, it is typed two lines below the inside address. Any enclosure notations are typed two lines below the identification line.

Hanging Indented

The use of the hanging-indented letter format is reserved for sales or advertising letters. This unorthodox format, shown in Sample Letter 4.6, is believed to attract the attention of the reader.

SAMPLE LETTER 4.5.   Example of an official-style format letter.

December 1, 19X6

Dear Ambrose:

Your article that appears in December's <u>Guam City Magazine</u> made good reading. It was informative and well written for the layman like me.

On behalf of Alan, Mike, and Gus, whom you cited in the article, as well as the whole crew here at Natick Nautical, I want to thank you for including us in the article. The exposure is great, especially in such a well written and widely read piece.

Thank you again.

Regards,

Paul Pendelton

Mr. Ambrose Kemper
<u>Guam City Magazine</u>
One Symphony Place
Guam City, Arizona 72177

PP:js

The first line of each paragraph of the hanging-indented letter is flush with the left margin. The remaining lines of that paragraph are indented five spaces. Single-spacing is used within paragraphs and double-spacing between.

The dateline is flush with the right margin and typed three lines below the letterhead. The inside address and salutation are flush with the left margin and blocked exactly as in the block format discussed earlier in this chapter. The complimentary close, signature block, and all subsequent notations are positioned similarly to the way they are placed in the semiblock letter format.

The main difference between the hanging-indented format and the semiblock format is the difference in the indentation of paragraphs. If there is a postscript in a hanging-indented letter, it is also typed with the first line flush left and the remaining lines indented five spaces.

SAMPLE LETTER 4.6.   Example of a hanging-indented format letter.

December 21, 19X7

Ms. Jane Kenney
1978 Malden Place
Summit, New Jersey 01005

Dear Ms. Kenney:

For a very limited time—and only to a select, qualified group—I'm
    authorized to send the next issue of The Armchair Reader's Review
    absolutely free.

Reply by March 1, 19X8, and you'll receive—without risk or obligation—
    the one publication dedicated to giving the inside knowledge on the
    latest in economic developments.

Mail the enclosed postage paid reservation card by March 1, 19X8, and the
    next issue of The Armchair Reader's Review is yours free. At the same
    time, we'll reserve in your name a full year's subscription at a special
    introductory rate.

When you receive your free issue, read it and then decide. If you can do
    without The Armchair Reader's Review, write "cancel" on the bill when
    it comes. You'll owe nothing. Your first issue will be your last. Or you can
    pay just $11.95 for 11 more issues—saving $24.05 off the newsstand
    price, and enjoy the insight that each monthly issue of The Armchair
    Reader's Review delivers.

Remember that this is a special offer good for a limited time only. Please
    reply today.

Cordially,

Alan Sitton
Publisher

AS:JS

Enclosure

Length

The length of any letter affects its appearance. Professionals or customers who receive a lot of correspondence every day are not going to react favorably to lengthy three-page letters that could have been written in one page.

Come right to the point in your letters. They should be concise and limited to one page if possible.

Begin discussing the main topic or topics of your letter in the first paragraph. If you do, your reader will know what to expect as soon as he or she begins to read.

Planning and clarity in your ideas can help to limit the length of your letter. Paragraphs should not be too long and difficult to follow. You should not, however, use a string of one-sentence paragraphs, which can result in a staccato-like reading. A concise paragraph with a few sentences that come right to the point should keep the length of your letters manageable.

Envelopes

The appearance of the envelope adds to the overall professional appearance of your letter. The address should be typed in the approximate horizontal and vertical center of the business envelope. With the exception of using the two-letter abbreviation for the state, the address on the envelope should appear exactly as in the inside address of the letter (see Chapter 3). The use of the two-letter state abbreviation will expedite postal service. (See Appendix III for a list of two-letter state abbreviations.)

The addressee's name should be typed on the first line. If there is space, the addressee's title can be typed next to the name on the first line, separated by a comma. On the second line, a single-space down, the person's title is typed if it did not fit on the first line. If the company's name will also fit on the second line, type it next to the title, separated by a comma. A single-space below, the company name is typed if it didn't fit on the second line. The complete street address or post office box number, whichever is used in the inside address, is typed on the next line. The city followed by a comma, the two-letter state abbreviation, followed by two spaces, and the zip code are typed as the last line of the address.

If you are addressing a company rather than an individual, type the company's name on the first line and the department name or attention line on the second line.

The sender's full name and address should appear in the upper-left corner of the letter. Usually the business' name will be imprinted on the envelope.

The stamp is placed in the upper-right corner of the envelope. Any special mailing notations should be typed in all capital letters directly below where the stamp is to go. On-arrival notations should be typed in all capital letters about nine lines below the top left of the envelope, aligned with the end of the return address. Italics and script writing should not be used because they might confuse the postal service.

Memorandums

More often than not, memorandums are written as interoffice correspondence. Different businesses use different formats for their memos. Businesses often have preprinted memo forms that resemble the company's stationery. Usually these forms will feature the following information at the top:

TO:
FROM:
DATE:
SUBJECT:

In many word processing software packages, a memo feature allows the user to call up the above heading whenever he or she wants to write a memo.

When a business does not have preprinted memo forms available, a memo writer can use the above format on a blank piece of stationery. The memo's message is begun two to four spaces below the subject line of the memo heading.

When you consider writing a memo, remember:

1. *Write a memo only when it is necessary*. Professionals are already drowning in a sea of paper. Don't compound the problem by adding unnecessary missives to the flood. If you don't really need to write the memo, don't.
2. *Keep your memos as brief as possible*. The memo is the ideal place for the professional to show how competent a writer he or she is. The memo must be clear, concise, and to the point. The reader must be able to grasp the message quickly and clearly. Memos can run on to more than one page, but only when absolutely necessary.

Memos can be written for countless occasions. Sample Memorandum 4.1 will give you an idea of the format and length of a well-written memorandum.

SAMPLE MEMORANDUM 4.1.   Memo to employees about new benefits.

TO: Employees Participating in Disability Insurance Plan
FROM: Etsuko S. Yukki, Benefits Administrator
DATE: August 13, 19X0
SUBJECT: Long-Term Disability Plan

Your long-term disability insurance carrier until now has been Security of America. The cost to you for this coverage has been $.30 per $100.

As of August 1, we are pleased to announce that we have changed long-term disability carriers. As a result, your costs have been reduced by 25%. The new carrier on the long-term disability plan is Sambuki General Life Insurance Ltd.

Plan benefits through Sambuki General will remain the same, but rates have been reduced retroactive to August 1. As a result, you will see a rate reduction in your August paycheck. Your cost will be reduced to $.22 per $100 in monthly earnings. The company will continue to pay 50% of the cost of your plan.

Please call me in the New York office if you have any questions.

CHAPTER 5
Grammar and Usage

People who have difficulty writing are often so frightened about making a mistake they freeze. Grammar just might be the most frightening element of writing.

You can combat this fear. Relax and try to write as naturally as possible. You'll usually find any grammatical errors when you do a careful proofreading. When I asked one professional how she managed to write such good letters, she replied: "Simple. I have a good secretary." Her secretary filled the role of proofreader. Most people can correct their own errors, however, once they get something down on paper.

Relax. That's the key. If you find you have a real problem with grammar, there are many good, easy-to-understand grammar books that should help you alleviate any mistakes you might be making. You'll find a list of these books in the Bibliography of this book.

In the meantime, this chapter gives you the grammar basics you need to create a well-written letter.

Grammar

The rules of grammar define how to speak and write clearly. Most of these rules are logical. Some may not seem as logical as others, but, on the whole, following the rules of grammar helps your writing to be consistent and understandable.

Spoken language often is not as precise as written language. Keep this in mind when you are writing, but don't feel compelled to embellish your letter with forceful strokes of the pen. If you get the basics correct and write with clarity and precision foremost in your mind, you will most likely produce correctly written English.

All types of grammatical errors are possible. A list of several of the most common follows. Look over these errors. Try to detect them if they occur in your own writing. Remember, most errors you make—including those listed here—can be detected in a careful proofreading after you've finished the first draft of your letter.

Wrong Pronouns

Some writers have a tendency to want to write "I" instead of "me," even when the latter is correct. For instance, the sentence:

He gave the book to Eddie and I.

is incorrect. The sentence properly should be written:

He gave the book to Eddie and me.

The above error is common when the writer lists two people as the recipient of the action. If you find yourself having difficulty in such a case, simply say the sentence to yourself as if the pronoun were the only receiver of the action.

> He gave the book to me.

It is easy to add other receivers of the action after you have determined the proper pronoun to use. This is a simple way to avoid using the wrong pronoun.

Another way to avoid using the wrong pronoun is to remember that there are three "cases" of pronouns. The "nominative" case pronouns are the *subject* of the verb. The nominative case pronouns are:

Singular	**Plural**
I	we
you	you
he, she, it	they

You would never write:

> Her and me are going to the movies.

but rather:

> She and I are going to the movies.

In the above sentence, because "She and I" is the subject of the verb, the nominative case pronouns are used.

The "objective" case pronouns are used as the *object* of a verb's action or as the object of a preposition. The objective case pronouns are:

Singular	**Plural**
me	us
you	you
him, her, it	them

The object of the verb can usually be determined by asking "What?" or "Whom?" is the receiver of the verb's action. In the sentence,

> I gave it to her.

"her" is the object of the verb because it answers the question: "To whom did you give it?"

Remember that an objective case pronoun is *always* used as the object of a preposition, so when you see a sentence that includes a prepositional phrase such as "at him," "with her," or "about me," it should immediately trigger your memory to use one of the objective case pronouns.

"Possessive" case pronouns indicate *possession* and are used incorrectly far less often than are the nominative and objective case pronouns. The possessive case pronouns are:

Singular	**Plural**
my, mine	our, ours
your, yours	your, yours
his, her, hers, its	their, theirs

Another common error involving the use of pronouns occurs when the words "than" or "as" precede an incomplete sentence construction. For example, take the sentence

Mr. Bradford is richer than I.

To determine the proper pronoun to use, complete the sentence:

Mr. Bradford is richer *than I am*.

Use the pronoun you would use if the construction were not incomplete.

There are many more rules governing the proper use of pronouns. Those listed here represent a few that remedy some recurring problems. If you are unsure of the pronoun to use, you can usually determine whether or not your sentence is correct by listening to how the sentence sounds once you have written it. If you remain unsure, check the rules I've noted or consult a grammar reference.

Pronouns and Antecedents

The most common mistake concerning pronouns and their antecedents occurs when it is unclear to what or whom a pronoun refers. To avoid any confusion in your letters, make sure than when you begin a sentence or a clause in a sentence with he, she, it, or other pronouns, it is absolutely clear to whom or what these pronouns refer.

A couple of simple examples of unclear references involving pronouns and antecedents are:

Loren Gary and Guy Martin prepared the advertising presentation and visited the customer's new office building. It was a handsome piece of work. [What *was a handsome piece of work? The advertising presentation? The office building?*]

Brian Palay spoke with Robert Long about the possibility of working together. He thought it was a good idea. [Who *thought it was a good idea? Brian? Robert?*]

Subject and Verb Agreement

Sentences consisting of a disagreement in number (plural versus singular) between subject and verb often result from quick, careless writing.

A word that is said to be singular in number refers to only one person or thing, whereas a word that is plural in number refers to more than one person or thing.

Singular	Plural
check	checks
this	these
loan	loans
client	clients

Remember these two basic rules:

1. Singular subjects take singular verbs.

    The check is here.
    This is unsatisfactory.
    The loan is adequate.
    The client coughs a great deal.

2. Plural subjects take plural verbs.

> The checks are here.
> These are unsatisfactory.
> The loans are adequate.
> The clients cough a great deal.

In a simple sentence, making subjects and verbs agree is not too difficult. But when a phrase appears between the subject and the verb or a word whose number you are unsure of is in a sentence, it becomes more difficult.

Remember that the verb must always agree with the subject. No matter how many words separate the subject and the verb, check to make sure they agree.

> The cancellation was final.
> The cancellation of the contracts was final.

Even though "contracts" would take a plural verb if it were the subject of the sentence, it only modifies a singular subject in the sentence above. "Cancellation" is still the subject, so you still use a singular verb.

When you use an indefinite pronoun as the subject of a sentence, it is sometimes difficult to tell whether the pronoun is singular or plural. Some take a singular verb while others take a plural.

These indefinite pronouns take a singular verb:

> anybody
> anyone
> each
> either
> everybody
> everyone
> neither
> no one
> one
> somebody
> someone

These indefinite pronouns take a plural verb:

> both
> few
> many
> several

With the following indefinite pronouns you must judge from the context of the sentence whether to use a singular or plural verb:

> all
> any
> most
> none
> some

For example:

1. All of the secretaries *are* talented.
   All of the money *is* green.

2. Any desk *is* fine.
   Are any of the proceedings to be taped?
3. Most of my days *are* busy.
   Most of my dinner *is* cold.
4. None of the stores *were* open.
   None of the ledger *was* saved.
5. Some of our orders *are* processed incorrectly.
   Some of the order book *is* missing.

Another simple rule to remember is that *compound subjects always take a plural verb*.

Mr. Hemingway has arrived.
Mr. Hemingway and Mr. Grimes have arrived.

When "or" or "nor" connects the two subjects, however, a singular verb is used.

Neither Mr. Hemingway nor Mr. Grimes has arrived.

If you carefully check to make sure that the subjects and verbs of the sentences you write agree in number, you will most likely not make any errors. Sometimes, however, when it is difficult to determine whether a singular or plural verb should be used, a quick reference to my pointers above or a grammar book will set you straight.

Dangling Modifiers

When a phrase doesn't clearly refer to the word it is modifying, it is said to be "dangling." The sentence

Preoccupied with the business negotiation, her secretary surprised her.

is unclear. What does the phrase, "preoccupied with the business negotiation," modify? It is a dangling modifier. It appears to modify "secretary," but it's more likely that it's meant to modify the "her" of the sentence. A word that the modifier can refer to sensibly in the sentence is needed:

Because she was preoccupied with the business negotiation, she was surprised
by her secretary.

When you write a sentence that contains a modifying phrase, always make sure that it clearly modifies what it is supposed to. Most dangling modifiers result from carelessness. You can usually tell after a careful proofreading of your letter whether or not the sentences you have written make sense.

Split Infinitives

Splitting infinitives is not always wrong. Some people will go to such great lengths to make sure infinitives are not split that the sentences they write are awkwardly constructed.

As a rule of thumb, you should not split an infinitive when the splitting results in an awkwardly constructed sentence. For example, the infinitive "to pass" is awkwardly split in the following sentence:

The legislation is the proper one to, whether or not you approve of deficit
spending, pass in the upcoming session.

A better way to write the above sentence is:

> Whether or not you approve of deficit spending, the legislation is the proper one to pass in the upcoming session.

If splitting an infinitive is less awkward than leaving it intact, however, it is acceptable to split it. For example:

> For the client *to* never *lose* is unusual.

Parallel Structure

Probably the most common error involving parallel structure occurs with lists. When you write a sentence that consists of a list or series of items, make sure they are written in the same grammatical form. The use of parallel structure makes your writing more consistent and clearer to your reader.

> Faculty parallel structure: To sell her proposal, the marketing director presented her marketing plan, asked for reactions to her presentation, and many other things to involve her audience.

> Better: To sell her proposal, the marketing director *presented* her marketing plan, *asked* for reactions to her presentation, and *did* many things to involve her audience.

> Faulty parallel structure: The personnel director was requested to handle terminations of employees as well as writing commendations.

> Better: The personnel director was requested *to handle* terminations of employees as well as *to write* commendations.

Faulty parallel structure can be corrected no matter what part of speech the items in a series are. The important thing to remember is to be consistent with the grammatical form you use for writing items in a series.

Usage

From time to time you've probably read a letter and thought that the way in which the person has worded whatever he or she has said didn't sound correct. The standard that sets how we speak or write as educated people is called "usage."

Usage guides us in the correct way of writing. Usage is not static. What is accepted as correct today may be obsolete fifty years from now. Slang words that might not even have been created yet may be acceptable to use as good English ten or fifteen years from now. To write effectively, you should be aware of current English usage.

One of the classic books on usage is William Strunk Jr. and E. B. White's *The Elements of Style*. Although there are more thorough usage references available, such as Theodore M. Bernstein's *The Careful Writer,* Strunk and White's book is straightforward, simple to use, and helpful as a reference on any professional's desk. (See the Bibliography for more about usage references.)

Some words are commonly misused by many letter writers. You will find a list of some of them in Appendix I.

Punctuation

Punctuation is used in writing to distinguish or separate one group of words from another to convey some meaning to a reader. The use of punctuation creates pauses and stresses where the writer feels they are necessary.

Appendix II goes over various aspects of punctuation that will help you use it correctly and effectively in your letter writing.

The most important thing about punctuation is using it consistently. Ralph Waldo Emerson might have thought that "foolish consistency is the hobgoblin of little minds," but you can rest assured that consistency in the use of punctuation is not foolish. It helps to clarify your message to your reader. By the same token, avoid overpunctuation; it impedes understanding.

Capitalization

Capitalization is another area that calls for consistency. Obviously you should capitalize the beginning of sentences as well as proper nouns and proper adjectives. There are, however, many quirks to the proper use of capitalization. When in doubt, it is usually best to lowercase or to check a reference such as a dictionary. For a discussion of proper capitalization within the various letter formats, see Chapter 4.

Spelling

Many books have been written to help writers with spelling problems. Most often, however, the best help is a dictionary. To avoid careless spelling mistakes, a writer should look up those words about which he or she has the slightest doubt. The two best tools to guard against spelling errors in your letters are care in writing and a dictionary at your side.

Most word processing software packages feature a "spellcheck" function. If you have any doubts about your spelling ability, a spellcheck can be a saving grace. It will highlight any misspelled words and help you choose a correctly spelled alternative. Spellchecks will not, however, catch misused words (e.g., *cat* for *can* or *lamb* for *lamp*). A careful proofreading is still the best guard against misuse.

Jargon

Jargon is a curse to any writer who wants to get a clear, precise message across to a reader. The word "jargon" has two meanings. The first is "incoherent language." The second is "the technical language of a profession." Usually both of these types of jargon should be avoided in letter writing. Of course the first, incoherent language, must be avoided at all costs. Technical language should be kept to a minimum in your letters to avoid confusing your reader.

A person who writes jargon is usually more impressed with the way the words sound than with getting a message across. You are writing to convey a message, not to impress your reader with how many big words you know. People who write in lofty language or jargon will often string together complex words that sound great but mean nothing.

Avoid pretension and strive for clarity in your letter writing. Forget about using jargon.

Use simple language if you can. Your reader will appreciate it.

Clichés

Clichés are words or expressions that become stale from overuse. Clichés often take the form of metaphors or comparisons, such as "big as an ox" or "slept like a log." They are trite and show a lack of originality in writing.

In business, expressions such as "put on the back burner" and "caught between a rock and a hard place" have been used so often that they can be considered clichés. Nothing is grammatically wrong with these trite expressions. They are just so stale that they really have lost the power to convey much meaning to the reader.

Avoid clichés by writing exactly what you want to convey. Make every word in your letters mean something. After you've written your first draft, clarify your message by deleting any clichés or trite expressions.

Be original in your letter writing. If you need to make a comparison, try to make an original one. Avoid drawing from the stock of clichés that have been used for years.

Wordiness

In Chapter 2, I warned that if you don't write what you mean, your writing will be full of ambiguity. I can't emphasize this point too much. Write what you mean, not what you think sounds good.

The following pointers may be helpful in guiding you away from the curse of wordiness. Remember the following "five avoids" and you will be on your way to writing in a clear, direct style:

1. *Avoid pretentiousness.* Don't overcomplicate your writing by trying to impress the reader with your vocabulary or your great literary style. Write simply, clearly, and directly.
2. *Avoid redundancy.* Don't use superfluous or repetitious words. Write what your reader needs to know and he or she will most likely get the message. There is no need to repeat your message over and over.
3. *Avoid padding.* Be direct in your letter writing. Strike out all unnecessary words or sentences. If you write more than you have to your reader might become impatient. Strive for clarity and precision.
4. *Avoid weak intensifiers.* Words like "very," "quite," and "completely" usually add little or nothing to the meaning of your sentences.
5. *Avoid unnecessary definitions or explanations.* Explain only what absolutely needs to be explained. Don't insult your reader by explaining something he or she obviously would already know.

Revisions can help you eliminate any problem with wordiness you may be having. In the revision process you should (1) reread the letter to make sure you've said what you wanted to say; (2) edit out all unnecessary words and phrases; and (3) clarify until your letter is precise enough to get the proper message across.

CHAPTER 6
Word Processing

Try as some might to fight it, the day of the word processor has arrived. What many have found, much to their surprise, is that word processors actually can simplify work without taking away any of the user's individuality or creativity.

Typing Skills Are Key

The biggest difficulty for many first-time users of word processors is not learning how to turn on the machine, nor is it formatting a disk or learning how to boot the system. For many users, the most difficult aspect is never having learned to type. Perhaps this is why many writers, although they fought the age of the computer as much as any other group, have been admirably successful in getting up to speed on word processing skills. They already knew how to type.

Using the Machine

Some argue that because word processors are computers, it is essential to learn how the computer works to be able to use it effectively. This includes learning to program and presumably learning how to add a chip or two to the inside of the machine should you want to upgrade its capabilities. While those who wish to tackle this endeavor have admirable ambitions, I am among those who hold to the argument, "I'm not really concerned with how it works. I just want to be able to use it."

I have a coffee maker that I can time to brew the coffee just before I wake up in the morning or just around the time I think my dinner guests may want a cup of coffee. But I don't have any idea how the timing mechanism in the machine works. All I know is that I put the coffee, filter, and water in the machine, press a few buttons, and I'll have coffee when I set the timer to make it.

It's similar with my computer. I know how to get it to do what I want it to do, but I've very little idea about what a chip is made from, or how all the boards inside the computer are wired.

Word Processing Software

As those of you who have been using word processors for some time already know, as you use your machine more and more you will learn new things. Barry, the salesman who sold me my machine, kept telling me about the learning curve that's

42

implicit in learning how to use a word processor. In the first several months of using a machine, you'll learn more and more and more. But after six months, you'll know probably 80 percent of what you'll ever have to know to use the machine as a word processor.

There are many different types of word processing software packages available. While some may be more frequently used than others, if you are in a larger business, the chances are you'll probably be subjected to the software that someone else chose. While some software packages are easier to use than others because their instructional literature is more clearly written, they don't involve many multiple key hits to get the software to do something, or their bells and whistles are fancier, most word processing packages will get the job done when you want to use them for letter writing.

Using Model Letters

The same letter is often written to different business customers. Rather than retype the letter every time you want to use it, you can store those letters you use frequently on a computer disk and call a letter up each time the appropriate situation to send it out arises.

Take, for example, the letter in Sample Letter 6.1, which is sent to a customer when a new account is opened. Rather than have the same letter retyped each time a customer opens a new account, you can simply call up the letter from a master file of letters you have stored, either on a floppy or hard disk, and tailor it to reflect the particular situation. Since most word processing software packages feature what is called a "mail merge" function, you can often simply type in a coded name and address, instruct the machine which letter you want it attached to, and create a custom-tailored letter.

SAMPLE LETTER 6.1.   New-account thank-you letter.

May 9, 19X8

Ms. Kate McGuffie
Vice President
McGuffie-Modugno Enterprises
43 Fletcher Street
Punxatawney, Pennsylvania 43434

Dear Ms. McGuffie:

Thank you for opening your charge account at Elite Garment Shop. We will mail your monthly account statements, which will provide you with current outstanding charges and interest charge information.

We value your business and will do our best to give you accurate and responsive service. Please call me at 382-5968 or use our toll-free number, 1-800-266-6866, if you need additional assistance or information.

Sincerely,

Alan Maxil
Senior Vice President

am/js

There are dozens of letters in this book that are suitable for tailoring to your needs and storing on a master disk for frequent use. Since each business' needs are different, you'll want to go through the letters to determine which ones are appropriate for storage in your system.

Remember, however, that one of the goals of letter writing is to give the impression that there is an actual person writing the letter specifically to the person addressed. Simply printing out the same letter to customer after customer is not always appropriate. There are other solutions.

For instance, one newly formed business decided to create a "private" file and a "public" file on its computer system. The company "networked" five personal computers together to a hard disk. Each terminal user can access anything on the public file. But if that user wants to tailor a letter or memo to reflect his or her personality, or to add specific items he or she believes to be necessary, or just to duplicate a few paragraphs to be used in a different letter, the user can copy the document from a public file onto a private file, which can be accessed only if the user types a personal code into the system. No one else can tamper with the changes that person made in his or her private file. But each user has access to whatever model letters are stored in the public file. The user is able not only to use a model letter, but also to add a personal touch.

This system is particularly useful with form letters. In the past, form letters included multiple paragraphs, covering all contingencies, and the sender checked off those paragraphs that applied to the situation. Now, letters can be individually tailored, with only the relevant paragraphs included. The result will be a letter that is shorter and easier to understand.

One of the critical things to remember about word processing is that no matter how proficient you become with the machine, it is not a substitute for good writing. The letters you send out will not be magically transformed into good prose by the mere fact that you are using an expensive machine to create or retrieve them. The letters you retrieve will only be as good as the letters that were stored in your system in the first place.

Word processing may not be the answer for every professional who reads this book. For those who wish to use it as a book of model letters on which to base their own, this book will prove very useful.

But for those who are committed to automating their offices and increasing their efficiency without losing their personal touch, *The AMA Handbook of Business Letters* should prove a helpful tool when it comes to setting up a database of frequently used model letters that can be called up by all users and tailored to particular needs.

PART II
THE LETTERS

A basic structural design underlies every kind of
writing. The writer will in part follow this design, in
part deviate from it, according to his skill, his
needs, and the unexpected events that accompany
the act of composition.

William Strunk, Jr., and E. B. White
From *The Elements of Style*

You have learned the basics. From planning and structure to appearance and grammar and usage, you have learned what it takes to write a good letter.

Part II of *The AMA Handbook of Business Letters* takes you a step further. In Chapters 7 through 17 you will see the basics of letter writing at work in more than 270 business letters.

These letters, which show you the application of the basics discussed in Part I, were chosen for two major reasons. First, this sampling of letters gives you access to many of the more common letters written in everyday business. Second, the letters are particularly well written examples upon which you can model your own letters.

Many of the letters in Part II can be used as form letters or as prototypes on a word processing system (see Chapter 6). If names, numbers, and addresses are changed in these letters, they can be used for many different customers.

All of the letters in Part II are models of good letters. By reading them you will learn how effective letters in various business settings should be written.

The captions to each of the sample letters give you a concise description of their purpose. The narrative interspersed among the letters gives you a brief analysis of each letter's strong points.

I don't expect many readers to diligently read through every sample letter in every chapter of Part II. Read those sample letters that can best help you improve or increase the scope of your letter writing. Study them and, if you apply the basics learned in Part I, you'll be well on your way to writing better, more effective letters.

CHAPTER 7
Sales, Marketing, and Public Relations Letters

The object of a sales, marketing, or public relations letter is to elicit a positive response from your reader toward the product or service you are trying to market. Successful sales, marketing, and public relations letters must therefore grab readers' attention and convince them that your product or services will satisfy their needs or desires.

Use a friendly, personal tone. Customers, whether they are consumers or business users, crave personal attention, and a very formal letter suggests just the opposite.

While all the letters in Part II could be considered sales and marketing letters in the broad sense that they are trying to convince a reader to take some sort of action, the letters in this chapter are sales and marketing letters in a more literal sense. They were written specifically to market a product or service to the reader.

Letters of Introduction

Sample Letters 7.1 through 7.5 are all forms of letters introducing salespeople or companies.

Sample Letter 7.1 was written by a salesman to an existing customer informing him that the salesman is being promoted and will be replaced by a new saleswoman. The current salesman comes right to the point in announcing his promotion and replacement. He then seeks to set up an appointment with the customer so the customer can meet the new saleswoman. Finally, he expresses his confidence in his replacement, stressing the service she will continue to give the customer's business.

SAMPLE LETTER 7.1.   Letter introducing new salesperson (full-block format).

May 10, 19X7

Mr. Lawrence Volpe, Treasurer
Boonton Medical Center
100 Harlan Drive
Milwaukee, Wisconsin 54321

Dear Mr. Volpe:

Last week I mentioned to you that I am being promoted to vice president at Gleechie Medical Equipment Supply Company. Taking over my territory as your sales representative will be Felicia Mamet. Felicia has been with Gleechie for four years in our Indiana office.

Felicia and I will be in your area on May 25 and 26. We would like to take some time on one of those two evenings to take you and Mark McIntyre to dinner and a baseball game. I'm hoping that this will give both of you the chance to get to know Felicia.

Larry, Felicia is my handpicked replacement. I know she will give Boonton Medical Center the attention it deserves. I have little doubt that you will be pleased with my choice.

I look forward to hearing from you to confirm our meeting.

Best regards,

Ambrose Kemper
Sales Representative

AK:js

cc: Mark McIntyre
    Felicia Mamet

    Sample Letter 7.2 was written by a new sales representative to an existing customer. Like Sample Letter 7.1, the letter immediately gets to the point by introducing the new salesperson and explaining who she will be replacing. The writer goes on to instruct the customer how she may get in touch with the salesperson and expresses a desire to set up a meeting so the two can become acquainted.

SAMPLE LETTER 7.2.   Letter from new salesperson (block format).

January 29, 19X1

Ms. Patsy Palay
Palay Sporting Goods
139 Howard Place
Carfer, West Virginia 26000

Dear Ms. Palay:

I am your new Glorious Racquets sales representative. I arrived in the
territory about a month ago and have been working with my predecessor,
Bob Sheffield, to familiarize myself with both the territory and all of the
dealers in it.

If you should ever need to reach me when I am on the road, feel free to
have me paged. The phone number for my paging service is 617-222-3232.
To have me paged:

>   Dial the pager number on a touch-tone telephone.
>   When you hear the tone, punch in your telephone number.
>   After you have entered your number, push the pound (#) button.
>   Hang up your telephone.

Your message will be transmitted to my pager. You can also call my
personal extension at Glorious Racquets, which is 222-2345, and leave a
message for me.

I look forward to meeting you and all of the people at Palay Sporting
Goods. I'll call soon to set up a mutually convenient meeting time. Thanks
for your patience in the transition to a new sales representative.

Cordially,

Bethany J. Cole
Sales Representative

bjc:nlc

Sample Letters 7.3 through 7.5 all introduce companies to customers. Sample
Letter 7.3 introduces a new company to a customer. The writer announces the new
company in the opening paragraph and spends the rest of the letter detailing the

company's chief employees, the desire to provide services to the reader, and the desire to set up a meeting with the reader.

Sample Letter 7.4 was written to a prospective customer by an existing company official. In the letter she explains what the company does and how it might benefit the reader. The letter elaborates on specific services provided as well as services that may be of particular interest to the party addressed.

Sample Letter 7.5 also introduces an existing company, but this letter is sent as a follow-up to a brief meeting. Like the earlier letters, this one gets right to the point by clearly indicating why it is written—to inquire about the recipient's public relations needs. The letter continues with a brief description of the writer's company, indicates that a press kit is enclosed with the letter, and closes by stating that the writer will get in touch with the reader.

SAMPLE LETTER 7.3.   Letter introducing new company (full-block format).

February 26, 19X8

Mr. Adam Leigh
186 Alpine Rock Road
Boston, Massachusetts 02125

Dear Adam:

I've enclosed a copy of our new corporate image brochure for our financial planning company. New Bedford Financial Planning Services Inc. provides complete financial planning consulting services through our staff of 50 financial services professionals.

The individuals who run this company have extensive experience in all forms of financial planning. They and other senior staff members have done financial planning for some of the country's largest corporations, including: Mom's Bagel Company, General Hospital, Broughton & Brady Corporation, STL Hotels, and a host of others. They have also completed financial planning services for many fast-growing small to midsize companies.

Adam, we would be pleased to provide whatever financial planning services you may need or, even on short notice, we will be pleased to offer you competitive quotations for your entire financial planning program or any portion of it. We are certain that we can earn the privilege of being your financial planning provider if you give us the chance to compete.

At your convenience I would like to introduce you to some of the key members of our staff. Please let me hear from you if you'd like to find out more about New Bedford Financial Planning Services and what we can offer you.

Regards,

Quentin Compson
President

QC/js

Enclosure

SAMPLE LETTER 7.4.   Letter introducing existing company and its services (semiblock format).

March 23, 19X7

Ms. Eliza Gruber
Long & Berrigan
200 Andover Street
Bar Harbor, Michigan 67892

Dear Ms. Gruber:

I am pleased to enclose a copy of a recently published "tombstone" advertisement covering selected corporate finance transactions completed during the past year by our corporate finance department. As indicated in the advertisement, we provided a variety of services to our Michigan public and private clients, including:

1. Underwriting common stock and debt offerings
2. Handling private placement of debt securities
3. Managing corporate sales and acquisitions
4. Providing financial advice, including opinion letters, in connection with various other merger and acquisition and leveraged buyout transactions

As you may know, our company is one of the securities industry's largest and most preeminent international firms. The objective of our Detroit corporate finance department is to combine the capital resources and specialized skills residing within the firm with the financial expertise and experience of the Detroit department to provide an exceptional level of corporate finance service to Michigan public and private companies. The advertisement reflects the diversity of our activities during 1986.

Ms. Eliza Gruber   - 2 -   March 23, 19X7

   I thought you would find this advertisement and the introduction to
our Detroit corporate finance department to be of interest. We would
welcome the opportunity to become acquainted with you and your
company and to be of service in achieving your corporate and financing
objectives. The objectives for the management of a company such as yours,
which has gone public during the past several years, may include:

1. Raising additional equity or long-term debt capital to support
   continued corporate growth
2. Pursuing growth through selected acquisitions
3. Increasing corporate exposure to the institutional and retail
   investment community

   Please don't hesitate to call me if we can be helpful to you in any way.
I look forward to discussing any aspects of our activities of particular
interest to you, as well as any other issue in which we may be of
assistance.

                         Kindest regards,

                         Susan Crooms
                         Vice President

SC/mn

Enclosure

SAMPLE LETTER 7.5.   Short letter introducing existing company (simplified format) as follow-up to brief meeting.

August 14, 19X7

Peter Velasquez
President
Commonwealth Pro Systems
54 Garland Drive
Hamilton, California 00012

PUBLIC RELATIONS NEEDS OF COMMONWEALTH PRO SYSTEMS

Not too long ago I had a brief discussion with Jennifer Silex about your company's public relations needs. Commonwealth Pro is certainly an exciting company with an interesting history. It's a public relations professional's dream.

I thought it might be appropriate to introduce my company to you to consider, should you decide to enhance your current marketing program with public relations. Berenson Public Relations specializes in marketing for clients in the sporting goods industry.

I've enclosed our press kit. It will help familiarize you with us. After you've had time to look through the enclosed material, I would like to make an appointment to meet with you and Rhonda Berringer, your marketing director.

Thank you, in advance, for your time. I'll call next week to arrange an appointment at your earliest possible convenience.

MACK NESINE
PRESIDENT

Enclosure

mn/ph

Sales Letters

Sample Letters 7.6 through 7.19 are all directly selling something.

Sample Letter 7.6 was written to sell a consumer product. The writer makes a special offer to a previous customer. The offer is established in the first paragraph of the letter, followed by suggestions about how to take advantage of it. The writer winds up the letter cross-selling other products the company offers, backs up her offer with the company's money-back guarantee, and closes with the date by which the offer must be taken. By being direct, enthusiastic, and personable in the letter, the writer clearly gets her sales point across to the prospective consumer.

Sample Letter 7.7 was written to sell a business product. The author of the letter makes clear what he is selling in the first two paragraphs of the letter. The next paragraphs detail the features of the product and spell out its convenience and results-oriented nature. The writer then offers the reader a no-risk trial period, and closes with a reminder to order the product today.

Sample Letter 7.8 was written to sell a consumer service. Like the earlier product sales letters, the author here clearly establishes what is being sold in the first paragraph. The next paragraph emphasizes the competitive qualities of the service and the convenient method of signing up. The letter closes by referring to an enclosed brochure and encouraging the reader to call and sign up now.

SAMPLE LETTER 7.6.   Letter selling consumer product (full-block format).

May 12, 19X9

Warren Laylor
78 Andover Street
Alabaster, Kansas 90909

Dear Mr. Laylor:

Because you're a valued customer, I've been authorized to make you this very special offer:

> For a limited time only, you can save 50% when you buy 4 pairs of Slacks Favorites slightly imperfect men's slacks!

That's right. Usually you save 40% when you buy 4 pairs of slightly imperfects. But we've slashed our prices, so now you pay only half the normal first-quality price.

Take advantage of these low prices to try some spring and summer favorites like Slacks Favorites Cotton Twills at only $22.99 per pair, or Summer Slacks at just $19.99 per pair. With prices this low, you can try several different colors to go with every conceivable outfit.

Page 2
Warren Laylor
May 12, 19X9

And it's the perfect time for you to stock up on your favorite slacks styles, like:

Slacks Favorites all cotton work pants   only $15.99 per pair.

Slacks Favorites cotton/polyester blend dress slacks—only $17.99 per pair.

Slacks Favorites bestselling durable casuals—only $18.99 per pair.

Remember Slacks Favorites, Inc. guarantees your satisfaction—no matter what. If you are not completely satisfied, just return the item for a full refund or replacement, whichever you prefer.

I only have authority to extend these special half-off prices through July 31, 19X9, so I urge you not to delay. Order now and stock up on your favorite Slacks Favorites styles at these super-saver prices.

Sincerely,

Lorraine Gabor
Vice President, Marketing

ls

enc.

SAMPLE LETTER 7.7.   Letter selling business product (full-block format).

November 9, 19X8

Mr. John Hill
327 Richmond Avenue
San Diego, California 90006

Dear Mr. Hill:

The AMA Handbook of Business Letters contains virtually every business letter you'll ever need to write—more than 270 model business letters in all.

Page 2
Mr. John Hill
November 9, 19X8

The new edition of The AMA Handbook of Business Letters shows you how
to write effective letters and memos that get the results you want. By
taking advantage of our 15-day free trial offer, you can see those results
immediately.

You'll get dozens of new sales, marketing, and customer service letters that
are ready to use. The AMA Handbook of Business Letters covers the broad
range of correspondence handled in almost every business setting. There
are tools for salespeople, personnel directors, secretaries, and managers.
This convenient and comprehensive guide will help you, your staff, and
your colleagues write results-oriented letters quickly and correctly.

These are actual letters used by businesses that are proven effective. Each
sample was selected for its ability to generate positive results, as well as
for its use of language and correct format and grammatical structure.

A brand new section in this edition shows you how to use a word
processor and make short work of routine correspondence by setting up
your own database of frequently used letters. You'll also learn how to tailor
form letters that make it easier for your customers to respond to your
requests.

In addition to the many sample letters, The AMA Handbook of Business
Letters provides information on the fundamentals of good letter writing—
from planning and formatting to phrasing and closing letters. You'll learn
techniques that enhance and improve communication and make all of
your correspondence more effective.

The appendixes are packed with practical aids that are useful to all letter
writers—the Grammar Hotline Directory, tips on correct usage of
commonly confused words, rules of punctuation, and a list of abbreviations
used in business.

The AMA Handbook of Business Letters is convenient, comprehensive, and
can help you get the results you want from your letters and memos.

Send for your 15-day free examination copy today. Just mail in the
enclosed order card to receive your copy. Use it for 15 days and see for
yourself how much time you save and how easy it is to write letters that
produce positive results.

You are under no obligation to purchase the book during the examination
period. If you are not convinced that it will improve the quality of your
writing and save you time, simply return the book to us and owe nothing.

Page 3
Mr. John Hill
November 9, 19X8

Should you decide to keep the book, approve the invoice for $49 plus shipping and handling.

Start getting the response you want from your letters and improve your communication skills by ordering your copy of The AMA Handbook of Business Letters today.

Sincerely,

Maury Notches
Publisher

jls

Enclosure

SAMPLE LETTER 7.8.   Letter selling consumer service (semiblock format).

March 31, 19X8

Mr. Jack Wagner
456 Allegheny Road
Southside, New Jersey 09090

Dear Mr. Wagner:

There is not a single reason why you should now be using Blotto Laundry Service. Because anything Blotto can do, Spotless Laundry's professionals can do better—for less. And if you switch to Spotless before April 30, 19X8, you'll receive a free week of laundry service.

Why would you want to pay the high cost of Blotto's weekly pickup and delivery service? Come over to Spotless. You'll get the best laundry service at the best price and you won't give up a thing.

Our complete fleet of trucks operated by professional drivers will give you the service you deserve. Our brand new state-of-the-art industrial

Page 2
Mr. Jack Wagner
March 31, 19X8

laundry facilities increase the efficiency of our operations, allowing us to give you the highest quality service at the lowest prices available.

Spotless Laundry is fully equipped to provide all the services you'd expect—even morning pickup and same afternoon delivery. And our quarterly billing plan is the ultimate in making it easy for you to pay for the service without receiving a pile of bills every week.

Rest assured that once you sign on with Spotless, there'll be no interruption of your laundry service and no inconvenience to you whatsoever.

Read the brochure enclosed with this letter. It includes our menu of services and prices. Then return the authorization form without delay so you don't miss out on our special offer of a free week of laundry service.

Better yet, get Spotless quality, savings, and service right now by calling us toll-free. We're waiting to hear from you at 1-800-776-8537.

Sincerely,

Beverly G. Krauss
Vice President
Sales and Marketing

bgk/lls

Enclosure

Sample Letter 7.9 was written to sell a business service. Unlike the previous product and service sales letters, here the author decides to create the perceived need in the reader's mind before even mentioning the company's name. While it is clear from the opening paragraph the type of service being sold, the first two paragraphs are used to raise questions in the reader's mind. In paragraph 3, the writer presents his service as the solution to the customer's problems. The letter continues to elaborate on the company's no-risk guarantee and its specialization with the reader's type of business, and closes with a special offer.

Sample Letter 7.10 was written to sell a subscription to a publication. To get the reader's attention, the writer used the hanging-indented format, a letter format used almost exclusively for sales letters as an attention-getting device. The writer here pulls no punches, but gets right to the subscription offer in the first paragraph. In the first four paragraphs, the writer clearly explains the offer to the reader. In the closing paragraph he reminds the reader that the offer is for a limited time so she should reply today. Like the earlier sales letters, Sample Letter 7.10 does not try to sell by bamboozling the reader with an array of sales offers. Sales letters work best when the reader knows what is being offered, how it can help him or her, and how to take advantage of the offer.

Sample Letter 7.11 is a brief letter selling a subscription renewal to a subscriber. Paragraph 1 explains the letter's purpose. Paragraph 2 highlights some benefits of renewing soon. And paragraph 3 explains how to renew.

SAMPLE LETTER 7.9.   Letter selling business service (semiblock format).

May 20, 19X8

Ms. Beatrice Alexandria
Office Manager
Pixadiddle & McCormick, Inc.
34 Runter Road
Luckier, New Mexico 34321

Dear Ms. Alexandria:

Have you ever wondered why every time your copy machine goes on the blink your copier service company's phone is busy or the repairperson won't be able to get to your business for at least a week?

If your company is like most, every lost day of your copying capabilities can spell headaches, delays, and increased expenses from having to send materials out to be copied.

Rest easy. Anderson Copy Repair guarantees you that when you use us as your copier service company, we'll be there when you need us with the solutions to your copier problems. Our trained staff of service repairpeople has years of experience under its belts, experience that gets your machine off the blink and back into A-1 condition.

What's more, there's no risk that you will be without a machine for long. While our servicepeople are servicing your machine, we'll provide you with a temporary machine until yours is up and going. Most repairs will take less than an hour. But just in case, there will be a top-of-the-line machine at your disposal.

Anderson Copy Repair specializes in servicing small businesses like yours. I've enclosed a partial list of our current clients. Feel free to check our reputation with any of them. I think you'll find the response is unanimous praise.

Page 2
May 20, 19X8
Ms. Beatrice Alexandria

As a special offer to new customers, we are offering a 6-month contract for copy repair service at our 3-month rates. But the offer's only good if you sign up by May 31. Simply fill out the enclosed postage paid card, mail it back to us, and we'll get you started on worry-free copier service.

Act now to get the special introductory offer.

Sincerely,

Ralph L. Anderson

rla/jls

enc.

SAMPLE LETTER 7.10.   Letter selling a subscription (hanging-indented format).

December 21, 19X7

Ms. Jane Kinneally
1978 Malden Place
Summit, New Jersey 01005

Dear Ms. Kinneally:

For a very limited time—and only to a select, qualified group—I'm
    authorized to send the next issue of The Armchair Reader's Review
    absolutely free.

Reply by March 1, 19X8, and you'll receive—without risk or obligation—
    the one publication dedicated to giving the inside knowledge on the
    latest in economic developments.

Mail the enclosed postage paid reservation card by March 1, 19X8, and the
    next issue of The Armchair Reader's Review is your free. At the same
    time, we'll reserve in your name a full-year's subscription at a special
    introductory rate.

When you receive your free issue, read it and then decide. If you can do without The Armchair Reader's Review, write "cancel" on the bill when it comes. You'll owe nothing. Your first issue will be your last. Or you can pay just $11.95 for 11 more issues—saving $24.05 off the newsstand price—and enjoy the insight that each monthly issue of The Armchair Reader's Review delivers.

Remember that this is a special offer good for a limited time only. Please reply today.

Cordially,

Mark Naddes
Publisher

MN:JS

Enclosure

SAMPLE LETTER 7.11.   Letter selling subscription renewal (block format).

May 20, 19X1

Mr. Erik Hane
1045 Snarcross Plaza
Roswell, Georgia 11583

Dear Mr. Hane:

Our message to you is brief, but important: Your The Armchair Reader's Review subscription will expire soon and we haven't heard from you about renewing.

We're sure you don't want to miss even one issue. Renew now to ensure that your subscription will continue uninterrupted. You'll guarantee yourself continued delivery of the excellent features, fiction, and insight that make The Armchair Reader's Review the fastest growing journal in America.

To make it as easy as possible for you to act now, we've enclosed a pencil for you to complete the postage-paid reply card enclosed. Simply send back the card today and you'll continue to receive your monthly issue of The Armchair Reader's Review without any interruptions.

                                        Best regards,

                                        Thomas Strout
                                        Circulation Director

TS/ny

Enclosure

Sample Letter 7.12 was written to welcome a new subscriber to a publication. It could be written as a follow-up to a successful subscription sales letter. The letter briefly welcomes the new subscriber, asks her to check her invoice for accuracy, and instructs her of the procedure for forwarding or holding her publication should she be out of town for any period of time. By showing a concern for the subscriber and letting her know how the system works, the publisher builds goodwill and subscription renewals are more likely.

   Sample Letter 7.13 was written to sell an educational seminar. Since seminars are intangible, the writer sells the benefits of attending the seminar. The first paragraph briefly paints the scenario of a time when the content of this particular seminar is more important than ever. It is followed by a paragraph announcing that a seminar is here to address the complex issues recounted in the opening paragraph. The close allows the prospective attendee to have a say in some of the issues covered. Being responsive to the customer's needs is the cornerstone of successful sales.

SAMPLE LETTER 7.12.   Letter welcoming new subscriber (full-block format).

August 23, 19X7

Ms. Jane Thomson
Brian, David & Lauren, Inc.
55 Congregation Drive
Boonton, Massachusetts 12543

Dear Ms. Thomson:

We're delighted to welcome you as a subscriber to The Armchair Reader's Review.

Please take a moment to review the enclosed invoice to make sure we have recorded your name and address properly. If any corrections are necessary, please make the changes on the portion of the invoice you return with your payment.

If you plan to be away for a month or longer, we will be glad to change your address label so you'll receive The Armchair Reader's Review at your temporary address. Delivery can always be suspended for a week or so while you are away and started again when you return. We'll credit your subscription so you receive every issue you've paid for. Let us know about three weeks before you leave and we'll make the necessary arrangements to ensure that you receive the Review when you want it where you want it.

Thank you for your subscription. We are glad to be able to serve you.

Sincerely,

Yvonne Surrene
Associate Publisher

ys/nw

Enclosure

SAMPLE LETTER 7.13. Letter selling an educational seminar (block format).

May 2, 19X8

Mr. Samuel Johnson
Auditor
Missoula Accounting Services
Missoula, Montana 89898

Dear Mr. Johnson:

Never before have accountants faced so many compliance issues. Countless questions have arisen and often accountants have difficulty knowing where to turn for correct answers to these questions.

To meet that challenge of compliance, you should plan to attend the Tenth Annual Southwest Accountants Group Compliance Seminar. Our compliance committee has developed a program that will answer many of your questions and help you establish personal contacts for future assistance.

We have also enclosed a survey form to determine the issues you would like covered in the afternoon session. Your responses will determine the make-up of that session. Complete the form and send it back with your registration.

We look forward to your participation.

Sincerely,

Jim Boswell, Chairman
SAG Seminar Committee

jb/js

Enc.

Sample Letters 7.14 through 7.19 are all sales letters that were written to market membership in one form of club or another.

Sample Letter 7.14 extends an offer of membership in a professional organiza-tion. It is written as a follow-up to an inquiry from a member of the profession. The letter acknowledges the inquiry, lists the services the professional will receive, details the costs of membership, and expresses a desire for the prospect to join the association.

Sample Letter 7.15 is written to a prospective member of a local professionals' organization. The letter is a follow-up to someone who attended one meeting as a guest. It is brief but to the point, expressing pleasure at having the prospective member attend the meeting, and offering him membership in the organization. Because the prospect attended a meeting, he has a fair idea of the type of issues that will be covered in the business club meetings, so a detailed analysis would be unnecessary.

In Sample Letter 7.16 the purpose is to sell membership in a local health club. First, the writer welcomes the reader to the community. In the first paragraph, he associates his health club with the community by expressing his fondness for the city. The next paragraph describes the benefits of the club. It is followed by an offer of special membership rates. The organization of the letter builds goodwill toward the customer and the community and leaves the reader with an impression that this organization really wants to serve her and her new community.

SAMPLE LETTER 7.14.   Letter extending membership (semiblock format).

September 21, 19X2

Mr. Joseph Y. Smith
Ventilating Experts
45 Archie Way
Elizabeth, Pennsylvania 34343

Dear Mr. Smith:

Thanks for your inquiry about membership in the Associated Ventilators of America. In the interests of providing more adequate services to AVA members, the National Plumbers Club has assimilated the AVA membership as a special division of NPC.

As a ventilation professional you will receive not only all of the NPC services, but also special market information and other news relating specifically to ventilation. You will also have an opportunity to be listed in the Plumbing Professionals Directory for a small fee.

If you wish to join the AVA division of the NPC, your dues will be $50, plus a one-time initiation fee of $15. A brochure describing the activities and services of the National Plumbers Club and an application form are enclosed. To qualify for the AVA division of NPC you must apply for professional membership.

If you have any further questions, please call on me. We look forward to having you as a member.

Best regards,

Bud Gener
Executive Director

bg/mn

Enclosures

SAMPLE LETTER 7.15.   Follow-up membership offer (block format).

March 12, 19X7

Mr. Rodney McDonnell
McDonnell Associates
11 Tepler Drive
South Zane, Illinois 45454

Dear Rodney:

It was a pleasure to see you at the South Zane Chamber of Commerce's
Business After Hours Club (BAHC) cohosted by South Zane Inn and the
East Zane Medical Group. The BAHC is one of our most successful
programs. It was created to provide a relaxed social atmosphere in which
our members can network with other professionals.

We have many more exciting new programs planned for our membership
during 19X7. We would love to have you as a member. I've enclosed an
application. If you have any questions, I'd be happy to talk with you.

I look forward to hearing from you.

Sincerely,

Zoe Nelson
Program Manager

zn/mn

enc.

SAMPLE LETTER 7.16. Letter selling membership in health center (semiblock format).

December 1, 19X1

Ms. Ellen P. Thrall
908 Visitation Drive
Hawthorne, Massachusetts 09087

Dear Ms. Thrall:

Welcome to Hawthorne. I sincerely hope that you will enjoy your new community. We at The Hawthorne Fitness Club feel that Hawthorne is a great place to live and work.

The Hawthorne Fitness Club has been part of this community for more than 25 years. Our facilities include two gyms, an Olympic-size swimming pool, two weight rooms (one especially designed for women), a Nautilus Center, locker rooms for men, women, and children, a jogging track, six racquetball and handball courts, four squash courts, an exercise studio, and a drop-in nursery and preschool center. We have more than 100 program offerings from which to choose.

To help you meet new friends and get started in a program of health, fun, and fitness, we are offering you a free 30-day family or individual membership. Just fill out the enclosed application, bring it to the Club, and receive your complimentary membership card and schedule of activities. Then you can begin to enjoy your new membership.

Again, welcome to the Hawthorne area. If you need additional information, please phone me at 555-6666.

Sincerely,

Simon Thorn
Executive Director

st/mn

Enc.

Sample Letter 7.17 was written as a follow-up to Sample Letter 7.16, offering congratulations to a new member for joining up. The letter opens with a repeat of the club's benefits and its commitment to helping its members.

Sample Letter 7.18 is a health club membership renewal letter. The letter's purpose is clearly stated in the opening paragraph. A reminder of the club's benefits follows. The methods of payment available are highlighted in the next paragraph. The final paragraph urges the member to continue to take advantage of the club's offerings.

Sample Letter 7.19 is a second membership renewal notice written as a follow-up to Sample Letter 7.18. The letter writer clearly states that he is reminding the member to renew, highlights in greater detail the methods of payment available, and reminds the member not to let her membership lapse so she can avoid paying the application fee again. Rather than giving a hard sell pressuring the member to renew, the writer makes it clear he wants the member to continue reaping the club's benefits and reminds her not only of the ease of paying but also of the consequences of letting her membership lapse.

SAMPLE LETTER 7.17.   Follow-up letter to 7.16 congratulating person on new membership (semiblock format).

January 1, 19X2

Ms. Ellen P. Thrall
908 Visitation Drive
Hawthorne, Massachusetts 09087

Dear Ms. Thrall:

Congratulations and welcome to a year of health, fun, and fitness as a new member of The Hawthorne Fitness Club. You're now one of the many individuals who have chosen The Hawthorne Fitness Club as the best way of feeling good through getting and staying fit, learning new skills, and simply having fun.

This year at the Club you can do it all. We look forward to helping you make good use of our facilities, try new programs, and meet new people. To help you make your program choices, please review the latest program schedule.

If at any time you have any questions, please feel free to call on me or any of our staff. The Club has earned its reputation as a "people place" because we're always listening to our members and making every effort to fulfill their needs and desires.

Sincerely,

Simon Thorn
Executive Director

st/mn

Enc.

SAMPLE LETTER 7.18.   Membership renewal letter (block format).

December 15, 19X2

Ms. Ellen P. Thrall
908 Visitation Drive
Hawthorne, Massachusetts 09087

Dear Ms. Thrall:

It's time to renew your membership at The Hawthorne Fitness Club. To keep yourself in top condition—physically, mentally, emotionally—to look good and feel good, you know there's no better way than the Club.

We offer you modern, clean, and well-equipped facilities, a friendly staff all dedicated to offering the widest range of sports, fitness, and relaxation facilities, and an interesting variety of instructional and recreational programs. The beauty of it all is that you can find it all in one convenient location for one low fee.

Renewing your membership is easy with a number of convenient payment methods from which to choose. We would suggest the monthly preauthorized bank draft. But you may also choose to charge the membership fee on your Visa or MasterCard or to send a check in the enclosed envelope.

Don't put off renewing your membership. We look forward to helping you enjoy another year of health, fun, and fitness at The Hawthorne Fitness Club.

Sincerely,

Simon Thorn
Executive Director

st/mn

Enc.

SAMPLE LETTER 7.19.   Second-notice membership renewal letter (block format).

December 28, 19X2

Ms. Ellen P. Thrall
908 Visitation Drive
Hawthorne, Massachusetts 09087

Dear Ms. Thrall:

I just wanted to make sure that you have not overlooked your first membership renewal notice. We look forward to you continuing your membership at The Hawthorne Fitness Club for another year. There are several payment options:

   *Monthly bank draft with no time commitment. We will continue your
    membership indefinitely. Should you wish to cancel at a later date let
    us know prior to the first of the month.

   *A discount for cash. Paying up-front you will receive the lowest rate
    possible.

   *MasterCard and Visa are both accepted.

Remember, if you renew now you will avoid having to again pay the $30 application fee should you cancel and pay at a later date.

We look forward to having you continue your activities at The Hawthorne Fitness Club.

Sincerely,

Simon Thorn
Executive Director

st/mn

Enc.

Letter Accompanying Renewal Notice

Sample Letter 7.20 was written as a renewal notice to someone whose annual insurance payment was due. While the letter writer is blessed with a seemingly automatic sale, since most drivers are obligated to renew their insurance, she is concerned that the reader check over the facts in his previous year's application for accuracy. She clearly states the letter's purpose in the first paragraph, explains the consequences of not checking the application, and closes with an offer of assistance to the insured.

SAMPLE LETTER 7.20. Letter accompanying a renewal notice (block format).

May 18, 19X3

Mr. Harold Lester
100 Newton Street
Binghamton, Maine 90009

Dear Mr. Lester:

Your automobile insurance renewal application is enclosed. While your insurance will be automatically renewed, it is important that you review the application to make sure that all drivers are listed and the coverage is adequate.

In the event of a serious accident, you may be held personally liable for damages that exceed the bodily injury and property damage limits on your policy. To avoid financial risk, we recommend that you review your coverage and call or write us to make whatever changes are necessary.

Please call or come into our office if you have any questions or wish to make any changes. If you have no questions, simply complete, sign, and return the renewal application in the enclosed return envelope.

Sincerely,

Bethany J. Cole
Vice President

mn

Encs.

Letter Announcing a Special Presentation

Sample Letter 7.21 was written as a letter to prospective customers announcing a special presentation of product offerings. The letter writer announces the success of this event in the past and invites the recipient and any friends to attend an upcoming presentation. The letter clearly explains how to register for the special presentation and makes it clear to the reader that this will be a wonderful opportunity to preview the products of this company.

SAMPLE LETTER 7.21.   Letter announcing a special presentation (simplified format).

March 31, 19X8

Mr. Alan D. Simpson
1980 Svenson Avenue
Biloxi, New Jersey 89898

SPECIAL SLIDE PRESENTATION OF PRODUCTS

Mr. Simpson, our Stradivarius Violin Slide Show Tour of the Factory was extremely well received. In fact, we've had so many requests for a repeat performance that we're having another presentation so that other family members and friends can attend.

Please register for the presentation on April 14 by filling out the enclosed form indicating what time of day you would like to attend. Also include the names and addresses of friends you would like us to invite to this or future presentations.

Feel free to call me any time I can be of further help to you.

JOHN SAVITHSON
VICE PRESIDENT

js/mn

Enc.

Catalog Letters

Sample Letters 7.22 through 7.24 were all written to accompany catalogs.

Sample Letter 7.22 was written to accompany a professional catalog. The writer first introduces the company, then highlights the enclosed catalog, and closes with an offer to help the prospective customer with any business products she might need.

Sample Letter 7.23 was written as a response to a request for a professional catalog. The letter writer first acknowledges the request, then mentions a specific product the prospective customer asked about, and offers special help to the prospect. The letter is short and to the point, and addresses the needs of the prospect.

Sample Letter 7.24 was written to accompany a consumer catalog. This letter is longer than the previous two were, and it is written with a more folksy style to attract its target market. While the style is different, the clarity is comparable. The writer mentions the catalog's highlights, describes a special offer as an incentive to get the customer to order early, and closes with information on how to order.

SAMPLE LETTER 7.22.   Letter accompanying a professional catalog (semiblock format).

January 29, 19X2

Mrs. Bess Cooperburg
Cooperburg Department Stores
One Park Place
Sibling, Ohio 02202

Dear Mrs. Cooperburg:

Bertram and Bertram Store Displays is a full-service company offering store layout and designs as well as fixtures and supplies.

Enclosed are our current catalog and price list. If you look through our catalog, you will find that our prices are competitive. We also offer quantity discounts.

If there is something you are looking for and you do not find it in our catalog, please call me. We'd be glad to fill your needs. Our phone number is 1-800-734-5467.

Yours truly,

William Berran
Vice President

wb:gm

Enc.

SAMPLE LETTER 7.23.   Short letter responding to request for a
professional catalog (block format).

April 16, 19X7

Mr. Justin Longen
Hartford Longs Department Store
186 Grampian Way
Dorchester, North Carolina 23232

Dear Justin:

I've enclosed a copy of our catalog and the flyer on wire grid cubes that
you requested. As I mentioned on the telephone, the wire grid cubes are an
excellent way to display blouses and sweaters and will add a high-tech look
to your stores at a low cost.

Please get back to me, Justin, and I will work out special prices on our
whole line of display fixtures for Hartford Longs stores.

Kindest regards,

Alison Kraw
Sales Representative

ak/mn

Encs.

SAMPLE LETTER 7.24.   Letter accompanying a consumer catalog
(semiblock format).

December 20, 19X2

Mr. Greg Dendrinos
1966 Myron Boulevard
Goddard, New Jersey 57000

Dear Mr. Dendrinos:

In the enclosed catalog for Mead's Seeds, we have a greater variety of
vegetable and flower seeds than ever before.

We have spent the entire season poring over a variety of seed

Page 2
Mr. Greg Dendrinos
December 20, 19X2

offerings. You will find a grand selection of new products as well as your old favorites.

This year we feature more than 100 varieties of the world's most beautiful flowers and tasty vegetables. What's more, you get the same quality products, good value, and super service that Mead's Seeds has offered for more than 100 years. And, as usual, you get our money-back satisfaction guarantee.

If you order before March 30, 19X3, you get something more: a $5 savings on your total order. Just enclose the coupon from the catalog with your order and deduct $5 from the total where indicated on your order form.

You can use the coupon to load up on the seeds that will blazen your garden with color this summer: blue ribbon asters, ultra crimson petunias, bronze giant mums. Choose your family's favorite vegetables from among the hundreds in our catalog.

Since this is a preseason catalog, nearly all the seeds are priced 20 to 25 percent lower than the prices in our spring and summer catalogs. So send in your order today for even more savings.

If you wish to order by telephone, call our toll-free number: 1-800-733-3733, Monday through Friday, 9 A.M. to 9 P.M., eastern time. You can charge your order to any major credit card. You won't be billed until April, when your seeds are shipped.

Best wishes for a glorious spring and summer of planting.

Sincerely,

Cyndee G. Mead
President

cgm/bjc

Enc.

Sales Inquiry Response

Sample Letter 7.25 was written as a response to an inquiry about a particular product. The author clearly addresses the prospective customer's question and follows by stressing his company's reputation. He closes by extending an offer of assistance to the prospect in making purchase decisions.

SAMPLE LETTER 7.25.   Letter responding to an inquiry (full-block format).

August 31, 19X7

Mr. Ned J. Waggoner
Keith, Simons, and Underthal
343 Twilite Drive
Encino, Oregon 09876

Dear Mr. Waggoner:

Thank you for your interest in FLOORBOARD™ products and systems. We have enclosed the information you requested for your review.

Since 1886, the M. L. Nilgest Company has provided quality construction products to the industry. We would like to provide any assistance you might require in your project.

If you have any questions, please feel free to call our office at 617-666-6666.

Best regards,

Martin Nilgest
Sales and Marketing Manager
Architectural Products

mn/js

enclosure

Appointment Requests

Sample Letters 7.26 through 7.29 were all written to request sales appointments with prospective customers.

Sample Letter 7.26 is a very short letter telling the prospect that the letter writer will be in his area and would like to set up an appointment when she is in town. The letter writer makes it clear what procedure she will take to set up the appointment and leaves little doubt whose court the ball is in.

Sample Letter 7.27 was written as a follow-up to a brief discussion. The letter writer thanks the reader for his time, refers to the reader's colleagues who recommended him, and closes by saying he will call at the end of the week to set up a meeting at a mutually convenient time.

After being referred to yet another person, the writer of Sample Letter 7.27 wrote Sample Letter 7.28. He recounts his history with the company, mentions the referral, and closes by requesting a meeting. Again, the letter writer makes it clear when he will call to set up a convenient meeting.

Sample Letter 7.29 was written to inform the reader of a rescheduled trip and requests a specific meeting time with the reader. The writer and reader had been in contact before the letter was written and this letter confirms the actual date the writer will be in town for a possible meeting.

SAMPLE LETTER 7.26.   Short letter requesting an appointment (full-block format).

August 19, 19X6

Mr. Simon Rone
Acme Film Labs
Cosgrove, Idaho 88899

Dear Mr. Rone:

I plan to be in Cosgrove on September 1, and would like to discuss the possibility of working with you on the Bimini project.

I'll give you a call next week to see if we can set up a convenient time to meet.

Sincerely,

Alice Berg
President

ab/rb

SAMPLE LETTER 7.27.   Letter requesting an appointment after initial
discussion (block format).

July 14, 19X7

Mr. Ralph Hamill
Thomson Enterprises
111 Prospect Street
Hamilton, California 89898

Dear Mr. Hamill:

Thank you for taking the time to talk to me last Friday.

Alice Crafton suggested that I meet with you and Sondra Narsak to discuss
the public relations needs of Thomson Enterprises. I have enclosed copies
of the publicity we've been able to secure for one of our high-tech clients—
Wheaton Softprodisk. Building an image through publicity is one part of
the marketing services we can offer Thomson Enterprises.

At your earliest convenience, I would like to meet with you and Ms. Narsak
to learn about your company and its public relations goals. I will call at
the end of next week to see when a meeting might be possible.

Congratulations and best of luck. I know your company will be well
received in the Hamilton community.

Yours sincerely,

Gene O'Connor

go/mn

encs.

SAMPLE LETTER 7.28.   Follow-up to Sample Letter 7.27, requesting meeting with appropriate person at company (full-block format).

August 6, 19X7

Mr. Loren Gray, President
Thomson Enterprises
111 Prospect Street
Hamilton, California 89898

Dear Mr. Gray:

Alice Crafton recommended I meet with Ralph Hamill and Sondra Narsak to discuss the public relations needs of Thomson Enterprises. In a recent discussion, they told me that you are handling the review process. I understand that the materials I had sent to Mr. Hamill were passed along to you.

At your earliest possible convenience, I would like to meet with you to learn about your company and its public relations goals. Enclosed is some recent publicity one of our software clients received in Hamilton magazine's August issue. The story focused on how to choose a software supplier.

I will call you at the beginning of next week to check your schedule. Thank you, in advance, for your consideration.

Cordially,

Gene O'Connor

go/mn

encs.

SAMPLE LETTER 7.29.   Letter requesting an appointment after
rescheduling a trip (block format).

January 5, 19X4

Bethany J. Cole
Bootbakers of America
4545 Razzen Way
Ft. Wayne, Illinois 45321

Dear Ms. Cole:

I have rescheduled my trip to Ft. Wayne and hope it will be possible for you
to meet with me on January 22. Would it be possible for me to meet you at
your office about 6 o'clock in the evening?

Please let me know if this is convenient for you.

Sincerely,

William Berry
Vice President

wb/mn

Letters of Interest

Sample Letters 7.30 and 7.31 were written as letters of interest in a project. These
are sales letters whose mission is to get attractive projects for the writers' companies.

Sample Letter 7.30 is also written to a specific prospect, but here the letter
writer not only introduces himself and explains what he is after, but also attempts to
set up a meeting with the prospect.

Sample Letter 7.31 is a follow-up letter of interest to a prospect with whom
the letter writer had met. The letter writer expresses a strong interest in a project
discussed and encourages the prospect to send along any material he has. The letter
writer then highlights the benefits of working with his company and closes by
reiterating his desire to see the prospect's material. The letter serves not only to
reinforce the letter writer's interest, but also to present his company as an ideal
match for the prospect's work.

SAMPLE LETTER 7.30.   Letter of interest in project and request for
meeting (semiblock format).

December 26, 19X6

Dr. James Wagon
Joe Bing College
47 Bing Boulevard
Noreaster, Maine 58585

Dear Dr. Wagon:

I am the program coordinator for Andoris Seminar Productions. It
has come to my attention that you are an authority in the area of
personnel management. We are interested in running seminars in your
specialty area.

I would welcome the opportunity to discuss your program with you
as well as the field of personnel management in general.

At present, I am planning to be at Joe Bing College on January 21,
19X7. Perhaps, if it is convenient for you, we could meet on campus. I will
be arriving in Noreaster on January 20 and will be staying at the college's
guest quarters.

I am looking forward to meeting you. In the meantime, if I can be of
any assistance to you, please feel free to call upon me.

Cordially,

Archibald Roberts
Program Coordinator

ar/mn

SAMPLE LETTER 7.31.   Strong letter of interest in project (block format).

July 14, 19X0

Mr. Paul Jensen
Sunvale Enterprise College
98 Bethany Road
Sunvale, Maryland 90909

Dear Mr. Jensen:

I was glad to have had the opportunity to meet with you when I was at
Sunvale Enterprise last month. Thank you for sending me a proposal
letter for the seminar we talked about having you run.

Your project sounds very interesting. We would like to know more about it.
I understand you have some sample material prepared, which we would be
interested in seeing. I would be happy to send you the comments and
suggestions of our board of advisors. I trust that you will find these
recommendations to be helpful as your work progresses.

Mr. Jensen, I know you are very interested in having your seminars
produced. As a prospective seminar leader, you will undoubtedly consider a
number of criteria in selecting who you would like to work with in putting
on the seminar. These might include sales, advertising, promotion, and
content development assistance. In all of these aspects, Andoris Seminar
Productions stands alone. For more than 25 years, Andoris has specialized
in three things: performing extensive market analysis designed to develop
a limited number of quality seminars; maintaining very high content
standards built on years of experience; and reaching a maximum market
for its seminars through a concentrated promotion policy.

I look forward to hearing from you and seeing your material. In the
meantime, you have my best wishes for continued progress on your work.
If I can be of any assistance to you, please do not hesitate to call upon me.

Best regards,

Martin Night

mn/js

Letter to Difficult-to-See Prospect

Sample Letter 7.32 was written to a prospect with whom the letter writer has been having trouble getting in touch. The letter writer clearly explains his predicament in the first paragraph by mentioning how many times he has tried to call the prospect. He does this in an inoffensive way by expressing his understanding of how busy the prospect must be. The letter writer realizes the prospect is short on time, so he wastes none of it and gets right to the point in his second paragraph. Here, he briefly explains what his company can do for the prospect. He closes by saying he will once again call the prospect to set up a meeting. But having written this letter, he has laid the groundwork for more successful results.

SAMPLE LETTER 7.32. Letter to a sales prospect who is difficult to see (full-block format).

May 12, 19X3

Mr. Allen Kenney
Volt & Wattage Company, Inc.
78 Alma Road
April, Iowa 09090

Dear Mr. Kenney:

I have tried to call you several times during this past month, but have had no success in reaching you. I can appreciate how busy you must be handling the installation of a new computer system at your company.

Palay Insurance Benefits Company is keenly aware of the heightened competition in insurance and is committed to responding with more creative and attentive servicing to corporate customers such as you. We combine the personal touch and convenience of a local insurance firm with all of the sophistication of the major insurance companies in our city.

I will call you in the near future to try to schedule a visit at your convenience. I look forward to meeting with you.

Sincerely,

Bridget Palay
Vice President

bdp

Letters Confirming Proposals

Sample Letters 7.33 through 7.35 were written to confirm sales proposals that had been made to customers. All followed some initial contact with the prospect.

Sample Letter 7.33 was written after the letter writer had a phone conversation with a prospect about his need for insurance. The letter writer opens by recounting the conversation and mentioning a mutual acquaintance who suggested the prospect to the letter writer. The next paragraph gives a capsule review of the proposal, followed by instructions to the prospect on how to go forward.

Sample Letter 7.34 was written to confirm a proposal for use of a function hall and catering facilities. The letter writer immediately acknowledges the prospect's reservation, reiterating what she has told him about her needs. He follows by explaining costs and procedures for securing the room and encloses sample menus to help her decide on her menu for the function.

Sample Letter 7.35 is written as a follow-up to action taken as a result of Sample Letter 7.34. After the customer has confirmed the room and chosen a menu, the letter writer writes to confirm the menu and instructs the reader on the procedure for informing him of an exact head count for the function. The letter writer, who wrote the letter shortly before the function, extends his offer of help should the reader need it before the function.

SAMPLE LETTER 7.33.   Letter confirming proposal for services (semiblock format).

November 30, 19X7

Mr. Ed Devick
RR & Associates
56 Downside Street
Cambridge, Alabama 45454

Dear Mr. Devick:

I just wanted to send you a brief note to tell you that I truly enjoyed speaking with you and look forward to advising you in the area of insurance and fringe benefit planning. Tracey Hunt speaks very highly of you.

I've enclosed a proposal and application for John Jay Insurance Company for the following disability insurance coverage:

$2,900 per month benefit
60-day waiting period
Payable to age 65
Coverage in your <u>own</u> occupation
Cost of living adjustment, which keeps pace with inflation
Future insurance option

I feel extremely comfortable with John Jay's proposal and recommend that we apply for it. Please sign where indicated (two times) on the enclosed application and mail it back to me in the envelope provided with a check payable to John Jay Insurance Company for $733.25.

Thanks in advance for the business. I hope to meet with you in person soon.

Cordially,

Lauren Gary
Principal

LG/mn

Enclosures

SAMPLE LETTER 7.34.   Letter confirming proposal for services (simplified format).

September 23, 19X5

Ms. Nancy Armitage
186 Stanfield Road
Sibling, Ohio 80976

SUBJECT: ARMITAGE/CATTON WEDDING

Nancy, I am delighted to acknowledge a reservation for the Armitage/ Catton wedding from 1 to 5 P.M. on Saturday, January 18, 19X6 in the Great London room of the Hopscotch Hotel. We will set the room for a reception, luncheon, and dance and understand that you expect you will be having 75 guests.

The rental for the room is $300, reduced by $100 for each $1,000 you spend on food and beverages.

I have enclosed a copy of this letter that, when signed and returned to my office, will confirm your tentative reservation. We also require that a deposit of $300 accompany your confirming copy and that it be returned within 14 days.

Full payment of your estimated bill, based on the guaranteed figure, will be required the day of the function. All payments should be made to our banquet manager prior to the start of the function in cash or certified check. Kindly make your check payable to The Hopscotch Hotel, Inc.

I have also enclosed our menus for your perusal and would appreciate hearing from you within three weeks about your menu selection.

We look forward to the opportunity to serve you. I can assure you that we will do our utmost to make this event a success.

DAVID L. BIXTON
DIRECTOR, SALES AND MARKETING

dlb/ajm

Enclosures

SAMPLE LETTER 7.35.   Follow-up to response to confirming letter in Sample Letter 7.34 (simplified format).

January 7, 19X6

Ms. Nancy Armitage
186 Stanfield Road
Sibling, Ohio 80976

SUBJECT: ARMITAGE/CATTON WEDDING

Nancy, with your upcoming function soon at hand, I am pleased to enclose the finalized copies of the menus and arrangements for your wedding for your verification. To help us proceed with the arrangements, would you kindly sign and return the original copy to us, making any notations or changes that you desire.

We will require that you furnish us with a guaranteed attendance number two business days prior to the function by noontime. Should a count not be received, your highest estimate will be used when we determine the final bill.

We look forward to the pleasure of serving you. If, in the interim, I can be of any assistance to you whatsoever, please do not hesitate to call on me.

DAVID L. BIXTON
DIRECTOR, SALES AND MARKETING

dlb/ajm

Enclosure

Follow-Up Letters

Sample Letters 7.36 through 7.41 were all written to follow up on a sales call to a prospect.

Sample Letter 7.36 was written to follow up on a meeting with a prospect. This letter writer briefly expresses thanks for the meeting, explains in capsule form what his company can do for the prospect, and closes by expressing a desire to work with the prospect.

Sample Letter 7.37 was written to follow up on a phone conversation. Here, the letter writer gets right to the point when he writes that he has enclosed the materials requested by the prospect in their conversation. He closes by reminding the reader of a meeting they have set up and thanks him for his interest in the company's services.

Sample Letter 7.38 was written as a follow-up to a former customer who had decided to go with the competition. The letter writer follows up a conversation he had with someone at the reader's company who told the writer why they made the shift to a new company. First the letter writer sets up the situation in the letter. Then he announces how his company is able to meet and surpass the competition when it comes to supplying the former customer's needs. He closes by expressing a desire to serve the reader and encourages him to call should he need any help.

SAMPLE LETTER 7.36.   Follow-up letter to meeting (semiblock format).

August 7, 19X1

Mr. Gerald Johanson, Chairman
State Oil Refinery
75 Mascot Place
Alderbine, Georgia 89898

Dear Mr. Johanson:

Thank you for taking time out of your schedule to meet with me at the Racquet Club last Thursday. It was a pleasure for David Paly and me to meet with you and the other partners of your organization to discuss your company's data processing needs. I hope this is just the beginning of a solid relationship between our two companies.

As I told you at our meeting, our company specializes in servicing the data processing needs of companies like yours. Please feel free to call on me at any time to discuss your data processing needs. I would be glad to meet with you or your partners to review any needs you would like to discuss.

Thank you again for the meeting. I hope to be able to work with you in the not too distant future.

Sincerely,

Alan Ross
Vice President

ar/fk

cc: David Paly

SAMPLE LETTER 7.37.   Short follow-up letter to phone conversation (block format).

September 22, 19X7

Mr. Walter B. Jingle
Christophers, Leighs & Plummers
P.O. Box 45
Menahagon, Washington 98765

Dear Mr. Jingle:

I've enclosed a copy of our press kit, which you requested when we spoke on the telephone yesterday. Among other things, the press kit contains articles I've written, stories in which I've been quoted, biographies of me and our senior staff, and a client list.

I look forward to meeting you the week of October 5. Thank you very much for your interest in NES Public Relations. I'll speak with you soon.

Yours truly,

Mack Nilton

mn/mv

Enclosure

SAMPLE LETTER 7.38.   Letter following up on lost sale (semiblock format).

May 21, 19X0

Mr. Carl B. Replick
Myers and Myers, Inc.
456 Merrimac Place, Suite 4B
Williamsburg, New York 34345

Dear Mr. Replick:

Checking through my records, I noticed that you were no longer an active customer of Zyblick Office Supplies. When I called your office, I was informed that your company is now using our competitor from a few counties over. Your office manager, Zed Globonk, was refreshingly forthright in telling me how Zyblick fell short of the mark in keeping your business.

I'm pleased to tell you that we have set up a whole new line of filing supplies, which Mr. Globonk expressed a desperate need for. We feature a wide array of legal and letter size folders, as well as a variety of color-coded hanging folders.

I thought you'd also be interested to know that we've established same-day delivery service and overnight billing, features Mr. Globonk mentioned would really help your business. These services are not offered by any of our competitors.

Mr. Globonk told me that you make all purchasing decisions at Myers and Myers. If you need additional information from me, Mr. Replick, please feel free to call. I welcome the opportunity to serve your company once again. I will do my best to ensure your satisfaction.

Sincerely,

Robert Kemprel

rk/js

Sample Letter 7.39 was written as a follow-up to a previous sale. The letter writer opens his letter by thanking the customer for her prior business and reassuring her that his company will continue to provide quality products and services. He closes by mentioning a listing of products he has enclosed with the letter and encouraging the reader to call him should she have any questions.

Sample Letter 7.40 was written as a follow-up letter to an active customer who had attended the letter writer's exhibit at a trade show. The letter writer reminds the reader about the trade show and then elaborates on a new product his company is offering. He closes by expressing his appreciation for the reader's business. The letter serves not only to sell the customer on the company, but to keep him informed.

Sample Letter 7.41 was written as a follow-up to a referral made by an associate of the reader. The letter writer immediately identifies the situation by mentioning the referrer's name in the first paragraph. If the prospect recognizes the name as someone he trusts, he is more likely to read on. The letter writer next explains what his services are, mentions an enclosed brochure, and closes by encouraging the reader to get in touch with him.

SAMPLE LETTER 7.39.   Follow-up letter to previous sale (block format).

March 20, 19X6

Ms. Bethany J. Cole
Academy Services, Inc.
P.O. Box 3456
Latin, Kentucky 54433

Dear Ms. Cole:

Thank you for purchasing your computer equipment at Diskquick Services earlier this year. My associates and I at Diskquick would be pleased to provide any services we can to your company, or act as a sounding board on your hardware and software needs. We do business with many professional services in the Latin area and are familiar with the trials and tribulations of operating a company such as yours.

To familiarize you with Diskquick, I enclose a copy of our latest product listings. Please feel free to call me or any of my associates on the enclosed list any time. I'll call you within the next few days to introduce myself over the phone.

I look forward to meeting you.

Sincerely,

Alan Macalester
Vice President

am/mn

Enclosures

SAMPLE LETTER 7.40.   Follow-up to exhibit visitor (simplified format).

April 1, 19X7

Mr. Lawrence Z. Weimer
Weimer Images
454 Main Road
Transit, Pennsylvania 34343

SUPPORT MATERIAL FOR NEW PRODUCTS

Larry, at the trade show in March, we announced that we would be
introducing a new line of medium-sized photography enlargers. The
response we received at the show was tremendous and, in order to help
you present the enlargers better, we are enclosing a selection of new sales
literature.

In addition to the introduction of the new enlarger, we are making other
changes. We're now better equipped than ever to respond to your needs and
the needs of your customers. You may already have noticed faster handling
of orders. More improvements in service are on the way!

This promises to be an exciting year for us and we're glad you're part of it.

MICHAEL KERRY
VICE PRESIDENT—SALES AND MARKETING

MK

Enclosure

SAMPLE LETTER 7.41.   Follow-up to referral (full-block format).

October 20, 19X6

Mr. John Nivas
Marketing Director
Nivas, Royal, Lauten, Inc.
681 Line Hill Avenue
Norstar, Massachusetts 09999

Dear Mr. Nivas:

Beatrice Clonig suggested I write you because she thought you might be interested in the unusual services that I provide corporations.

I perform magic at sales meetings, trade shows, and corporate parties. I also work with companies to use magic in promotions and new product introductions. Magic is used to support the theme of the introductions, to support the theme of the meeting, and to reinforce key marketing points and product attributes in an entertaining presentation. Each show is specially designed to highlight the client's program objectives.

For your information I have enclosed one of my promotional brochures. It should give you a better indication of my capabilities and expertise.

If you think that corporate magic might be something that Nivas, Royal, Lauten, Inc. would be interested in exploring, please do not hesitate to get in touch with me. I hope to hear from you soon.

Cordially,

Ray Fontmore

rf/jm

Enclosure

Letter to Renew Contact

Sample Letter 7.42 was written to a prospect whom the letter writer knew when the reader was at another company. The letter writer congratulates the reader on the new position, reminds her who he is, and offers any help the reader might need in choosing services that his company provides.

SAMPLE LETTER 7.42.   Sales letter to renew contact (semiblock format).

June 13, 19X8

Dr. Lindsey Harl
Executive Vice President
Emerson, Waldo & Associates
One Divinity Place
Coopers, Ohio 98989

Dear Lindsey:

I was pleased to hear that you have become an associate of Emerson, Waldo & Associates. Please accept best wishes from all of us at Ambrose Trucking Company.

You may remember that we had several phone conversations when you were vice president of operations at Grimes and Grimes. Since that time my duties have changed at Ambrose Trucking Company from handling long-term fleet leasing arrangements to handling the accounts of large wholesale firms like Emerson, Waldo.

Please let me know if I can be of assistance to you or help you better serve your clients. We at Ambrose Trucking are committed to providing the quality trucking services that wholesalers require to run a successful business.

Again, I wish you continued success.

Kindest regards,

C. C. Lange
Vice President

ccl/jlb

Letter Welcoming New Client

Sample Letter 7.43 was written to welcome a new client. The letter writer opens by welcoming the client, and follows by telling him who will be handling his account, how the company will help him, and what he should expect from the company. The letter writer closes by informing the reader that his account representative will be calling him to set up a meeting. Writing a brief, but informative, welcoming letter serves not only to remind the new client of what services the company will provide, but more importantly to assure him that the company cares enough about him to take the time to welcome him after he has already agreed to give the firm his business.

SAMPLE LETTER 7.43.   Letter welcoming a new client (semiblock format).

September 8, 19X7

Mr. Alexander Hayes
Rightaweigh, Inc.
98 Bolivia Avenue
Cortland, New Jersey 54545

Dear Mr. Hayes:

We're pleased to welcome you as a new client and want to take this opportunity to thank you for your selection of Nilges and Crowbaker, CFPs to handle all of your financial planning needs. You have chosen a firm that is committed to providing you with excellent service and superior professional counsel.

We have assigned Greta Lockin as your personal financial planner and primary liaison. Of course, Greta will work closely with our entire staff of specialists to ensure that you will receive the best guidance on all matters.

Our firm specializes in strategic financial planning to help you and your company prosper. We address your future potential as well as assess your past financial performance. What's more, we provide ancillary services that can be vital to your success, such as complete management of all your financial software needs.

As a client of Nilges and Crowbacker, CFPs, you will receive monthly newsletters with the latest tax and financial information available. You will also be invited to special seminars we regularly conduct on financial matters of interest to our clients.

Greta Lockin will be calling on you shortly to arrange an initial appointment. Should you have any further questions on any or all of our services, please do not hesitate to call Max Nilges or me.

Again, welcome to Nilges and Crowbacker.

Sincerely,

Niles Crowbacker
Principal

nc/mr

Letter Asking for Referral

Sample Letter 7.44 was written to an existing customer with whom the writer has recently met. The writer first takes care of business by telling the reader that his application has been received. Next the writer asks the reader for possible referrals who might be interested in his services. He describes the type of clients he is looking for and suggests that he call the reader to see if he is willing to recommend some people. The tone of the letter is congenial, not at all pushy. The letter writer makes it clear that it is entirely up to the reader if he wants to recommend possible referrals.

SAMPLE LETTER 7.44.   Letter asking for a referral (semiblock format).

May 20, 19X5

Mr. Geoffrey Spaulding
Animal Crackers, Inc.
45 Marx Drive
Chico, California 32345

Dear Mr. Spaulding:

It was great meeting you for lunch at the Racquet Club last week. I've received your first premium check and your application for the disability insurance policy I recommended to you. I'm glad I was able to fill your needs with this policy. I trust you'll be as pleased with this product as you have been with insurance products you have purchased through me in the past.

At lunch you mentioned that you run into a good number of small-business owners in your business dealings. If you think it is appropriate, I would welcome the opportunity to furnish these people with the same quality of service that I and my colleagues at Pacific Insurance Benefits, Inc. have supplied you.

As I mentioned to you, Pacific Insurance Benefits has been getting more and more into the area of fringe benefit and insurance planning for small-business owners. Would you consider thinking of a few business owners you know who could use my services?

I'll call you next week to see if you'd be willing to refer me to these people. A referral from you would go a long way in opening new doors for me and my colleagues.

I look forward to talking to you next week.

Best regards,

Gino Inatreck

gi/js

Letter Promoting Special Sale

Sample Letter 7.45 was written to promote the special sale of a product that unexpectedly came to market. The letter writer explains the situation and the product available in the first three paragraphs, then closes by telling the reader how she can take advantage of the offer if she is interested. The writer clearly points out why the offer is a special one and how the reader can benefit from it.

SAMPLE LETTER 7.45.   Letter promoting special sale (semiblock format).

January 2, 19X8

Ms. Zoe Patterson
34 Laramy Street
Apriori, Utah 38928

Dear Ms. Patterson:

You now have an opportunity to step in and build a house where the preparatory work has already been done!

Due to the owner's serious illness, the construction of a house in the prestigious Township section cannot be completed. The owner would like to sell the site as is for $79,900—less than the appraised value.

The property includes a secluded one-acre lot, blueprints for a 3,400 square-foot house, all necessary building permits, a cleared home site and driveway, in-place footings, termporary water hookup, temporary electricity hookup, and $2,500 worth of building materials on the lot.

If you are interested in additional information, please call me at 888-8888. We plan to list the property with a real estate agency as of January 25, 19X8, so please call soon if you are interested.

Sincerely,

Max Jeffries
President

mn

Public Relations Letters

Public relations is a marketing tool used by many professionals to build public awareness of their business. Sample Letters 7.46 through 7.51 are examples of public relations letters that were written for a variety of purposes.

Sample Letter 7.46 was written to a group of journalists inviting them to a special screening of a production that was being underwritten by the letter writer's company. The writer makes the invitation in the first paragraph, follows that with a brief description of the production, mentions the resources from her company that will be available at the screening, and closes by telling the reader she will call to see if she can attend the event. The letter is informative and clearly written so the reader knows exactly what is being offered.

Sample Letter 7.47 is written as an invitation to the press to attend an annual professional conference. Like Letter 7.46, this letter clearly establishes what is being promoted. The writer first makes the invitation, elaborates a bit on what can be expected at the conference, mentions special services that will be available to the press, and closes by encouraging the reader to respond soon to take advantage of local accommodations.

Sample Letter 7.48 was written to promote the formation of a new company. The writer directs his letter to a member of the press suggesting a possible story angle.

SAMPLE LETTER 7.46.   Letter inviting people to special screening (block format).

December 22, 19X7

Ms. Patricia Pauly
The Flushing Herald
134 Howard Place
Flushing, Connecticut 09087

Dear Pat:

Please join us for breakfast on January 6 at 9 A.M. to screen a unique new television series on personal financial planning. The screening will be hosted by The Crayon Financial Group, a local affiliate of ours, at 45 Adamant Drive, in Flushing.

The six-part series, "How to Plan Your Finances," will air in the Flushing area beginning January 5, 19X8, on the Consumer Cable Station (CCS). Using real-life examples and a panel of noted financial experts, the series addresses a baffling, yet common, financial mistake: People often confuse investing with financial planning. As a result, they have a lot of investments, but no long-term strategies to reach their financial goals.

Representatives from The Crayon Financial Group and our firm, the series producer and sponsor, will be available at the screening to answer your questions about the program as well as other financial planning issues you might be interested in.

I'll call next week to see if you'll be able to join us. We look forward to meeting with you soon.

                                        Sincerely,

                                        Belinda J. Carlson
                                        Public Relations

bjc/jls

SAMPLE LETTER 7.47.   Letter inviting press to conference (simplified format).

July 22, 19X7

Ms. Nancy Kenworthy, Editor
Hamilton Financial Journal
54 Garland Drive
Hamilton, California 00012

ANNUAL CONVENTION OF THE NATIONAL INVESTMENT ADVISORS GROUP

Ms. Kenworthy, you are cordially invited to be the guest of the National Investment Advisors Group at its Tenth Annual Convention and Exposition on October 5–8 at the Idaho World Trade Pavilion in Bilink, Idaho. As our guest, join us for all of the educational and general sessions, the exhibitions, and all scheduled meals. A special reception to honor the media is scheduled for Tuesday, October 6. For your convenience, registration will be in the press room at the World Trade Pavilion.

Some 2,000 investment advisors are expected. The four-day event features three general sessions and more than 100 education sessions in 10 major subject areas conducted by key industry leaders. The exhibition features more than 300 financial product and service companies. Detailed information is featured in the enclosed brochure.

Page 2
Ms. Nancy Kenworthy, Editor
July 22, 19X7

Keynote speakers include Alice Tanner Nyquil, one of the nation's leading
commentators on investments, and a four-person panel debating the
future of the investment advisory industry. The closing session will
feature Thomas Thomas, the leading commentator on personal finance in
the country.

Interviews can be arranged during the week with speakers, industry
leaders, attendees, and NIAG officers to meet your editorial needs and
deadline. My staff and I would be glad to help you line up any interviews
we can.

To better ensure your preference of accommodations and rates, I suggest
you complete the enclosed registration form and return it to my attention
by August 30. Feel free to call me with the information.

The 19X7 NIAG Convention and Exposition is filled with more
information on the investment advisory industry than you will find
anywhere else. We look forward to hearing soon that you can be with us.

PAMELA A. HOAN
PUBLIC RELATIONS DIRECTOR

PAH/trw

Enclosure

SAMPLE LETTER 7.48.   Letter introducing company (semiblock format).

September 28, 19X8

Mr. John Hill, Editor
Local Business Chronicle
San Anamant, California 43456

Dear Mr. Hill:

When the Sibling International Commerce Club opened last summer
at the Sibling International Center on San Anamant Wharf, it was yet
another significant indication that San Anamant has truly become a city
of international scope. Local Business Chronicle readers might be

interested to know that membership in the Sibling International
Commerce Club opens new international opportunities to them as well.

San Anamant's Sibling International Commerce Club joins more than
50 other clubs throughout the world in offering a host of business and
social amenities to members. These clubs have become "homes away from
home" for frequent business travelers, places where not only can they
relax and enjoy fine food and spirits, but also where they can arrange for
translator services, receive discounts at hotels, and have access to
temporary office space and secretarial services. These reciprocal
memberships at Clubs in nearly every major commerce center throughout
the world offer central staging areas to conduct both business and
personal affairs while on the road.

Because the global marketplace is shrinking daily, we thought a
profile of the Sibling International Commerce Club and its activities would
provide valuable information for your readers.

Thank you, in advance, for your consideration of an article on the
Sibling International Commerce Club. I'll call you next week for your
feedback.

Sincerely,

Alan Harlan

ah/mn

Sample Letter 7.49 was written to a business acquaintance by someone who
decided to form his own business. The writer announces his new business in the first
paragraph, follows that with a brief description of the type of work the business
does, and closes by encouraging the reader to meet with the writer should he ever
be in the writer's area. While the letter writer is not making any direct sale with the
letter, he is building an awareness that may pay off in the future.

Sample Letter 7.50 was written to accompany information that a professional
organization was offering as an educational tool to consumers. The letter writer sets
up the reasons for the need for the information in paragraphs one and two, follows
with a description of the material enclosed with the letter, and closes by offering to
set up interviews with members of the professional group should the reader want to
pursue this information.

SAMPLE LETTER 7.49. Letter announcing the formation of new business (block format).

December 28, 19X7

Mr. Samuel Johnson
19 Court Road
Lichfield, Georgia 08765

Dear Sam:

In August I left my position as manager of consulting at Boswell and Boswell, Inc. to establish my own consulting business. I would like to take this opportunity to pass along my business card and to tell you a little bit about my business.

My practice will deal with automating accounting firms and small businesses. My services will focus on three primary areas:

*Consulting services to CPA firms on use of computers in audit, tax, and management; client computer consulting; and special financial analysis;

*Consulting services to small businesses that are considering automation;

*Training seminars on specific computer software packages including: Lotus 1-2-3, Wordstar, TimeLine, FAST, and MS-DOS.

The last four months have been quite rewarding professionally. Business has taken me to New York, Boston, and Europe.

If you are in the New York or Boston area and would like to get together, please call.

Sincerely,

Robert Lang
Principal

rl/js

SAMPLE LETTER 7.50.   Letter accompanying industry information
(simplified format).

December 15, 19X7

Mr. Jacob Wirth
Wirth & While Journal
45 Boston Place
Nashville, Massachusetts 90876

HELPING CONSUMERS COPE WITH STOCK MARKET CRASH

The aftereffects of the October stock market plunge have left consumers
confused and uncertain over both the economy's future and their own
financial situations. Frankly, consumer confidence has been shaken.

What can consumers do now to calm their fears and restore optimism to
their financial outlook?

This question and others are answered in the enclosed background
information, which provides practical advice for consumers in coping
with their finances. The information comes from the National Investment
Advisors Group (NIAG), the 10,000-member professional organization in
the investment advisory industry.

Overall strategies are provided in this material to help consumers protect
and build their investments to better prepare them to meet their short-
and long-term objectives.

Leading professionals in the investment advisory industry are available to
talk about what consumers can and should be doing now to meet their
immediate and long-term goals. If you would like more information or to
arrange an interview with an investment advisor, please do not hesitate to
call me or Athena Chin at 212-555-6767.

PAMELA A. HOAN
PUBLIC RELATIONS DIRECTOR

PAH/trw

A good public relations tactic is to keep abreast of prospectives' status in the professional market. The letter writer of Sample Letter 7.51 used the occasion of the reader's new position as an excuse to not only congratulate the reader but also to briefly promote the writer's services. The letter clearly focuses on the congratulations, but by briefly reminding the reader about the letter writer's capabilities, he increases the chances that should she need such services, she will remember his company.

SAMPLE LETTER 7.51.   Letter congratulating customer on promotion (full-block format).

September 20, 19X2

Ms. Pamela Chin
Seimor & Simons
45 Tewksbury Road
Alexandria, Michigan 34321

Dear Ms. Chin:

Congratulations on being named an associate at Seimor & Simons. While I realize that you are limited in the amount of insurance business you handle for clients, I would be glad to help you in any way I can.

Savin Hill Benefits Group tailor makes insurance programs for professionals like you. We also have a fast response time for any business referrals.

Good luck with your new responsibilities. I hope I can be helpful to you with any service or question you have.

Sincerely,

Albert Flynn
Vice President

af/cc

CHAPTER 8
Customer Service Letters

Customer service letters are some of the most important letters you will write. Serving the needs of customers is a sure way to capture their loyalty to your business. Even when sticky issues such as complaint resolutions or price increases arise, handling these issues with respect for the customer is crucial in maintaining the integrity of the business and in achieving some desirable results.

All of the customer service letters in this chapter were written with the customer in mind. Many were designed to win over or strengthen the loyalty of customers. Others were crafted to achieve a desired goal without alienating existing customers.

Complaint Resolution Letters

Sample Letters 8.1 through 8.6 were all written to deal with complaints issued by customers.

Sample Letter 8.1 was written to acknowledge receipt of a customer complaint. The letter writer acknowledges the complaint in the first paragraph, informs the customer that a credit will be issued to her account while the complaint is being investigated, and finally lets her know how to get in touch with her customer service department should she have any further questions.

Sample Letter 8.2 was written to a customer who had complained about an incorrect billing that appeared on his charge account statement. In this letter, the letter writer explains what further information the customer service department needs to explore the discrepancy. In the first three paragraphs the letter writer clearly spells out the steps the customer should take to help speed up the investigation. The letter writer closes by thanking the customer for his help and encourages him to call if he has any questions while the problem is being cleared up.

Sample Letter 8.3 was written to inform a customer that all the information necessary to resolve a complaint had not been received. The letter could be written as a follow-up to the information requested in Sample Letter 8.2. The writer recaps the complaint, explains that the temporary credit is being rescinded, and asks the customer to call if he has any other questions. The reference line on this letter matches the one on Sample Letter 8.2, indicating they both refer to the same account.

SAMPLE LETTER 8.1.   Letter acknowledging receipt of complaint
(semiblock format).

March 1, 19X8
A-564-654567-90000

Mrs. Alison Q. Rumpole
546 Haversford Drive
Massapequa, New York 94032

Subject: Incorrect Charge Query

Dear Mrs. Rumpole:

You recently inquired about the charges on your monthly bill from
Henderson & Henderson Department Store. We have written the store
management to try to resolve the discrepancy. As soon as we receive their
reply, we will write you again.

While we are conducting our investigation, we are issuing a
temporary credit on your charge account for $86.81.

If you have any questions or if we can be of further service, please call
me or another customer service representative at the telephone number
listed on your monthly billing statement.

Cordially,

(Mrs.) Leslie T. Waters
Customer Service Manager

ltw/jls

SAMPLE LETTER 8.2.   Letter instructing customer on procedure to clarify
billing (block format).

November 26, 19X7
A-456-8765-87777

Mr. Simon F. Wallace
43 Douglas Road
Far Hills, Pennsylvania 23234

Dear Mr. Wallace:

In order to trace the payment of $20.95 you recently called us about, we
need a copy of the front and back of your cancelled check. If the
information on the copy is not readable, please handwrite it so that it is
legible.

If your check has not yet cleared, simply stop payment on it and send us a
replacement check. We have enclosed a return envelope for your
convenience.

While waiting for this matter to be resolved, we are issuing a temporary
credit to your charge account. If we do not receive the above item from you
by December 7, 19X7, we will remove the temporary credit and charge
your account again.

We appreciate your help in resolving this situation quickly. If you have any
questions or if we can be of further assistance, please call me or another
customer service respresentative at the telephone number listed on your
monthly billing statement.

Cordially,

(Mrs.) Leslie T. Waters
Customer Service Manager

ltw/jls

SAMPLE LETTER 8.3.   Letter notifying customer that necessary information for complaint resolution was not sent. Could be sent as follow-up to Sample Letter 8.2 (full-block format).

December 15, 19X7
A-456-8765-87777

Mr. Simon F. Wallace
43 Douglas Road
Far Hills, Pennsylvania 23234

Dear Mr. Wallace:

You recently called us about the payment for $20.95 not credited to your charge account.

When we could not locate the credit, we asked you to send us more information. Since we have not received the necessary information from you, we are removing the temporary credit we had issued to your account and will be charging you again for the amount.

If you have any questions or if we can be of further service, please feel free to call me or another customer service representative at the telephone number listed on your monthly billing statement.

Cordially,

(Mrs.) Leslie T. Walters
Customer Service Manager

ltw/jls

Sample Letter 8.4 could also be sent as a follow-up to Sample Letter 8.2, but here the letter writer agrees with the customer's complaint and attempts to resolve the issue. The letter writer addresses the problem immediately in the letter, explaining what caused the problem, lets the reader know how it will be resolved, and apologizes for the mishap. The letter is short, but clarifies the problem and should set the reader's mind at rest.

Sample Letter 8.5 was written to disagree with a customer complaint. In the first paragraph of the letter, the letter writer refers to the complaint and disagrees with the customer about a product defect. The writer then explains to the reader that he may return the product for a refund if he is dissatisfied with it for any reason, and closes by explaining the appropriate procedure for future complaints.

Sample Letter 8.6 is a more detailed complaint resolution written to clear up some problems the client had with the letter writer's services. The letter writer begins by apologizing for the displeasure, then details the problem, explaining how it occurred. The letter writer proceeds to offer a solution to the problem, telling the client that he will pay for any problems that were caused by his error. He also clearly spells out how much cost there will be to the client as a result of the suggested resolution. He then asks that the client call him to give him the go ahead with the approach he has recommended.

SAMPLE LETTER 8.4.   Follow-up letter to 8.2, agreeing with customer's complaint (block format).

December 31, 19X7
A-456-8765-87777

Mr. Simon F. Wallace
43 Douglas Road
Far Hills, Pennsylvania 23234

Dear Mr. Wallace:

We have found that we inadvertently applied a payment for $20.95 to another charge-account holder's account. We have now transferred it to your account, and it will appear on an upcoming statement.

We apologize for any inconvenience this may have caused.

If you have any questions, or if we can be of further service, please call me or another customer service representative at the telephone number listed on your monthly billing statement.

Cordially,

(Mrs.) Leslie T. Waters
Customer Service Manager

ltw/jls

SAMPLE LETTER 8.5.   Letter disagreeing with customer (semiblock format).

May 20, 19X8

Mr. Elmore T. Holstein
56 Trueblood Terrace
Minerva, Washington 34345

Dear Mr. Holstein:

In response to your letter of May 12 about your purchase of Dandy Wanda's Clam Sauce, while we appreciate your concerns, I assure you that we have taken all necessary steps to ensure that the product meets the highest nutritional standards.

If you are dissatisfied with this product, however, we will be pleased to refund your money for your purchase.

For future reference, please direct any specific concerns about return of products to the store from which you purchased the goods.

Cordially,

James T. Lardley
Customer Service Manager

jtl/jl

SAMPLE LETTER 8.6.   Complaint resolution letter (full-block format).

September 24, 19X7

Ms. Millicent Conroy
Conroy & Smyrna, Inc.
678 Boxford Street
Taylor, New Jersey 09876

Dear Millicent:

I am sorry that you are not pleased with the copies of your company press clips that we sent you. Alice Farning, from your office, sent me a copy of each press clip. After reviewing them for context, here are my suggestions.

Page 2
Ms. Millicient Conroy
September 24, 19X7

Four of the clips are fine. They are enclosed with this letter. There is nothing missing from the clips, nor is anything taken out of context.

Six of the clips are out of context. As I explained, these copies were made from my portfolio boards. They are a compilation of quotations your company received, highlighted for our presentation purposes. For your purposes, I agree, they should be complete articles in case a client or prospective client decides to read one.

I have the originals for all of the articles. To make a complete set, we must copy 23 additional pages, 500 copies of each page. We also must consider that the longer pieces have advertisements surrounding the editorial content. I recommend that we hire a paste-up person to cut and paste the pages, thus combining columns and eliminating the advertisements. This will lessen the number of pages and make for better presentation. I will get an estimate for this work if you agree that this is the way to go. Then I'll know exactly how many pages will have to be copied, and I can get a final quote.

We have spent $595 plus tax for the initial group of 5,000 copies. Farran Public Relations is responsible for paying $210 for the initial 6 pages that weren't acceptable. We will also pay for those 6 pages to be redone. This leaves an additional 17 pages, 500 copies each ($8,500 \times 7$ cents), before any advertisements are removed and columns combined by a competent paste-up artist. While the number of pages will be reduced by this process, the artist's time will be an additional cost.

Millicent, I'm sorry to waste your time with these details. But my responsibility to your company is to get approval on any expense beyond our fee. These expenses for copying could total as much as $800 to $1,000 for the project. I don't want to proceed without your authorization.

This project is not a simple copy job. It requires careful thought and organization to provide Conroy & Smyrna, Inc., with great presentation materials. We emphasized the value it will provide your company through third-party credibility. It will be well worth our efforts, and should help to provide your company with a competitive edge, especially in new-business situations.

Please give me a call about how you'd like to proceed. I appreciate your

Page 3
Ms. Millicient Conroy
September 24, 19X7

patience and understanding. I am confident this project will prove to be a rewarding investment.

Sincerely,

Mack Nothrop
Account Executive

mn/pb

Encs.

Apology Letters

Sample Letters 8.7 through 8.10 are all examples of letters of apology.

Sample Letter 8.7 is a general letter of apology written to express regrets over a problem caused a customer. Because of the general nature of this letter, it is easily tailored to any situation where a letter of apology is needed.

Sample Letter 8.8 was written to express apologies about an employee's rudeness. The letter writer acknowledges the customer's complaint, apologizes for the treatment he received, stresses that it does not reflect the typical quality of service of the company, indicates she has spoken to the rude employee, and closes by again apologizing for the inconvenience.

Sample Letter 8.9 is an apology for a product defect. The letter writer expresses regrets over the customer having had to return the product, but assures him that the product will be repaired or replaced to the customer's satisfaction. The letter writer continues by mentioning the terrific reputation of the particular product and extends an offer of assistance should the customer have any other questions.

Sample Letter 8.10 was written to apologize for a delayed shipment. The letter writer tells the customer when she can expect the product and then explains what caused the delay. He continues to apologize for the inconvenience and explains that the company has taken an extra effort to get the replacement shipment there on time.

SAMPLE LETTER 8.7. General letter of apology (semiblock format).

December 23, 19X6

Mr. Harold T. Harigold
56 Yorkshire Terrace
Columbus, Michigan 34343

Dear Mr. Harigold:

Please accept our deep and sincere apologies. On behalf of the Hoodle Company, I wish to express our regrets and assure you that all efforts have been made to rectify your situation.

Please call or write me personally if you have any further questions or comments about this situation. Thank you for your kind understanding.

Sincerely yours,

James Elwood
Customer Service Manager

je/jl

SAMPLE LETTER 8.8. Letter apologizing for employee's rudeness (semiblock format).

May 23, 19X8

Mr. Zach Rendell
56 Biscayne Drive
Florina, Florida 34345

Dear Mr. Rendell:

I am writing in response to your letter of May 15, 19X8, in which you described your frustrations in dealing with one of our employees.

I apologize for the treatment you received and want to assure you that it does not reflect the quality of service we strive to maintain. I have spoken with the employee and am confident this will not occur again.

Please accept my apology. We appreciate your business and look forward to continuing our relationship in the future.

Sincerely,

Barbara T. Blazen
Customer Service Manager

BTB:jk

SAMPLE LETTER 8.9.   Letter apologizing for product defect (semiblock format).

May 24, 19X0

Mr. Harold P. Winkle
67 Yorkey Place
Fenway, Nebraska 43456

Dear Mr. Winkle:

We regret that the stereo system you purchased from our Sherman Oaks store was returned because of a defect. We assure you that your system will be repaired or replaced as soon as possible.

The Z-186X system is one of the finest available, and the Z Company one of the most reputable and quality conscious. The Hoodle Company stands behind these products and will take whatever steps are necessary to guarantee your satisfaction with this product.

Please call my office if you have any further questions about this problem.

Sincerely,

Hans N. Sociates
Customer Service Manager

HNS/jl

SAMPLE LETTER 8.10.   Apology for delayed shipment (semiblock format).

May 24, 19X9

Ms. Carlisle P. Hunneycutt
Haskins, Haskins & Sony, Inc.
34 Radcliff Road
Cambridge, Kentucky 34345

Dear Ms. Hunneycutt:

I have seen to it that the computer tables you ordered on May 1 from us have been loaded on our truck. The shipment should arrive in Cambridge by Thursday of this week.

After receiving your letter of May 15, I checked our warehouse and found that the original shipment of computer tables was mistakenly returned to us. I apologize for the error and hope that this replacement shipment will reach you in time to meet your needs.

Ms. Hunneycutt, I realize that there is little hope that we can make up for the inconvenience the delivery mishap caused you. I hope that this rush shipment will make up for some of it.

Please call me if you have any questions or problems. Again, sorry for the delay.

Best regards,

Armand L. Newport
Vice President

aln/jls

Letter Acknowledging Order

Sample Letter 8.11 was written to acknowledge an order and explain how it will be shipped. The letter writer clearly explains how much of the order is being shipped and how much has been back ordered, and thanks the customer for his business.

SAMPLE LETTER 8.11. Acknowledging an order (full-block).

June 24, 19X0

Mr. Simon Legyern
Legyern Cabinetmakers, Inc.
45 Merrimac Trail
Williamsburg, Colorado 32345

Dear Mr. Legyern:

Thank you for your order of 12 cases of wood glue from our company. The invoice for $288 is enclosed.

A portion of your order—8 cases—was shipped out this morning and should reach you within 10 days. We regret that to fill your order, we depleted our stock and must order the remainder of the glue from the manufacturer. You should receive the remainder of your order within 2 weeks. We apologize for the delay, but as a result of a special bulk rate we offered on this particular type of glue, we sold much more than we had anticipated. We are, of course, offering you the same savings that were featured in the sale.

Thanks for your order. We look forward to doing more business with you in the future.

Sincerely,

Kate Narconi

kn/js

enc.

Letter Correcting Wrong Shipment

Sample Letter 8.12 was written to clarify an incorrect product shipment. The letter writer immediately explains that the correct product is being shipped express. He apologizes for the error and asks the customer to return the wrong product at his convenience and at the company's expense.

SAMPLE LETTER 8.12.   Letter correcting shipment of wrong merchandise
(block format).

December 26, 19X1

Mr. Robert R. Noren
Big Bank School
56 Teller Place
Island, Hawaii 32345

Dear Bob:

We've shipped two cases of <u>The Commercial Accounts Kit</u> to you by
overnight express mail. These forms will replace the shipment of <u>The
Retail Accounts Kit</u> we sent you by mistake.

We apologize for the error we made in shipment, Bob. Your order for two
cases of the forms was clear in stating the amount, title, and date on
which you needed the forms for use in teaching your commercial accounts
seminar on January 5, 19X2.

I am pleased that the correct forms will arrive in time for you to use in
your seminar. When you have time, will you send <u>The Retail Accounts Kits</u>
back to us? We will, of course, pay for the shipping charges.

Again, I apologize for any inconvenience we may have caused. I hope this
year's sessions go well.

Sincerely,

Merlin L. Nesgas

mln/jls

Product or Service Information Letters

Sample Letters 8.13 through 8.17 are examples of product or service information
letters.

Sample Letter 8.13 was written in response to a customer's request for a
duplicate copy of his charge account records. The letter writer explains that he has
enclosed the copies and offers any help he may be able to give to the customer.

Sample Letter 8.14 informs the customer that the entire amount of product
she ordered is not in stock and that partial payment is being returned.

Sample Letter 8.15 informs the customer that the product she ordered could not be located. The letter writer offers to help her find any other product she might need.

Sample Letter 8.16 was written to inform the customer that the product offered is out of stock, but the letter writer suggests a substitute for the desired product. The letter writer explains that the substitute has been used by many others who also use the primary choice product. He asks that the customer let him know if he'd like the substitute product in place of the original order.

Sample Letter 8.17 was written to inform a customer about the reasons for the damage to a shipment of products the company made to the customer. The letter writer takes the blame for the damage to the shipment, offers a solution to the problem, and thanks the customer for his patience.

SAMPLE LETTER 8.13.   Responding to customer's request for information (full-block format).

April 20, 19X7
A-354-29

Mr. Alexander Campbell
Bethany Bagel Company
14 Pendleton Road
Scots, Pennsylvania 00012

Dear. Mr. Hamilton:

The records you requested are enclosed. Because of the technical difficulties we have in processing microfilm, I am unable to provide better quality copies.

I am sorry for any inconvenience this may cause. If I can be of any further assistance, please call me or another customer service representative on our toll-free number.

Sincerely,

Ambrose Kemper
Customer Service Representative

jls

Enclosure

SAMPLE LETTER 8.14.   Letter informing customer item is out of stock
(semiblock).

October 20, 19X7

Mr. Jackie Mustang
Whist, Inc.
98 Primiano Place
Rockefeller, Massachusetts 03234

Dear Mr. Mustang:

I hope your shipment of garland arrived in good shape. Since we did
not have the full quantity you ordered, I am enclosing a check for $8.76 to
cover the difference.

I'm looking forward to seeing you in November at the dealer's show in
Penob City.

Yours truly,

Kate Peterson

kp/jb

enc.

SAMPLE LETTER 8.15.   Letter informing customer that item ordered could
not be located (block format).

August 19, 19X7

Miss Diantha Roen, Buyer
Roen Sporting Goods
98 Headley Drive
Loom, Virginia 87765

Dear Miss Roen:

Thank you for your inquiry about undershirt and brief racks. I'm sorry to
say that I was unable to locate the specific racks you wanted.

If there is anything else you might need, please call me.

Sincerely,

Kate O. Peterson
Account Representative

kop/job

SAMPLE LETTER 8.16.   Letter suggesting a substitute (semiblock format).

February 3, 19X1

Ms. Alicia T. Hansdale
67 Utica Road
Ithaca, Connecticut 34345

Dear Ms. Hansdale:

Thank you for your recent order for 500 Acmeplus 320 double-sided, double-density computer disks. Unfortunately, that item is out of stock.

In the past, many of our customers have used our All-Star 782 disks in place of Acmeplus 320s, and have found them completely satisfactory.

I would be happy to send you the All-Star disks on a no-risk trial basis. If you do not find them completely to your liking, simply return the unused disks and we will refund your money.

Please let me know if you would like to try the All-Star product. If you do, I'll ship them out immediately.

Thank you for your order. I look forward to hearing from you.

Sincerely,

Mark E. Mathews
Account Representative

mem/jk

SAMPLE LETTER 8.17.   Letter apologizing for damaged shipment
(semiblock format).

May 24, 19X8

Mr. Alan T. Quizone
Back Bay Secretarial Services, Inc.
306 Dartmouth Street
Trenton, Pennsylvania 85643

Dear Mr. Quizone:

After receiving your letter today, I instructed my warehouse foreman
to load a new shipment of computer tables onto one of our trucks to be
sent to you. You should have the tables by the time this letter reaches you.

The damage to the first batch of computer tables was almost
undoubtedly the result of the poor handling it received from the shipping
service we used. We will arrange to pick up the damaged tables from your
office at a time that is convenient to you.

I apologize for the inconvenience this matter has caused you. I am
sure that the computer tables you receive on the second go-round will
meet with your approval.

Thank you for your patience.

Sincerely,

Oscar E. Renter
Account Executive

oer/mln

Thank-You Letters to Customers

Sample Letters 8.18 through 8.22 were all written to thank customers. Sample
Letter 8.18 was written to thank a customer for a testimonial about a company's
products. Sample Letter 8.19 thanks a customer for a referral to a prospective
customer. Sample Letter 8.20 thanks a customer for supporting a new business.
Sample Letter 8.21 thanks a customer for continued business support. Sample Letter
8.22 thanks a customer for repeat business.

All five letters express sincere thanks to the customer for a different reason.

But in each, the letter writer lets the customer know how important he or she is to the company. Thank-you letters to loyal customers can go a long way in ensuring that their loyalty will continue for some time to come.

SAMPLE LETTER 8.18.   Letter thanking someone for a testimonial (full-block format).

May 9, 19X6

Ms. Nancy Lang
Business Enterprise College
186-A Storming Hill Road
Grampian, Pennsylvania 32456

Dear Ms. Lang:

Thank you very much for the kind words you said about Andoris Company. Your testimonial lets us know that we are doing something right and that our customers appreciate it.

Rarely does someone take the time to write us about the good job she thinks we are doing. We appreciate the time you took to express your pleasure.

I am glad that the software that we sold you fit the bill perfectly for your work on account management. We think the software is among the best, if not the best, easy-to-use software available today on account management.

Thanks again for your kind words. If we can be of help in the future, we'd consider it a pleasure to serve you.

Sincerely,

Manuel L. Narciega
President

MLN:jls

SAMPLE LETTER 8.19. Letter thanking customer for a referral (block format).

June 2, 19X5

Mr. Jeffrey R. Krauss
Krauss Associates
25 Huntington Avenue, Suite 408
Boonton, New Jersey 07005

Dear Jeffrey:

Thanks for referring me to Kate Paul, who you thought might be in need of insurance planning. I called on Kate last Wednesday and enjoyed meeting with her and her partner at Kate Paul & Helen Louise Enterprises, Ltd.

You were quite correct in assessing Kate's insurance situation. I am sure my firm can meet her insurance needs and help her plan for the future.

Thank you for calling Kate ahead of time to let her know I'd be calling on her. She told me how positive you were about my services. That endorsement from you was an incredible boost to my credibility before I even walked in the door.

Thanks again for the referral and your kind words.

Sincerely,

Greg B. Luzinski
Principal

gbl:jlh

SAMPLE LETTER 8.20.   Letter expressing appreciation for support
(semiblock format).

July 15, 19X8

Mr. Edward J. Cole
Baning Consulting Group
301 Morlan Road
Bethany, West Virginia 26032

Dear Mr. Cole:

The time has simply flown by, but on July 31, 19X8, Parpubris Company will celebrate five years in business. We're proud of the office equipment and office design services we've provided and the reception we've received in the marketplace, all in five short years.

Much of the credit for our success has resulted from the support of loyal customers like you who have consistently come back to us to place orders. It's friends like you who have put Parpubris on the map as the supplier of office equipment and design services to businesses throughout the tri-state area.

Thank you for your support over the last five years. We plan to continue to provide the products and services that have satisfied you in the past. We look forward to a prosperous future made possible by customers who've stuck with Parpubris since its humble beginnings.

Thanks again.

Best regards,

Mary L. Neals
President

mln/jls

SAMPLE LETTER 8.21.   Letter thanking customer for business (full-block format).

August 25, 19X0

Mr. Dave Wallace
Parthenon Products
45 Alenton Road
Washington, D.C. 03040

Dear Dave:

I wanted to let you know how much we at NES Products, Inc., appreciate your business and the opportunity to be able to serve you. I hope that this is the beginning of a long and beneficial relationship for both you and NES Products.

If there is anything I can do for you and Parthenon, please give me a call. When you're in the area, make sure to drop in and say hello.

Sincerely,

David St. Simon
Sales Representative

ds/mn

SAMPLE LETTER 8.22.   Letter thanking customer for repeat business (semiblock format).

December 26, 19X6

Ms. Rachel Victoria
39 Tide Place, Suite 654
Boonton, New Jersey 07005

Dear Ms. Victoria:

   I wanted to take the time to thank you for the way you have handled your business dealings with us. This note is written just to make sure that you know how high a value we at Graham Products place on our relationship.

We are trying to do a good job for you and will always welcome your suggestions. If you like our service and products and the way we do business, we hope you will recommend us to your friends and acquaintances. If not, we hope that you will tell us why.

Please feel free to call upon us whenever we can be of service. We want you to feel that Graham Products is always responsive and eager to give you the best service and products in the business.

Yours very truly,

Miles Cannon
President

mc/mn

Pricing Letters

Sample Letters 8.23 through 8.25 all deal with pricing of products. All three letters clearly lay out the issues and leave little doubt in the customers' minds about how the company is planning to deal with these particular pricing questions.

Sample Letter 8.23 announces to a retail customer that the wholesaler will be raising its prices on goods. The letter includes a list of products and the percentage price increase to which they will be subjected.

While the primary purpose of Sample Letter 8.24 is to announce a freeze on price increases, the writer takes the opportunity to introduce several new products to a company's line. The letter serves not only as a customer service letter, but also as a sales letter.

Sample Letter 8.25 informs the customer that the product he desires is in stock and that quantity discounts on the merchandise and shipping costs are available. He asks the customer to let him know how much of the product he would like so he can calculate the discount.

SAMPLE LETTER 8.23.   Letter informing customer of a price increase
(simplified format).

January 26, 19X7

Mr. Paul Vanice
Vanice Camera Shop
96 Pauline Drive
Oshkosh, Wisconsin 43456

PRICE INCREASE ON BLACK AND WHITE PHOTOGRAPHY PRODUCTS

Mr. Vanice, effective February 26, 19X7, we will be raising prices on black
and white products by the following percentages:

PAN F, FP4, HP5, PAN films all types	3.6%
XP-1 film except 36 exposure	3.6%
XP-1 film 35mm, 36 exposure	12.0%
Bornesprint paper	5.0%
Bornesobrom paper	8.0%
Multigrade II, Multigrade FB, Bornespeed papers	4.0%
All liquid chemicals	3.5%

We are happy to announce that all film and paper powder chemicals will
be significantly reduced in price. Watch your price list for details. New
catalog pages will be mailed to you before February 26, 19X7.

We at Bornes Photo Corporation would like to thank you for your past
support and wish you continued success in 19X7.

MAURY SIMONS
VICE PRESIDENT, MARKETING

MS/js

SAMPLE LETTER 8.24.   Letter notifying customers that prices will not be raised (block format).

February 1, 19X8

Ms. Zoe Jeffries
Laramy Equipment Company
34 Main Street
Apriori, Utah 35436

Dear Ms. Jeffries:

Just a quick note to send you the 19X8 Extendacord price list. Please note that we have held our 19X7 prices. We will continue to do so for as long as possible.

Extendacord, Inc., has a new look and several new cords and covers for home appliances for 19X8. We have redesigned the fold-a-way cord, wrap-a-round cord, and retractable cord. Three new additions to our line of appliance covers are the Heatshield 1000, the ProTouch, and the Keepitwarm Mit. We have also enhanced the entire Extendacord look with colorful accents on all of our products.

You can see all of this for yourself in the enclosed Extendacord catalog or during the February Home Appliance Show in Salt Lake City. Come visit us in booth B-444.

See you in Salt Lake City.

Cordially,

Keye Quinn
National Sales Manager

kq/mn

encs.

SAMPLE LETTER 8.25.   Letter informing customer about volume discount
(semiblock).

September 23, 19X7

Mr. Ambrose Kemper
Kemper Construction Company
Box 8765
Encino, Arkansas 98765

Dear Mr. Kemper:

Thank you for your inquiry about our drywall products. We do have
drywall in stock. It can be shipped from here or directly from Little Rock.
The cost per sheet is $39 plus $20 for crating. If you order 40 sheets or
more, the price will be less.

I understand that you are interested in buying 15 sheets. Delivery of
this size order usually averages two to three days. I should also mention
that Washington Freight System does allow a 50% discount on freight
charges. This is a considerable savings. The cost to ship 15 sheets would be
approximately $207.50 less 50%, or $103.75.

Once you decide how much drywall you need and how you'd like it
shipped, please get in touch with me. We look forward to filling your order.

Yours truly,

Max Martinson
Vice President

mm/sf

Change-in-Location Letter

Sample Letter 8.26 was written to inform customers of a change in location of repair
services. The letter clearly and briefly gives the customer the information necessary
for her to continue to use the services.

SAMPLE LETTER 8.26.   Notice of change in location (semiblock format).

February 9, 19X8

Ms. Zelda Jeffries
Laramy Equipment Company
34 Main Street
Apriori, Utah 35436

Subject: New National Service Update

Dear Ms. Jeffries:

We are pleased to announce that as a result of our recent expansion into our new facilities in Boonton, New Jersey, we are now performing all repairs of household appliance products sent directly to New National from the following two locations:

New National Corporation   New National Corporation
312 West Main Street   43 Lorraine Terrace
Boonton, New Jersey 60070   Diego, California 417729
ATTN: Appliance service   ATTN: Appliance service

The only exceptions to this policy are discontinued products for which parts are no longer available. Should we receive a product that we are unable to repair due to lack of parts, we will return it to you unrepaired, at no charge.

An estimate of repair costs will continue to be sent to you for approval prior to the start of any repair. To save repair time, preapprovals will be honored if a letter of authorization accompanies the product.

Thank you for your cooperation and support. We remain committed to providing you with the finest service available.

Cordially,

Martin North
Director of Operations

mn/lh

Project Status Letters

Sample Letters 8.27 through 8.30 all involve questions of project status.

Sample Letter 8.27 requests a response to a project proposal. It is a brief letter written as a follow-up to a phone conversation. The letter writer gives the reader a cutoff date by which he would like to have a response and explains why time is of the essence.

Sample Letter 8.28 was written to inform a client about the status of services provided to the client. The letter writer clearly details all of the work he has done for the client and asks for the client to indicate if he is pleased with the results.

Sample Letter 8.29 informs a client about the status of contracts that were to be sent him. Because the letter writer is taking longer than he thought he would have to in ironing out the details of the contracts, he sent this letter to assure the client the matter is under control.

Sample Letter 8.30 is an abbreviated version of the type of letter illustrated in Sample Letter 8.28. Here the letter writer quickly lists some of the work done to date on the client's account. As in Sample Letter 8.28, the letter writer here asks for a reaction to the work done.

SAMPLE LETTER 8.27.   Letter asking for response to project proposal (block format).

November 3, 19X7

Ms. Nancy Kenworthy
56 Yount Street
Berkeley, California 34321

Dear Nancy:

It was good to speak with you earlier today. Sheila Morlan and I are eager to go forward with the screenplay of The Man Who Lived in the Adirondacks. Therefore, I must ask that I hear from you within the next three weeks—no later than Monday, November 24—about any possible revisions to the agreements I sent you. If we have not heard from you by then, I would like all of Sheila's materials returned to me so that we can pursue our own efforts.

Nancy, considering the amount of time that has passed on this project, I'm sure that you understand our concern. I look forward to hearing from you and getting the agreements signed very soon.

Best regards,

Pamela Yale

py/ph

cc: Sheila Morlan

SAMPLE LETTER 8.28.   Letter to client about status of project—services rendered to date (full-block format).

August 4, 19X7

Mr. Goorgo Dondino
Dendrinos Fish House
1966 Jim Lewis Drive
Boonton, New Jersey 07005

Dear George:

I spoke with Alan Prestige, a freelance writer for The Daily Mail, and sent him the materials he needed to do a review. He planned to eat at Dendrinos Fish House last night.

Let me tell you about the other things I did for Dendrinos Fish House in July. I have, on a number of occasions, spoken to Regina Wheaton, food critic for The Blaze, about your expansion plans. Simon Grimes interviewed Deena Dendrinos for the October issue of Boonton magazine. Although the restaurant may not be mentioned in that story, this is a good way to introduce Simon to Dendrinos'. He works in the service features department, which is responsible for the annual "Best and Worst" listings. The other day I spoke with Marvin Allens about a story he's doing for The Daily Mail in September. It is a guide to restaurants for newcomers to the Boonton area. Dendrinos will be included.

I also recently sent The Blaze Bulletin Board a cover letter with all of your menus to tie into any possible stories they might be doing about restaurants. Regina Wheaton tipped me off to this possibility before she left for vacation. I've also spoken to Woody Woodson, who has a weekly food show on WBOK radio, and invited him to dinner at Dendrinos. I'll keep you posted on my progress with all of these people.

You mentioned the menu award Dendrinos received. I would be glad to send out a release with accompanying sample menus to the relevant local press and national trades. Information must be timely and salient to even stand a chance of getting publicity. Let me know the details as soon as possible.

I know you were disappointed about not being anointed as Boonton's best fish house in July's Boonton magazine. I was too. All I can say is: I know you'll be around for a long time to come. Your day will come; I'm sure.

I believe that covers the work we've done to date. I think my time was well spent. Quite a bit was accomplished in this past month. The results of it all will come later.

Page 2
Mr. George Dendins
August 4, 19X7

Let me know if you are pleased with our work so far. I look forward to hearing from you.

Sincerely yours,

Mary Nilthonson
Account Executive

mn/js

SAMPLE LETTER 8.29.   Letter to client about status of project—pending contracts (semiblock format).

September 23, 19X7

Mr. James Louis
312 Lathrop Avenue
Boonton, New Jersey 07005

Dear Jim:

I just wanted to let you know that the changes I am requesting in your new contract with Doris Corporation are more extensive than I had expected, and that it will take a bit longer than I predicted to get them down to you for your signing. I'm finishing up negotiations with Zoe North now, though, so it shouldn't be too much longer.

Thanks for your patience.

Best regards,

Beverly J. Carlson

bjc/ejc

SAMPLE LETTER 8.30.   Letter about status of project, including samples of
work to date (block format).

July 24, 19X7

Mr. Zack Romance
Romance & Romance, CPAs
54 Quickness Drive
Encino, Washington 34345

Dear Zack:

We're off to a good start. I've enclosed some of the things we've been
working on. Please look them over and give us your feedback. Here's what's
enclosed:

> *Samples of sales materials, including rough sketches for brochures
>   and collateral material
> *Marketing program memorandum—a draft of a memo that will come
>   from you and Jim about marketing plans for the company and the
>   employees' role
> *AICPA release—for your approval, then for release to the local and
>   trade press
> *Biographical information sheet—for employees to fill out to aid our
>   internal publicity program

I met with Alice Glipstein from your office this morning. I am assigning
her the duties you and I had previously discussed, such as preparing your
information package and understanding her role as a marketing/publicity
liaison.

I look forward to hearing your reaction to the status of our work so far.

Sincerely yours,

Melvin Nierce

mn/js

encs.

Product-Handling Letter

Sample Letter 8.31 was written to a customer informing him of proper handling
procedures for a company product. The letter writer clearly states the purpose of

the letter, instructs the reader that the information on handling is enclosed, and asks that it be passed on to the appropriate person within the firm.

SAMPLE LETTER 8.31.   Letter giving handling procedures for product (semiblock format).

November 4, 19X7

Mr. Loren Ray, Director
Humana, Humana & Kramden
45 Eufala Drive
Huntington, Massachusetts 03245

Dear Loren:

Enclosed is a material safety data sheet for propane gas that we supply to all of our customers. This information is part of our program to provide you with the health, safety, and environmental protection information that is necessary for the safe handling of propane.

Please direct this information to the person in your firm responsible for health and safety matters as well as employees handling propane. If additional material safety data sheets are required, or if you have any questions about the safe handling of our product, please call me at 323-908-7654.

Thank you very much for your business.

Sincerely,

O. C. Dillard
Operations Engineer

ocd/rgj

Enclosure

Letter Explaining Regulatory Impact on Client

Sample Letter 8.32 was written to a client informing him of the impact a regulatory change will have on his finances. The writer clearly states the intent of the letter in his opening paragraph. He then details the effect of the regulation and closes by suggesting the client set up an appointment to discuss how to plan under the new laws. The letter serves to warn the client of impending changes and, by doing so, lets him know that the letter writer is concerned enough about him to keep abreast of his personal situation.

SAMPLE LETTER 8.32. Letter to customer explaining how new regulations will affect him or her (block format).

September 19, 19X6

Mr. Brad S. Pale
65 Lincoln Drive
Grand Forks, North Dakota 32345

Dear Brad:

The enclosed reports are 19X7 and 19X8 income tax projections prepared for you to estimate the effects on your income tax of the proposed legislation recently approved by the House-Senate Conference Committee. While the reduction in individual tax rates is the cornerstone of this tax reform legislation, many tax deductions are also curtailed or eliminated.

Since these income tax projections are based on the facts as shown on your 19X5 income tax return, which we prepared, and not on current facts, they should not be viewed as tax planning projections. In addition, we made some key assumptions to complete this analysis.

Under the Conference Committee bill, your 19X7 federal income tax liability is $261.55 more than it would be in 19X7 under current tax law. The increase is due mainly to:

    *The partial elimination of passive losses of $36.05
    *The reduction of your IRA deduction of $1,815.41
    *The elimination of the sales tax deduction of $169.00
    *The partial elimination of consumer interest deduction of $149.10
    *The elimination of miscellaneous itemized deductions of $315.00
    *The increase in the marginal tax rate from 30% to 35%

Various deductions allowed under current tax law will be phased out gradually over several years under the Committee bill. Items scheduled for partial or complete elimination include the personal exemptions above certain income levels and the consumer interest, investment interest, and passive loss deductions. In 19X8, your federal income tax liability is $209.53 more than it would be in 19X8 under current tax law.

We will continue to monitor any changes that occur between the Conference Committee bill and the final tax law. Since your income tax

Page 2
Mr. Brad S. Pale
September 19, 19X6

situation is adversely affected by this tax reform proposal, we encourage you to contact us at your convenience to discuss tax planning strategies to minimize the impact of this proposal. To set up an appointment, please call us at 643-998-4533.

Best regards,

David Paul, C.P.A.

DP/JS

Enclosure

Subscription Response Letters

Sample Letters 8.33 through 8.37 were written in response to subscriber inquiries. Whether the letter writer is addressing a complaint or a positive inquiry, she treats each subscriber with courtesy, providing all of them with the information they need.

Sample Letter 8.33 was written to respond to a subscriber who wanted to know why a renewal notice was sent out so early in his subscription period. The letter writer acknowledges the question and clearly spells out the publication's policy on renewal notices.

In Sample Letter 8.34, a subscriber is offered either a refund or an extension to make up for an overpayment.

Sample Letter 8.35 was written to a customer to respond to an inquiry about back-issue sales. The letter writer clearly spells out the pricing structure for back issues and informs the reader that some issues will be facsimile copies, not originals. By explaining this to the reader, she diminishes the chances of a disappointed customer.

Sample Letter 8.36 was written in response to a subscriber inquiry about why a refund for a cancelled subscription has taken so long to be sent. The letter writer explains the hold up, apologizes for the delay, and assures the reader she will expedite the refund.

SAMPLE LETTER 8.33. Letter responding to question about subscription renewal notice (semiblock format).

June 1, 19X8

Mr. John T. Larry
65 York Place
Plattsburgh, Pennsylvania 32345

Dear Mr. Larry:

Thank you for your recent note about your renewal notice. The reason you received a renewal notice well before your expiration date is simple economics. Anyone in the subscription business learns two facts about renewals very quickly. First, the average subscriber needs several renewal notices before he actually subscribes. Second, renewal notices sent prior to the expiration of the current subscription are far more effective than those sent after expiration.

Putting these facts together results in a series of renewal notices beginning well before expiration to allow sufficient time between notices.

If you do not wish to renew in advance, you may wait until closer to your expiration. We will continue to send you notices.

Thank you for your interest in Business Life. We look forward to serving you in the future.

Best regards,

Harriet Tibbits
Publisher

ht:js

SAMPLE LETTER 8.34.   Letter written to subscribers notifying them of a
price decrease (block format).

December 26, 19X6

Mr. John R. Reynolds
67 Truscott Lane
Hudson, New Jersey 07005

Dear Mr. Reynolds:

Originally, we offered Parriston Company customers like you a
subscription to The Review for $87 a year. We have now reduced that price
to $75 per year. Therefore, we would like to offer you the opportunity to
extend your subscription for an additional 6 months—6 extra issues at no
charge.

If you prefer, we will send you a refund check for $12. Simply check off the
appropriate box on the enclosed questionnaire and mail it back to us in
the enclosed postage-paid envelope.

Thank you for your interest in The Review. We look forward to serving you
in the future.

Yours truly,

Glenda Allen
Publisher

ga/js

encls.

SAMPLE LETTER 8.35. Letter responding to question about back issues (semiblock format).

June 15, 19X8

Mr. Larry T. Lester
67 Farway Road
Bolovin, Mississippi 44345

Dear Mr. Lester:

Thank you for your letter inquiring about back issues of The Armchair Reader's Review. We have a limited supply of back issues. The cost of back issues is $7.00 per copy. With any order that exceeds 9 copies, this price is reduced to $6.50 per copy.

If we have the issue in stock, we will send you the actual printed issue. We will mail facsimile copies of the issues, however, if we are out of stock. The same price will be charged for these copies. We want people to understand our back-issue policy since some people would rather not receive a facsimile.

We have enclosed a postage paid envelope for your convenience in mailing your check. We've also enclosed an index for you to decide which back issues you'd like to receive. We regret that we cannot bill you for any back issues. Therefore, please be sure to include payment.

We look forward to serving you in the future.

Best regards,

Yvette Nelson
Publisher

yn/js

encs.

SAMPLE LETTER 8.36.   Letter written in response to cancellation and
refund query (full-block format).

May 9, 19X6

Ms. Letitia T. Ryan
56 Tyscott Road
Tucker, New Hampshire 34435

Dear Ms. Ryan:

We have sent your request for cancellation of your subscription to The
Review to our subscription service department and have requested your
refund from our accounting department. Both requests were forwarded on
April 15, 19X6. Upon checking with our accounting department, however,
we have found that your refund check is just now being processed.

Please accept our apologies. As soon as we receive your check from the
accounting department, we will immediately forward it to you.

Sincerely,

John Nelson
Associate Publisher

JN:js

        Sample Letter 8.37 was written to respond to a subscriber who claimed that he
had never ordered the publication and so was cancelling his subscription. The letter
writer expresses his concern over the reader's claim. She explains that a copy of the
order card with the reader's signature is enclosed, and offers this as the reason
the subscription was sent. The letter writer then offers to continue sending issues to
the subscriber with no obligation until the first invoice, at which time the subscriber
can cancel the subscription.

SAMPLE LETTER 8.37.   Letter written as a follow-up to subscriber who cancelled saying he never ordered subscription (semiblock format).

November 9, 19X5

Mr. Jack T. Wags
65 Yucaman Place, Apt. 5A
Boonton, New Jersey 07005

Dear Mr. Wags:

You recently returned an invoice for a year's subscription to <u>Home Life</u> marked "cancel." The reason given for the cancellation was that no subscription had ever been ordered by you.

I am writing you because I am concerned about our reputation. We are very proud of our long history of service to subscribers and do not want any misunderstanding to damage our standing with you. As you can see from the enclosed order card we received from you, we did have reason to believe you ordered a subscription. We are not in the practice of billing people for subscriptions without an order. Not only would that be ethically and legally wrong, it also would not make economic sense.

As a result, I have not cancelled your subscription. I will continue to send you copies of <u>Home Life</u>. Should you still wish to cancel because you don't like the publication, you are under no obligation to pay for these copies. They are yours to keep. I am sending them so that if you do wish to continue your subscription, you won't miss any issues.

On the enclosed postage paid card are spaces to check if you would like to continue your subscription or still cancel it. Please check the appropriate space and return this card to me.

Thank you for considering <u>Home Life</u>.

Sincerely,

Alan Tempor
Publisher

AT:JS

ENCL.

Letters to Stockholders

Sample Letters 8.38 through 8.45 were all written to stockholders. Sample Letter 8.38 was written to accompany a proxy statement. The letter writer explains the issues that will be covered at the company's annual meeting and urges the reader to complete and send in the proxy whether or not she attends the meeting. Sample Letter 8.39, which invites stockholders to the annual meeting, is a variation of the letter featured in 8.38. Letter 8.39 is a bit more formal invitation.

Sample Letter 8.40 was written to accompany an annual report. The letter writer clearly explains that the annual report is enclosed, writes enthusiastically of the company, and encourages the reader to review the annual report and call the company if he has any questions. Sample Letter 8.41 is a shorter version of a cover letter to an annual report. It states simply that the annual report is enclosed, makes a brief positive remark about the company's status, and encourages the reader to follow up if he has any questions.

Sample Letter 8.42 was written to accompany a balance sheet sent to stockholders. The letter writer clearly states what the balance sheet does and does not feature.

Sample Letter 8.43 was written to acknowledge a new stockholder. The letter writer welcomes the new stockholder, mentions the enclosed annual report, and extends an offer to set up a meeting for the reader with the company's executive officers.

SAMPLE LETTER 8.38.   Letter accompanying proxy for annual meeting of stockholders (semiblock format).

March 24, 19X8

Ms. Lauren J. Palle
54 Lincoln Drive
Grand Forks, North Dakota 32345

Subject: Notice of Annual Meeting

Dear Ms. Palle:

The annual meeting of stockholders of Dover Company will be held at Boonton Bandwagon Hall, 324 Lathrop Avenue, Boonton, New Jersey, on Wednesday, April 27, 19X8, at 11:00 A.M. to consider and act on the following matters:

1. Determination of the number of directors and election of directors for the ensuing year
2. Ratification of the selection of Rosenblatt, Talbnesor & Company as auditors of Dover Company for the current year

3. Any other matter than may properly come before the meeting or any adjournment

Whether or not you attend in person, it would be appreciated if you would fill in and sign the enclosed proxy and return it promptly in the enclosed envelope. If you attend the meeting, you may, of course, vote your shares even though you have sent in your proxy.

Sincerely,

Mel Palay, Clerk

mp/js

Enclosure

SAMPLE LETTER 8.39.　　Letter inviting stockholders to annual meeting (semiblock format).

March 24, 19X8

Mr. Alan Palay
45 Twilite Road
Simmons, Alabama 23456

Dear Mr. Palay:

You are cordially invited to attend the 19X8 annual meeting of stockholders of Parris Company on Thursday, April 28, 19X8, at 11:00 A.M. at Boonton, Bandwagon Hall, 324 Lathrop Avenue, Boonton, New Jersey.

The formal business to be considered and acted upon by stockholders at this meeting is the election of directors and the ratification of the selection of the company's certified public accountants. These matters are described in detail in the accompanying Notice of Annual Meeting and Proxy Statement. We will also use this opportunity to report to you on Parris' 19X7 performance and outlook for the future.

It is important that your shares be represented whether or not you are able to be there in person. I urge you, therefore, to register your vote now by completing, signing, and returning the enclosed proxy card promptly.

All stockholders will receive a report of the meeting in the mail.

Sincerely,

Mary Nachez, President

mn/js

Enclosures

SAMPLE LETTER 8.40.   Letter accompanying annual report (full-block format).

January 4, 19X5

Mr. Ryan D. Kenney
45 Trander Road
Elipses, New Jersey 32456

Dear Mr. Kenney

Enclosed is the MR. WONDERFUL Public Partnerships' Annual Report for 19X4. It contains important information about your investment.

I am very proud of the enclosed report because it clearly demonstrates that the limited partnerships formed by MR. WONDERFUL are producing and performing as anticipated.

We live in an economic environment that is becoming increasingly complex due in part to tax reform, deficits, and globalization of financial markets. It is, therefore, very gratifying to me to see the positive results of a simple investment concept: the free and clear ownership of commercial real estate properties producing monthly spendable income. For your information, we have reproduced a table on the back of this letter that summarizes the success of these public programs.

As our financial world becomes more complicated, the necessity of sound financial planning increases. I urge you to update your financial plan and review your long-range goals with your professional financial planner.

If you and your financial planner have any questions or need further information on the enclosed annual report or our continued investment programs, please feel free to call our investor/broker relations staff at the toll-free numbers listed below.

Yours truly,

B. R. Roenshoot
President

brr/mnn

Enclosures

SAMPLE LETTER 8.41.   Short cover letter to annual report (semiblock format).

March 23, 19X8

Mr. Lawrence D. Braden
Parks, Bryans, Alans & Sims
67 Gotshald Drive
Arcade, Maine 32456

Dear Larry:

You might find Arris Company's 19X7 annual report interesting. With a lot of hard work and good luck, the company had an excellent year. We are looking forward to continued progress.

Please give me a call if you have any comments.

Sincerely,

Maury Noblesse
President

mn/js

Enclosure

SAMPLE LETTER 8.42.   Letter to stockholders accompanying balance sheet
(simplified format).

March 9, 19X5

Mr. Paul W. Hudson
LKTY, Inc.
991 Hampton Road
Newfork, New Hampshire 60233

ARRIS COMPANY ANNUAL BALANCE SHEET

Mr. Hudson, we have compiled the accompanying balance sheet of Arris
Company as of December 31, 19X4, and the related statements of income
and expense and changes in financial position for the year then ended in
accordance with the standards established by the American Institute of
Certified Public Accountants.

A compilation is limited to presenting in the form of financial statements
information that is the representation of management. We have not
audited or reviewed the accompanying financial statements and,
accordingly, do not express an opinion or any other form of assurance on
them.

At management's election, these financial statements were prepared for
their internal use and therefore do not necessarily include all of the
disclosures required by generally accepted accounting principles. If the
omitted disclosures were included in the financial statements, they might
influence the user's conclusions about the company's financial position,
results of operations, and changes in financial position. Accordingly, these
financial statements are not designed for those who are not informed
about such matters.

SIMON NIELSON, C.P.A.

sn/js

Enclosures

SAMPLE LETTER 8.43.   Letter acknowledging a new stockholder
(semiblock format).

May 16, 19X8

Mr. Lester Cooper
345 Brooklyn Drive
Saunders, New York 12345

Dear Mr. Cooper:

It is a pleasure for me to welcome you to the growing list of stockholders in Arris Company. Since 19X4, it has been our privilege to manufacture quality furniture.

We are pleased to enclose a copy of our current annual report. It shows our strong financial condition and the many types of furniture we offer. It illustrates, through our board of directors made up of business and civic leaders, the position and support we enjoy in the community. We take pride in being a local business that supports its community and has the support of its community.

Please give me a call and I will arrange for you to meet with our executive officers. They and I would be glad to acquaint you with our business and how it plans to continue to grow in the future.

Sincerely,

Wayne Doxety
President

wd/bc

encl.

Sample Letter 8.44 was written to accompany an offering memorandum for stock. The letter writer clearly explains that she is enclosing the requested materials and instructs the reader which forms to fill out and send back.

Sample Letter 8.45 is a letter of confidentiality sent to a client who is interested in acquiring a company. The letter clearly details its intent and instructs the reader on the appropriate procedure to take in completing the confidentiality agreement.

SAMPLE LETTER 8.44.   Letter accompanying offering memorandum for
stock (full-block format).

October 19, 19X7

Mr. Thomas Alexander
Franroad and Libersmidt Corp.
45 Hope Park
Trintonite, New Jersey 79685

Dear Mr. Alexander:

I am enclosing two confidentiality letters and a confidential memorandum
on Fleitschmidt & Co. that you requested in our telephone conversation
today. As I explained to you, the management of Fleitschmidt has recently
become concerned about the level of stock held by certain investors.
Therefore, management is pursuing a course that allows it the
opportunity to control who its partner may be.

The management team at Fleitschmidt has positioned the company in the
microcomputer and peripherals market. It has a strategy for the future
that it would like to implement and is selectively approaching a few
companies that it feels may help it enhance and accelerate that strategy.

Please sign and return one of the confidentiality letters. We would then like
your thoughts on this opportunity after you have had a chance to review
the memorandum. Since time is an issue, I look forward to hearing from
you soon.

Best regards,

Rowena Guitterez
Vice President

rg/ms

Enclosure

SAMPLE LETTER 8.45.   Letter of confidentiality (simplified format).

October 19, 19X7

Mr. Thomas Alexander
Franroad and Libersmidt Corp.
45 Hope Park
Trintonite, New Jersey 79685

CONFIDENTIALITY AGREEMENT

Mr. Alexander, in connection with your possible interest in acquiring
Fleitschmidt & Co., Nilges Investment Bankers, Inc. and Fleitschmidt will
be furnishing you with certain materials that contain information about
Fleitschmidt that is either nonpublic, confidential, or proprietary in
nature. Such information, in whole or in part, together with analyses,
compilations, studies, or other documents prepared by Fleitschmidt or
Nilges Investment Bankers, to the extent such analyses, compilations,
studies, or documents contain or otherwise reflect or are generated from
such information, is hereinafter referred to as the "Information," and the
existence of any negotiations or discussions between us will also be
considered "Information." In consideration of furnishing you with the
Information, you agree with Nilges Investment Bankers and Fleitschmidt
that:

1. The Information will be kept confidential and will not, without prior
   written consent of Fleitschmidt, be disclosed by you, your agents or
   employees, in any manner whatsoever, in whole or in part, and will not
   be used by you, your agents or employees, other than in connection
   with the transaction described above. Moreover, you agree to transmit
   the Information for the purpose of evaluating your possible interest in
   acquiring Fleitschmidt to those who are informed by you of the
   confidential nature of the Information, and you will cause such agents
   and employees to comply with the terms and conditions of this
   Agreement. In any event, you will be responsible for any breach of this
   Agreement by your agents or employees.

2. The Information, including analyses, compilations, studies, or other
   documents prepared by you, your agents or employees, will be held by
   you and kept confidential and subject to the terms of this Agreement, or
   destroyed.

3. In the event that you or anyone to whom you transmit the Information
   pursuant to this Agreement becomes legally compelled to disclose any

Page 2
Mr. Thomas Alexander
October 19, 19X7

    of the Information, you will provide Fleitschmidt with prompt notice so
that Fleitschmidt may seek a protective order or other appropriate
remedy and/or waive compliance with the provisions of this Agreement.
In the event that such protective order or other remedy is not obtained,
or if Fleitschmidt waives compliance with the provisions of this
Agreement, you will furnish only that portion of the Information that is
legally required and in so doing you will not be in violation of this
Agreement.

The foregoing restrictions do not apply to Information that is or becomes
part of the public domain without your fault.

In accepting the Information, you are aware of the importance of
maintaining security surrounding all discussions in order to preclude the
possibility of premature disclosure to third parties, including
Fleitschmidt's customers.

If the above terms are in accordance with your understanding of our
agreement, please sign the enclosed copy of this letter and return the copy
to us.

ROWENA GUITTEREZ
VICE PRESIDENT

rg/ms

Enclosure

Accepted by: _____
This _____ day of _____, 19X7
By: _____

CHAPTER 9
Credit and Collection Letters

"Neither a borrower nor a lender be" might have been words Polonius could live by in Hamlet's Denmark, but such philosophy simply doesn't work in today's society. In our country, credit has become a standard way of doing business. We buy our homes on credit, start businesses on credit, stock our stores on credit, and so on. In the world of credit, the lender has to be particularly careful about the borrower's ability to pay back funds.

The letters in this chapter arm the lender with a variety of credit and collection letters that can be used to ensure that a solid relationship is built with a borrower. Should that relationship falter, the letters are here to help the borrower recoup the money that was lent. There are letters here that can also be used to help the professional set up credit arrangements with a company with which it does business.

The letters in this chapter will not help the professional avoid being a borrower or lender. But they just may make the roles a little bit easier to handle.

Letter Requesting Commercial Credit

Sample Letter 9.1 was written to a company with which the letter writer wanted to establish a business relationship. Fully aware that he will have to set up credit arrangements with the firm, he requests that the letter reader send him the forms that he will need to complete to establish commercial credit.

Credit Information Letters

Sample Letters 9.2 and 9.3 both involve credit information. The letter writer of Sample Letter 9.2 is writing to thank a customer for his order and to request that he fill out some standard credit information forms. The letter is courteous, brief, and clearly written.

Sample Letter 9.3 was written to send credit information that was requested. It could be sent as a response to Sample Letter 9.2. The letter writer wastes little space. He simply explains that he is enclosing the necessary materials.

SAMPLE LETTER 9.1.   Letter requesting commercial credit (full-block format).

June 15, 19X7

Mr. Renatto Kim
Kim Metal Products, Inc.
P.O. Box 3456
Tuscany, West Virginia 26032

Dear Mr. Kim:

After an extensive market survey, we have determined that your company's rolled steel products best meet manufacturing specifications required by our automobile factory. But before we begin placing orders -- which we anticipate will occur on a quarterly basis -- I am writing to inquire about your terms for granting commercial credit.

Since there is probably specific information that you require before establishing a credit account, perhaps it makes the most sense at this juncture for you to send me the necessary forms that we should fill out.

I look forward to hearing from you, and to establishing a credit relationship with your company.

Sincerely,

Lee I. Larroquette
Purchasing Manager

LIL:wlg

SAMPLE LETTER 9.2. Letter requesting credit information (semiblock format).

March 20, 19X0

Mr. Morton P. Stovak
VA Hospital
177 Varoom Street
Rockaway, New Jersey 43456

Dear Mr. Stovak:

Thank you for your recent order of prosthetic devices from Snug Fit Products, Inc. I note that this is the first order you have placed with our company, so let me take this opportunity to express our gratitude as well as to pledge our every effort to serve you in the future.

Before we can ship your order, however, there is some standard credit information we need. I have enclosed three forms that I would like for you to complete. Once we have these completed forms, we can set up your credit account and expedite your order with the least possible delay.

Sincerely,

Carmine D'Amato

cd/wg

encls.

SAMPLE LETTER 9.3. Letter sending credit information (block format).

May 13, 19X8

Mr. J. Lee Jumbuck
Matilda Corporation
12 Swagman's Way
Sydney, Hawaii 34345

Dear Mr. Jumbuck:

Enclosed in triplicate is the credit information that you requested. I trust that this data will satisfy any concerns you may have about our creditworthiness, and that it will lead to the establishment of a credit account for our organization.

Cordially,

Gajan Matoussamy

gm/wg

Letter Announcing Credit Policy Change

Sample Letter 9.4 was written to announce a credit policy change. The letter writer clearly announces his letter's purpose in the opening paragraph and offers a reason for the change in credit policy. He goes on to explain the specific changes and expresses appreciation to the letter reader for his continued support.

SAMPLE LETTER 9.4.   Letter notifying customer of credit policy change (semiblock format).

January 7, 19X9

Mr. Hiram T. Louis
Louis Construction Company
43 Treadway Drive
P.O. Box 4536
Newport, California 98765

Dear Mr. Louis:

After many years of service to you, we are forced to change our credit terms effective February 26, 19X9. Because of the increase in the cost of capital, changes in manufacturers' terms, and the general cost of doing business, we regret that this decision has become necessary.

Our new terms are: 2% discount if paid within 10 days from date of invoice and are net 30 days from date of invoice. The terms for all contracts are net 30 days from date of invoice, no retainage. A late finance charge of 2% (minimum charge $1.00) per month will be assessed on that portion of any account beyond 30 days. This is an annual percentage rate of 24%.

We appreciate your past patronage and trust you will understand and support our decision. We look forward to many years of satisfying your building material needs.

                            Sincerely,

                            BIG-TIME BUILDING SUPPLY

                            Dean Wheton
                            Credit Manager

dw/hs

Returned-Check Letters

Sample Letters 9.5 and 9.6 were both written as a result of returned checks. Sample Letter 9.5 was written from the debtor to the creditor informing him that his check had been returned. After telling the creditor this fact, the letter writer apologizes, offers to reimburse the creditor for any penalty charges, and assures the creditor this will not happen again.

    Sample Letter 9.6 was written to a debtor about a returned check. The letter writer states the facts in the first paragraph and explains what action he would like the debtor to take to resolve the problem.

SAMPLE LETTER 9.5.   Letter to creditor about returned check (simplified format).

May 23, 19X8

R. R. Shirley
Fly-By-Night Air Express
7201 Parisite Boulevard
Mesa, Arizona 34434

NOTIFICATION OF RETURNED CHECK

Mr. Shirley, we were just notified that the check we made out to you on March 15 (check number 2237 for $14,675) was returned by our bank for insufficient funds.

We are terribly sorry for the inconvenience this has caused you, and would like to reimburse you for any penalties you have incurred because of the returned check. We have subsequently made a deposit to our account sufficient to cover this draft.

Please be assured this will never happen again.

JASPER T. JONES
CONTROLLER

JTJ:wlg

SAMPLE LETTER 9.6.   Letter notifying debtor about returned check (block format).

August 6, 19X8

Ms. Joan B. Yennek
56 Malden Place
Medford, Wyoming 34345

Dear Ms. Yennek:

New Bank of Medford has returned your check #454 made out to Kemper Office Supplies, Ltd. for $565 to us. The check was stamped "NSF," indicating insufficient funds.

We have enclosed a postage paid return envelope in which you can send us a certified check, money order, or cashier's check for the $565. We ask that you do this as soon as you receive this letter.

If the lack of funds resulted from a mixup at the bank, we are sure you will clear up this matter by sending us a replacement check. If you are having some financial difficulty in meeting your monthly debt obligations, please call us to let us know. We'd like to work with you to come up with a solution. In either case, it's crucial that you call or write us immediately so that you can maintain your good credit standing.

Sincerely,

Alan T. Kicksad
Credit Manager

atk:jls

enc.

Credit Bureau Complaint

Sample Letter 9.7 was written to a credit bureau to complain about inaccurate information contained in the letter writer's credit history report. The letter writer clearly establishes the fact that he is writing to complain about the errors and asks that the credit bureau correct them in its file.

SAMPLE LETTER 9.7.   Letter complaining to credit bureau (semiblock format).

October 10, 19X0

Mr. Simon T. Legrey
Legrey Credit Bureau
56 Taxing Place
Huma, Arkansas 34345

Dear Mr. Legrey:

I recently received the copy of my history that I had requested from you three months ago. I am now writing to complain about the numerous inaccuracies that appear in that report.

The most glaring error is that I do not even have a credit card through the East Kebibble Bank of North Dakota. Thus, the history of late payments on this account should not apply to my credit history.

I have corrected the other errors that I found on your credit report and am returning the report to you so that you can enter the correct information.

Sincerely,

Webster L. Gray

wlg

enc.

Credit Reference Letters

Sample Letters 9.8 and 9.9 were written to get credit information from references. Both letters clearly ask for the information they need, providing blank spaces for the recipient to fill in.

SAMPLE LETTER 9.8.   Letter sent to credit reference (semiblock format).

March 20, 19X0

Ms. Beverly J. Coleman
Pink Flamingo Trading Co., Inc.
88 Latin Academy Road
Fenway, Massachusetts 56432

Subject: Credit Reference for Amlemper, Inc.

Dear Ms. Coleman:

Ambrose L. Kemper, president of Amlemper, Inc., has given us your company's name as a credit reference. Mr. Kemper has requested credit privileges for his company at Wharton Office Supply Ltd.

Would you kindly answer a few questions for us about Mr. Kemper? There are two copies of this letter enclosed. Please complete, sign, and return one copy in the postage-paid envelope provided.

What kind of credit terms did you give Mr. Kemper? _____
_____

How punctual was Mr. Kemper in making his payments? _____
_____

Do you have any reservations about Mr. Kemper's financial responsibility or stability? _____
_____

Thank you for your time. We will make sure that your comments are treated confidentially.

Sincerely,

Alan L. Shoester

als/jls

encs.

SAMPLE LETTER 9.9. Letter requesting employment information for credit applicant (simplified format).

November 23, 19X9

Ms. Trudy P. Reindollar
Director of Personnel
Farout Enterprises, Inc.
45 Trustme Lane
Far West, Florida 32345

VERIFICATION OF EMPLOYMENT OF MAXWELL L. SIDNEY

Ms. Reindollar, Mr. Sidney has made an application for a charge account. He has used you as a credit reference. Your prompt reply will be appreciated by us and your employee. It will be held in strict confidence.

1. Is the applicant employed by your company? _____
   If answer is no, please complete, the following:
   a. Date applicant left _____
   b. Reason for leaving _____
2. Base salary per hour _____ per week _____ per month _____
   per year _____
   Is all or part of salary in the form of a bonus or commissions? _____
   Overtime earnings? _____
3. How long has applicant been employed by your company? _____
4. What position does the applicant hold? _____
   _____
5. Are the applicant's services satisfactory? _____
6. What is the probability of the applicant's continued employment?
   _____
   Other remarks _____
   _____

Please sign and date the enclosed copy and return it to me. Thank you for your assistance.

RACHEL A. GRIMES
VICE PRESIDENT

rg/lg

enc.

Acknowledged by:

_____

Date: _____   _____
                                        Signature and Title

Letter Denying Credit

Sample Letter 9.10 was written to deny credit to someone who had requested it. The letter writer acknowledges the request for a credit, but then informs the customer why it cannot be set up. The letter writer clearly explains the reason credit has been denied and suggests that the customer reapply should the circumstances change.

Letter Granting Credit

Sample Letter 9.11 was written to inform a customer that he has been granted credit. The letter writer welcomes the customer, announces that his credit line has been approved, and then goes on to describe his company's services, the amount of the credit line, and the name of the letter reader's account representative. The letter's tone is enthusiastic and helpful.

SAMPLE LETTER 9.10.   Letter denying credit (full-block format).

May 20, 19X9

Mr. Alan T. Hinsdale
Hinsdale, Hinsdale, and Wanda, Inc.
43 Turnstable Road
Elmira, New York 90432

Dear Mr. Hinsdale:

Thank you for taking the time to apply for credit at Square Office Supplies, Ltd.

I'm sorry to inform you that we are unable to grant you the credit line you requested. We are grateful for your interest in our office supplies store and welcome your business, but I am afraid that your current debt situation suggests that your ability to take on additional monthly payments could put you in difficult financial straits.

When you have paid down some of your outstanding debt, or your cash flow situation changes, we would be glad to reconsider your credit application. We will, of course, welcome the opportunity to provide you with quality products and services and continue to do business on a cash basis.

Cordially,

William W. Donohoe
Credit Manager

wwd:jls

SAMPLE LETTER 9.11.   Letter granting credit (full-block format).

January 4, 19X8

Mr. Bertrand R. Levine
Lovinc's Lumber Land
P.O. Box 567
Richmond, South Dakota 34345

Dear Mr. Levine:

Welcome! Your account at Nilges Wood Supply has been approved. We are proud to have you as a customer.

Nilges Wood Supply is a 50-year-old company, with 85 stores in 9 Midwestern states. We supply a complete line of building products to our customers, including millwork, plumbing, electrical, paint, kitchen supplies, bath supplies, hardware, and tools. As a leader in this industry, we strive to provide the best service possible to our customers. Our goal is to be your most valuable supplier. Customer satisfaction is our number-one priority.

Your approved credit line is $2,000, with billing terms of Net 10th. Monthly statements are mailed on the first or second working day each month. A service charge is added to past-due balances that are not paid by the 25th day of the billing month.

We at Nilges Wood Supply welcome the opportunity to serve you and look forward to a long and prosperous relationship.

Your branch manager is Sheila McGulicuty. Her telephone number is 890-765-8765.

Yours very truly,

Larry E. Nilges
Vice President—Credit Sales

len/jls

Letter Raising Credit Limit

Sample Letter 9.12 is a brief letter informing a credit card customer that his credit limit has been raised. The letter writer makes the announcement in the first paragraph, thanks the customer in the second, and closes the letter.

SAMPLE LETTER 9.12.   Letter extending higher credit limit (block format).

May 17, 19X8

Mr. Loren T. Hinsdale
45 Alabama Place
Indian River, Colorado 34321

Dear Mr. Hinsdale:

Congratulations! Your credit card line has been increased to $2,600. Thank you for using our credit card. We have increased your line of credit so you can make more convenient credit card purchases.

We appreciate your business and hope you enjoy this extra purchasing power.

Sincerely,

Carla B. Torsolini
Credit Manager

cbt:jls

Disputed Items Cleared

Sample Letter 9.13 was written to inform a debtor that items he disputed in his credit file have been deleted. The letter writer clearly makes his point, offers to send the debtor or any of the debtor's creditors a copy of the corrected report, and closes.

SAMPLE LETTER 9.13.   Letter informing customer that disputed items have been deleted from his credit file (semiblock format).

June 15, 19X8

Mr. Jaime Chin
36 Levittown Place
Hopscotch, New York 32345

Dear Mr. Chin:

We have deleted information you disputed about your credit rating from our files. We have put a copy of your letter disputing these items in our files.

You have the right to make a written request that we furnish you with notice of the deletion, or a copy to anybody you specifically designate who has received a consumer report containing the deleted or disputed information within the preceding two years for employment purposes or within the preceding six months for any other purpose.

If you make such a request, we will advise you of any charges we will make prior to the time we furnish the notices.

Yours truly,

Colman Ling
Credit Manager

cl/bl

Stop-Payment Letter

Sample Letter 9.14 was written to a bank to ask it to stop payment on a check. The letter writer clearly indicates to whom the check was made out and how much it was made out for. He asks that the bank debit his account for the penalty charge.

SAMPLE LETTER 9.14.   Stop-payment letter (semiblock format).

August 3, 19X4

Mr. Leonard R. Coshatt
Large Bank
2666 Barbour Lane
Lugo, Alabama 32345

Please issue a stop-payment order on our company check number 722-311, written on June 30, 19X4, to Earle B. Lockwood Sod Farm for $2,545.

Please debit our account for the $15 fee assessed for issuing this stop-payment order.

Sincerely,

Ernest T. Bream

etb/wlg

Collection Letters

Sample Letters 9.15 through 9.24 are examples of collection letters.

Sample Letters 9.15 through 9.19 is a series of letters that can be used in sequence for collection purposes. This series features a first, second, third, fourth, and final overdue notice for payment due. While maintaining a level of decorum, the letters become increasingly less patient, until the final notice that the account will be turned over to a collection agency.

Sample Letter 9.20 is a brief collection letter that was sent along with a bill. The letter writer clearly explains to the reader how to figure out the amount due. This letter was written from a wholesaler to a retailer that purchased goods.

Sample Letters 9.21 and 9.22 are also examples of a series of collection letters. Sample Letter 9.21 was written as a second notice on charges due on an account. The letter writer states the amount overdue and expresses concern for the reader should he be having financial difficulty. The writer offers to help the reader deal with the overdue payment problem. Sample Letter 9.22 was written to the same person after no response was received to Sample Letter 9.21. The writer is less sympathetic and explains that he has had to notify various credit agencies about the delinquency. He offers some hope to the letter reader by explaining he can clear up his credit rating by filling out the enclosed reply card and making payment arrangements.

SAMPLE LETTER 9.15. Letter serving as first reminder after monthly statement (block format).

August 20, 19X7

Mr. Kyle T. Roading
Bolivian Import Merchants, Inc.
56 Trinity Place
Detroit, Illinois 34565

Dear Mr. Reading:

This is to inform you that we have not received the payment of $650 that appeared on our billing statement of June 8, 19X7. If you have already made the payment, please disregard this notice.

If there is any question about your bill, please call my office immediately.

Thank you for giving your prompt attention to this matter.

Sincerely,

Mark Hoddlecoock
Credit Manager

jl

SAMPLE LETTER 9.16. Letter serving as second overdue notice (semiblock format).

September 20, 19X7

Mr. Kyle T. Reading
Bolivian Import Merchants, Inc.
56 Trinity Place
Detroit, Illinois 34565

Dear Mr. Reading:

We are still waiting for the payment of $650 due since June 8, 19X7.

Failure to resolve this matter may result in the suspension of your credit privileges and can jeopardize your credit rating.

Sincerely,

Mark Hoddlecoock
Credit Manager

jl

SAMPLE LETTER 9.17.   Letter serving as third overdue notice (semiblock format).

October 15, 19X7

Mr. Kyle T. Reading
Bolivian Import Merchants, Inc.
56 Trinity Place
Detroit, Illinois 34565

Dear Mr. Reading:

Your account is overdue for $650, as we previously noted in our correspondence of September 20. We have had a long and pleasant business relationship in the past and hope to continue this relationship in the future.

If there is any reason you cannot make full payment on this account, please call my office immediately to discuss a new payment schedule.

Unless we hear from you, we will be forced to take other steps to remedy this problem. You will thereby be jeopardizing your credit rating.

I look forward to hearing from you this week.

Sincerely,

Mark Hoddlecoock
Credit Manager

jl

SAMPLE LETTER 9.18.   Letter serving as fourth overdue notice (semiblock format).

October 30, 19X7

Mr. Kyle T. Reading
Bolivian Import Merchants, Inc.
56 Trinity Place
Detroit, Illinois 34565

Dear Mr. Reading:

Despite three previous reminders about the $650 overdue on your account since June, we have received no response from you.

As previously noted, we will be pleased to discuss a revised payment schedule in order to help you resolve this matter. Unless we have heard from you within 5 days, however, we will find it necessary to turn your account over to a collection agency.

We thank you for turning your attention to this matter immediately.

Sincerely,

Mark Hoddlecoock
Credit Manager

jl

SAMPLE LETTER 9.19.   Letter serving as final overdue notice (semiblock format).

November 7, 19X7

Mr. Kyle T. Reading
Bolivian Import Merchants, Inc.
56 Trinity Place
Detroit, Illinois 34565

Dear Mr. Reading:

As of this writing, we have received no response to correspondence about payment of $650 due since June 19X7.

Therefore, we must send this final notice to inform you that your account will be turned over to a collection agency if full payment is not received by November 15, 19X7.

We urge you to give your prompt attention to this matter.

Cordially,

Mark Hoddlecoock
Credit Manager

jl

SAMPLE LETTER 9.20.   Short initial collection letter (block format).

November 29, 19X7

Mr. Peter T. Nobless
Nobless Hardware Store
P.O. Box 5432
Roanoke, Georgia 34321

Dear Mr. Nobless:

Enclosed you will find a statement with your September 19X7 charges. If you will total up all your charges and subtract your payments, you will arrive at your total due.

If you have any questions concerning your bill, I will be glad to help.

Sincerely,

Lois T. Handley
Credit Manager

lth:ltg

enc.

SAMPLE LETTER 9.21. Letter serving as second notice on charges due (semiblock format).

June 15, 19X3

Mr. Thomas T. Dialon
76 East Coast Drive
Sudbury, Vermont 43456

Subject: Credit Charges Due

Dear Mr. Dialon:

Is something wrong? A few weeks ago we sent you a notice that your charge account payment was past due for $575. In spite of this notice, we have received no payment from you. You should be acting now to preserve your good credit rating.

We will be understanding if there is a reason why you have not been able to make the payment. Call me to explain the circumstances. We always make every effort to accommodate our customers who are encountering financial difficulties, as long as they cooperate with us.

If you fail to either bring your account up to date or contact us to make some new arrangements, however, we will be forced to turn the matter over to our collection department and instruct them to inform the various credit reporting bureaus about your delinquent status.

Sincerely,

Simon L. Gree
Credit Manager

mls

SAMPLE LETTER 9.22.   Follow-up to no response to second notice
collection letter in Sample Letter 9.21 (semiblock format).

                                                        July 14, 19X3

Mr. Thomas T. Dialon
76 East Coast Drive
Sudbury, Vermont 43456

Subject: Credit Charges Due

Dear Mr. Dialon:

The payments on your charge account have become seriously
delinquent. The credit manager of Bixley Department Store has turned
your account over to us for collection.

You have already been sent a late payment notice, followed by a letter
from our credit department requesting payment. Both of these moderate
requests have remained unanswered by you. We have also attempted to
reach you by telephone, but have had no success in reaching you.

Because you have been unresponsive to those efforts to bring your
account up to date and to preserve your good credit rating, we have
notified various consumer credit reporting agencies of your present
delinquent status. We now intend to take every legal recourse we can to
collect from you the entire amount you owe, plus whatever late charges
and legal fees may be incurred.

It is still not too late to clear up this matter. You can still pay the
amount you owe and start restoring your credit rating at Bixley
Department Store by coming in personally, calling us, or using the
enclosed postage paid reply card to make arrangements for payment.

You must respond immediately or we will have to take corrective
action against you.

                                                        Sincerely,

                                                        H. N. Hart
                                                        Credit Manager

mls

enc.

Sample Letter 9.23 was sent as a follow-up collection letter to a debtor who had sent in payment, but was still delinquent on his account. The letter writer thanks the letter reader, but explains the delinquency that remains. He asks that the letter reader call to arrange an equitable payment schedule.

SAMPLE LETTER 9.23.   A follow-up collection letter (semiblock).

April 30, 19X7

Mr. Carl D. Weaver, Controller
Busalami Department Stores
28 Huntington Avenue, Suite 507
Brookline, Michigan 34356

Dear Mr. Weaver:

Thank you very much for sending March's payment. January, April, May, and June are still outstanding. Our purchase order number is 0254. Copies of the outstanding invoices are enclosed.

Could you please call us with a proposed payment schedule? It is important that we be able to anticipate our cash flow situation.

Sincerely,

Maxwell L. Nitten

mln/jls

encls.

Sample Letter 9.24 is a collection letter that was sent by a law firm after the creditor failed to collect money due from the debtor. The writer is clear and pointed in his language. He recaps the delinquency problem and closes by giving a payment due date, after which he will take legal action against the debtor.

SAMPLE LETTER 9.24.   Collection letter from a law firm (semiblock format).

December 26, 19X9

Querilous Office Supply, Inc.
43 Rustballic Road
Simondale, Kansas 34325

Attention: Mrs. Evelyn Z. Querilous

Subject: Balance Owed to Welan Rubber Stamp Company, Inc.

Dear Mrs. Querilous:

This law firm has been hired by Welan Rubber Stamp Company, Inc. to collect the balance that you owe it. We understand that as of November 25, 19X9, the balance owed was $2,354.65, reflecting charges for products sold by Welan Rubber Stamp Company, Inc. to Querilous Office Supply, Inc. We further understand that you wrote a check to our client dated November 10, 19X9, in payment of the balance, that payment was subsequently stopped on the check, and the check was returned to our client for insufficient funds.

This letter is being written to demand that you make full payment of the balance by Wednesday, January 18, 19X0. If payment is not made by that time, we will take appropriate legal action to collect the amount due.

Cordially,

Wesley T. Harding, Jr.

wth/wlg

cc: Mr. Simon B. Welan
    R. Stephen Levitz, Esq.

Credit-Suspension Letter

Sample Letter 9.25 was written to suspend a customer's credit after no response was received to earlier collection efforts. This letter could be written as a follow-up to the collection letters featured in Sample Letters 9.15 through 9.19. The letter writer informs the debtor that he has had to turn the account over to a collection agency and that his credit privileges have been suspended. He offers hope that credit privileges may be reinstated if the matter is resolved.

SAMPLE LETTER 9.25.   Letter suspending further credit. Follow-up to Sample Letters 9.15–9.19 (semiblock format).

November 30, 19X7

Mr. Kyle T. Reading
Bolivian Import Merchants, Inc.
56 Trinity Place
Detroit, Illinois 34565

Dear Mr. Reading:

We regret to inform you that the Hoodle Company has found it necessary to turn your account over to the Coin Collection Agency for collection of the $650 you have owed since June 19X7.

We must further inform you that all of your credit privileges with the Hoodle Company have been revoked as of the date of this letter.

Please resolve this matter immediately so that we may reinstate your credit privileges and continue our business relationship.

Cordially,

Mark Hoddlecoock
Credit Manager

jl

Letter Reinstating Credit

Sample Letter 9.26 was written after a delinquent customer paid the amount due on his account. The letter writer thanks the customer for his payment and announces that credit has been restored. This letter could be written as a follow-up to any of Sample Letters 9.15 through 9.19 after delinquent payment has been received.

SAMPLE LETTER 9.26.   Letter reinstating credit. Follow-up to Sample
Letters 9.15–9.19 (semiblock format).

December 15, 19X7

Mr. Kyle T. Reading
Bolivian Import Merchants, Inc.
56 Trinity Place
Detroit, Illinois 34565

Dear Mr. Reading:

    Thank you for payment of $650 on your account. We are pleased to
inform you that the Hoodle Company has reinstated your credit privileges.

    We look forward to continuing our business relationship and
providing you with all of your office supply needs.

Best regards,

Mark Hoddlecoock
Credit Manager

jl

Letters Accepting Partial Payment

Sample Letters 9.27 through 9.29 are acknowledgments of partial payment on a
delinquent account.
    Sample Letter 9.27 thanks the debtor for payment, tells him how much is still
due, and reminds him that the remainder must be received for credit to be
reinstated.
    Sample Letter 9.28 is written to acknowledge partial payment and that a new
payment schedule has been arranged.
    Sample Letter 9.29 is a shorter version of Sample Letter 9.27. Here the letter
writer simply acknowledges partial payment, reminds the letter reader how much is
still due, and asks that payment be made immediately.

SAMPLE LETTER 9.27.   Letter accepting partial payment (block format).

November 5, 19X7

Mr. Kyle T. Reading
Bolivian Import Merchants, Inc.
56 Trinity Place
Detroit, Illinois 34565

Dear Mr. Reading:

Thank you for partial payment of the $650 owed on your account. Please note that your balance is now $500, overdue from June 19X7.

While we appreciate this partial payment, it is essential that complete payment be received by November 15, in order for us to reinstate your credit privileges and continue our business relationship.

Sincerely,

Mark Hoddlecoock
Credit Manager

jl

SAMPLE LETTER 9.28.   Letter accepting partial payment (block format).

November 10, 19X7

Mr. Kyle T. Reading
Bolivian Import Merchants, Inc.
56 Trinity Place
Detroit, Illinois 34565

Dear Mr. Reading:

We received partial payment of $150 after you called us about your account and arranged a new payment schedule. We trust that this mutually agreed upon schedule will result in complete and timely payment of the $500 still due on your account.

Thank you for the partial payment. Please call my office if you have any questions about your account.

Sincerely,

Mark Hoddlecoock
Credit Manager

jl

SAMPLE LETTER 9.29.   Letter acknowledging partial payment (block format).

June 15, 19X9

Mr. Kyle R. Belter
67 Yorkway Plaza
Vesuvius, California 09876

Dear Mr. Belter:

You have responded to our request to bring your account up to date by making a partial payment of the amount due. To protect your good credit rating, we ask that you pay the entire past due payment of $575.

Please pay this amount immediately.

Cordially,

Alan T. Wirey
Credit Manager

jl

Letter Acknowledging Payment

Sample Letter 9.30 was written to a debtor after he had paid up all past invoices. The letter writer acknowledges payment, then recounts the new payment schedule he has arranged with the debtor.

SAMPLE LETTER 9.30.   Letter acknowledging payment (full-block format).

August 5, 19X7

Mr. Carl E. Twonby
The River Steak Houseboat
654 Pacific Avenue
Carlsbad, Iowa 56432

Dear Carl:

I received payment for all of the past invoices. Thank you very much.

We have two months left on our initial contract. Beginning with August, I will bill you at the end of each month. That way, I'll be able to adjust our fee to the work performed. The figure will not exceed the $1,700 we agreed upon earlier. Let me know if this meets with your approval.

Sincerely,

Mark L. Blinke

jls

Letter About Deposit Due

Sample Letter 9.31 was written to a prospective hotel guest to remind him that a deposit is due on a room he had reserved.

SAMPLE LETTER 9.31.   Letter reminding customer that deposit is due (full-block format).

December 5, 19X6

Mr. Simon T. Harsdale
45 Trustworthy Drive
Penobscot, Illinois 34321

Dear Mr. Harsdale:

Please refer to our acknowledgment of your request for reservations dated November 7, 19X6. As you will note, a $125 deposit per room is required to secure your reservation. This deposit was due within 10 days of the date of the acknowledgment of your reservation.

To date, we have not received your deposit and are anxious to make your reservation definite. Please forward your remittance by return mail in the postage paid envelope provided or telephone immediately to let us know your plans. Our toll-free number is 800-555-4545.

We are looking forward to hearing from you.

Cordially,

Beverly G. Krauss
Reservations Manager

bgk:lls

enc.

CHAPTER 10
Letters to Vendors and Suppliers

This chapter contains examples of letters that are commonly written to vendors and suppliers. The occasion for the writing of these letters varies from things as simple as placing orders to issues that must be carefully handled, such as complaints about salespeople or products. The letters here serve as models for professionals to use in their own dealings with vendors and suppliers.

Letter Placing Order

Sample Letter 10.1 was written to place a simple order with a company. The letter writer clearly spells out what he wants to order, listing the product name, quantity, and total cost. He also indicates that he is enclosing a check for the order, and instructs the letter reader about where to ship his order.

SAMPLE LETTER 10.1.   Letter placing order (semiblock format).

June 15, 19X8

Mr. Maxwell North
Andoris Publishing Company
312 West Main Street
Boonton, New Jersey 07005

Dear Mr. North:

Please send me the following books advertised in your Fall 19X8 catalog:

5 copies of The Commercial Loan	$245.00
6 copies of Banking Dictionary	294.00
3 copies of Bank Seller's Directory	105.00
Total	644.00
Less 10% discount on 10 books or more	64.40
Amount due	$579.60

I have enclosed a company check for $579.60. Please send the order to me at: Big Bank Company, 186-A Grampian Road, Gloucester, New Jersey 43456.

Thank you for your assistance.

                        Sincerely,

                        Larry T. Edsel
                        Training Director

lte:jls

enc.

Letter Requesting Free Materials

Sample Letter 10.2 was written to request free materials after the letter writer saw an advertisement. The letter writer clearly requests the material he wants, indicates how he came to know the reader's company, and explains that the free material might help him decide whether or not to buy the product.

SAMPLE LETTER 10.2.   Letter requesting free materials (full-block format).

December 25, 19X5

Mr. Edward T. Davis
Bimini Mining and Crockery Company
45 Transcome Road
Byntyne, Wisconsin 90434

Dear Mr. Davis:

I read with interest your advertisement for an exercise machine in the most recent edition of The Armchair Reader's Review. Please send me the brochure and videotape you mentioned in the advertisement.

I first came across your company's name a couple of years ago when a friend mentioned how satisfied he was with your company's equipment. I hope that your brochure and videotape will give me enough information to decide whether or not Bimini Mining makes the kind of equipment I am looking for.

Thank you.

Cordially,

Maxwell L. Ross

jll

Letter Requesting Distributor's Name

Sample Letter 10.3 was written to a company to request the name of a distributor in the letter writer's area. The letter writer explains that he came across the reader's product at a trade show. He asks for the name of a local distributor so he can look into buying the product.

SAMPLE LETTER 10.3.   Letter requesting name of dealer or distributor (semiblock format).

June 15, 19X0

Mr. Carl T. Pernicks
Vice President
Advanced Copiers In Offices, Inc.
76 Troden Road
Troden, Connecticut 43456

Dear Mr. Pernicks:

   I picked up your business card and a brochure for your company's copiers when I was at the Annual Office Supply Trade Show in Anaheim. I am very interested in buying a Mark-VG564 Copier that is advertised on page 5 of your brochure.

   Can you please send me the name of a distributor in my area from whom I can buy this copier? I would like to examine the machine to see if it is capable of meeting my business needs.

   Thank you.

Sincerely,

Alan T. Rylees

jls

Letter Seeking Information About Product

Sample Letter 10.4 was written by a professional whose office was in the process of evaluating a variety of copiers to make a purchase decision. The letter writer explains this situation and asks the letter reader to send information on his product. The letter writer briefly explains the type of office she runs so the letter reader might get an idea of her office's needs.

SAMPLE LETTER 10.4.   Letter requesting information about product
(block format).

May 24, 19X8

Mr. Vladimir Puchefsky
Vladimir's Copy Machines
45 Orange Road
Trinstale, Michigan 45456

Dear Mr. Puchefsky:

We are in the process of updating our copier equipment. Will you please send us information on the price, capabilities, and availability of your office line of copy machines?

Byron Public Relations, Inc. is a 50-person public relations company. We currently have two copy machines, which we plan to trade in. Because of the volume of copying our company does, we are considering purchasing four copy machines.

Please send us the information we need to evaluate whether or not your firm can supply us with the copiers we need.

Thank you very much for your help.

Sincerely,

Leigh Simons
Office Manager

ls/js

Letter Asking About Quantity Discounts

Sample Letter 10.5 was written to a business to request information about quantity discounts on a product the letter writer is interested in buying. The letter writer identifies the product, explains how many copies he would be interested in purchasing, and asks if the letter reader can give him quantity discount prices on the purchase. He closes by letting the reader know when he'd need the first of the product shipments so the reader will know that he would like to make a decision about the purchase soon.

SAMPLE LETTER 10.5.   Letter asking about quantity discounts (semiblock format).

September 4, 19X5

Mr. Nathan T. Bloom
Dover Products Company
312 West Main Street
Boonton, New Jersey 07005

Dear Mr. Bloom:

On a recent trip from New York to Boston, I picked up a copy of Jason Lang's book, <u>Marketing Financial Advisory Services: A Hands-On Guide,</u> at an airport bookstore.

I speak on the subject of financial services marketing frequently. After reading Mr. Lang's book, I thought it might make an excellent course book for some of the seminars I run. Do you offer quantity discounts on your books? If I were to order copies, my first order would be for a minimum of 100 books. My seminars are run quarterly, so I would probably order 300 more copies throughout the year.

Please let me know if you can offer me a discount on this large purchase. I have a seminar coming up the first week of November and need to make a decision soon about which text I will use.

Thank you for your help.

Sincerely,

Brandt T. Higginbottom

bth/jls

Letters Complimenting Vendors

Sample Letters 10.6 and 10.7 were written to compliment vendors. The writer of Sample Letter 10.6 took the time to write about the quality service he had been getting from his sales representative. A letter like this does a lot to build goodwill with the sales representative and with the vendor.

Sample Letter 10.7 was written to compliment a vendor on the job he had done. The letter writer is particularly pleased with the service that the vendor has provided and, in no uncertain terms, lets him know of his pleasure. He clearly indicates that part of the success of his company's product is due to the vendor's services. Like Sample Letter 10.6, this type of complimentary letter goes a long way toward building goodwill and a solid relationship with the vendor. It also helps the vendor since it will give him something to show to others who might be interested in using his services.

SAMPLE LETTER 10.6.   Letter praising supplier's representative (semiblock format).

September 9, 19X9

Mr. Richard H. Unimant
Branch Manager
Best Copy Service
412 Santiago Drive
Wonderland, New Jersey 09020

Dear Mr. Unimant:

I recently renewed our service contract on our copy machine for the third consecutive year. Our lasting business relationship has prompted me to write this letter.

I want to compliment your company on its most important commodity—your service representative, Peggy Fection. Peggy is a superior individual. She is always prompt, courteous, and diligent at her work. Her work is quick and professional and it cures whatever ails our tired old copying machine. She instills a quiet confidence in your company, which is one of the reasons we continue to do business with your company. When we decide to upgrade our copying system, we will call upon your company for further assistance.

People like Peggy are hard to find. It's not often I take the time to note this, but she's been so consistently outstanding that I just couldn't help myself.

Best regards,

Max Nightson

amb

SAMPLE LETTER 10.7. Letter complimenting supplier of services (block format).

May 23, 19X6

Mr. Brady D. Omram
Omram Design Studios
45 Andover Place
Breakstone, Montana 04325

Dear Brady:

Now that we've got our product—the Sunshield Sport Glasses—rolling off the production lines, I thought it appropriate to write you a note. Everyone in the company from the chairman of the board on down is extremely excited about the product. Your design of our packaging is above and beyond anything we ever expected.

I think we can credit Omram Design Studios' communication design approach with the success. Rather than designing a pretty box, your team created an "environment" for our product that truly communicates how special we feel the product and company behind it are.

The environment is being translated directly into a success at the wholesale and retail levels. When we started the project, Boonton Optical Company, Inc. was fairly new in the sunglass business. We did approximately $120,000 worth of business in sunglasses last year. Currently this year, after only three months of selling, we have actual sales of more than $500,000, and expect to hit $1.5 million before the year is over.

Since the product line, sales force, and advertising have remained the same, it looks like the packaging is communicating the right message to the retail trade.

Once again, thanks for a great effort. We are anxious to begin work on the next project. We like the way Omram Design Studios communicates Boonton Optical's products to the trade and the public.

Sincerely,

Zed B. Grusinki
Marketing Director

fwd

Letter Clearing Up Billing Error

Sample Letter 10.8 was sent to a vendor to clarify a billing error made by the vendor. The letter writer is stern, yet not insulting. He identifies the cancelled check he is enclosing to verify payment and suggests that the vendor should be sure it has not been paid before it threatens to turn over matters to a collection agency.

SAMPLE LETTER 10.8.   Letter to vendor clearing up billing error (simplified format).

January 31, 19X6

Ms. Patricia S. Paly
Customer Service Department
Grand Forks Office Supply Company, Inc.
Albion, New Mexico 23245

CLARIFICATION OF BILLING ERROR

Ms. Paly, I have enclosed a copy of the front and back of our check that was used to pay your invoice numbered 3352217. If you look at the copy of the back of the check, you will note that your company endorsed this check and that it was processed by your bank on January 5, 19X6.

I would suggest that your company evaluate the procedures it uses for processing payments on its account receivables. It seems to me that you should correct your problems prior to sending past due notices threatening to turn your customers over to a collection agency.

I trust that the enclosed copy of our check will clear up your processing error and put our account back on the paid-up status.

JAMES LONG
CONTROLLER

jl:rl

enc.

Letters Complaining to Vendors

Sample Letters 10.9 and 10.10 are examples of letters that were written to complain to vendors or suppliers.

Sample Letter 10.9 was written to a supplier of a business product. The letter writer clearly establishes his complaint and suggests the solution the letter reader should take. He explains that he would like to discuss the problem with the wholesaler since he has never had such a problem with the vendor before. The letter is clear and leaves no doubt about what the problem is and how the letter writer expects it to be resolved.

Sample Letter 10.10 was written to a vendor to complain about one of his sales representatives. The letter writer clearly explains that the sales representative is breaking the letter writer's company policy by directly approaching employees. After warning the sales representative and finding the situation has not changed, the writer finds it necessary to write the vendor to complain about the situation. The letter writer asks that the vendor speak to the sales representative to get him to cease breaking company policy.

SAMPLE LETTER 10.9.   Letter complaining about unsatisfactory products (full-block format).

May 24, 19X5

Mr. Lawrence E. Tribune
Tisk-a-Disk, Inc.
43 Software Center Turnpike
Framingham, New Hampshire 43456

Dear Mr. Tribune:

For the last several months, my customers at the store have been returning Tisk-a-Disk Double-Sided, Double-Density 5.25-inch floppy computer disks. Never before have I had such a problem with one of your products. The complaint is the same for virtually all dissatisfied customers: The casing for the disk falls apart soon after removing the disk from its sleeve.

Imagine the trouble this situation can cause my customers, Mr. Tribune. What if they lose valuable data that they have stored on these disks? Have you been getting similar complaints from other retail outlets? Perhaps the latest shipment of disks I received is an isolated case of poor craftsmanship. If not, then I will have to discontinue carrying your disks and stock another company's.

I've shipped to you what I had remaining in stock of disks. There are 100 packages with 10 disks each, which makes a total of 1,000 disks. I am returning these disks since I am concerned the same unraveling problem might occur. Since the wholesale price is 69.5 cents a disk, please credit my account for $695.

Please call me when you've assessed this problem and let me know Tisk-a-Disk's plans for correcting the situation. I look forward to hearing from you in the next couple of days.

Cordially,

Justin L. Raisch

jln/nls

SAMPLE LETTER 10.10.   Letter complaining about sales representative (block format).

May 25, 19X8

Mr. Oscar B. Crum
Crum Notepads, Inc.
467 Scholarly Way
Tuskin, Alabama 32345

Dear Mr. Crum:

As you are probably aware, The Armchair Reader's Review orders a significant amount of supplies from your company. We are pleased with the quality of the products, particularly the reporters' notebooks you manufacture. But I am writing you because of difficulty I am having with your sales representative assigned to our territory, Mack McIntyre.

While we do make frequent purchases from your company, we have time and time again requested that Mr. McIntyre deal directly with our office manager for product ordering. We have asked that he call to set up an appointment before arriving on the scene. On many occasions, Mr. McIntyre has simply shown up at our offices. Often, even when he has already met with the office manager, he approaches our writers and editors directly to encourage them to buy your products or have them ordered.

I must ask that Mr. McIntyre follow the procedure we have clearly outlined for him to use in approaching us for orders. His method of "cutting through the red tape" results in time away from work that our

Page 2
Mr. Oscar B. Crum
May 25, 19X8

writers and editors need to get done. By having our office manager handle the ordering, we have centralized that function. I am sure you can understand why this procedure is important to us.

While we let Mr. McIntyre know about the appropriate procedure when he first took on this sales territory, he has continued to fail to follow it. Many of our editors and writers are up in arms about the disruption and continue to complain to me about his direct sales approaches.

As I mentioned, we are very pleased with your products. We are also pleased with the speed and efficiency with which you handle orders. We are not looking to make life difficult for Mr. McIntyre. We simply ask that you speak to him about following the procedure that we have established here.

Cordially,

Kate McGuffie

km/js

cc:MN

Letter Canceling Contract

Sample Letter 10.11 was written to cancel a contract with a supplier. The letter is short, but the letter writer clearly explains that his company would like to cancel a contract coming up for renewal. He closes by requesting that the machine that was contracted out to his company be removed as soon as possible.

SAMPLE LETTER 10.11.   Letter to vendor canceling contract (full-block
format).

June 15, 19X8

Mr. Richard H. Unimant
Branch Manager
Andrews Copy Service
412 Santiago Drive
Wonderland, New Jersey 09020

Dear Mr. Unimant:

We do not plan to renew our contract for the use of a Copier 14X40
copying machine. The contract expires June 20, 19X8.

The copying machine is located at our downtown office in Melrose. We
would like to have the machine removed at your earliest possible
convenience.

Sincerely,

Phlange A. Indelible
Office Manager

PAL:jls

CHAPTER 11
Personnel Letters

A large volume of correspondence flows through the personnel department of every major business. Smaller businesses may also find their mailboxes and outboxes stuffed with personnel-related letters. Whether they are written by the business or by a prospective employee of the business, when personnel-related letters are written effectively they can do a good deal to enhance the credibility of both the business and the prospective employee.

Personnel letters may not secure business, but they will help ensure that you hire the best possible candidate for a job and maintain a good relationship with that candidate once he or she is on board. For the job-seeker, some of the letters in this chapter can be used as model letters for selling yourself to a prospective employer to get the job you want.

Many other personnel matters call for written communication, but usually not in letter form. Such issues as organizational changes, labor relations activities, changes in benefits, office closings, and other "in-house" matters are most often addressed in memorandums distributed to employees in the workplace. Since letters are rarely sent in these cases, they are not covered here.

Job Interview Request Letters

Sample Letters 11.1 through 11.5 were written by prospective employees to request job interviews.

Sample Letter 11.1 was written in response to an advertisement the letter writer had seen. The writer refers to the advertisement, mentions a bit about her background that is appropriate to the advertised position, asks for an interview, and gives the reader information about how to reach her during the day. She also indicates that she has enclosed a résumé for the letter reader's perusal.

Sample Letter 11.2 was written to request an interview after the letter writer had had a brief conversation with the addressee. The letter writer asks that his application be considered for a specific open position, gives the reader some information about his past work experience, and asks that his résumé be routed to the appropriate person at the company.

Sample Letter 11.3 was also written as a follow-up to a conversation, but here the letter writer is not applying for a specific position. Instead, she is asking that the addressee give her any advice on seeking a position at his company. She thanks him for the talk they had, mentions her professional background, asks if he might be able to refer her to any appropriate person within his company, and mentions when she will try to call him again.

SAMPLE LETTER 11.1.   Letter requesting job interview based on
newspaper advertisement (semiblock format).

                                                        January 9, 19X5

Mr. Jacob L. Rudman
Parris Sheet Metal Company
312 West Main Street
Boonton, New Jersey 07005

Dear Mr. Rudman:

    Enclosed is my résumé, which I am sending in response to your
advertisement in The Boonton Chronicle for a production engineer.

    I am currently employed at Heavy Sheet Metal Company as one of
three production engineers. I have complete responsibility for the sheet
metal fabrication process from beginning to end. As you can see from my
résumé, I have been a production engineer for the past five years.

    Please feel free to call me at my office during the day or at my home
in the evening. Both numbers are listed on my résumé. I will call you on
Tuesday, January 17, to arrange a convenient time for us to meet if I have
not heard from you before then.

    I look forward to speaking with you.

                                                        Sincerely,

                                                        Marie L. Dow

enc.

SAMPLE LETTER 11.2.   Letter requesting job interview as follow-up to
phone conversation (full-block format).

November 22, 19X5

Ms. Elaine Longworth
Personnel Director
Primary Textbooks Company, Inc.
One Parkway Plaza
Brighton, Oregon 89765

Dear Ms. Longworth:

Please consider my application for the humanities editor position in the
college division at Primary Textbooks, which we discussed during our brief
phone conversation earlier this week. I have enclosed a résumé for your
consideration.

As you can see from my résumé, I have been at Andoris Publishing
Company for four years. The work I have done there and at Andover Parris
and Cromwell & Fitch seems to mesh well with the qualifications Primary
Textbooks desires in a college editor. I would welcome the opportunity to
make a move into a larger publishing house with Primary Textbooks'
reputation.

Please forward my résumé to the appropriate people, and give me a call
should you need more information from me.

Thanks for your consideration. I look forward to hearing from you.

Sincerely,

Max Birney

enc.

SAMPLE LETTER 11.3.   Letter requesting job advice (block format).

November 22, 19X5

Mr. Orin P. Hikep
Vice President
Franing, Transcome & Lewis Company
12 Main Street
Boonton, New Jersey 07005

Dear Orin:

Enclosed is the copy of my résumé that I mentioned I would send you
when we talked earlier today. I appreciate your taking the time to look at
it. If there are any suggestions you can make to improve it, I would be very
grateful.

As you can see, I've been at Hungadunga & McCormick for almost four
years. The firm is a small typesetting company, which has offered many
opportunities for me to develop skills in composition. I now feel that it is
time for me to move to a larger company that will offer me more of a
chance to move into a management position.

If you know of any opportunites at Franing, Transcome & Lewis, please let
me know. Feel free to pass on my résumé to the appropriate division. I am
also sending a copy of my résumé to Larry Fenner in your personnel
department. I spoke briefly with him about a position at your company.

Orin, I know that you are very busy, and I just want to thank you again for
agreeing to look at my résumé and for being willing to help. I'll call you
after Thanksgiving to see if you have any suggestions.

Sincerely,

Carol Nesin

enc.

Sample Letter 11.4 was written to request a job interview on the basis of a referral.
The letter writer makes it clear in her first paragraph that she is writing at the
recommendation of a mutual acquaintance who told her the letter reader's company
was seeking to fill a position. She goes on to tell the reader a little bit about her
background, and closes by asking for an interview.

SAMPLE LETTER 11.4.   Letter requesting job interview on the basis of
referral (semiblock format).

November 22, 19X5

Ms. Kimberly Duachim
Pulverize Products, Inc.
23 Reply Place
Biloxi, Missouri 34325

Dear Ms. Duachim:

I am sending my résumé to you on the recommendation of Lawrence
Kernel of Splendid Paper Corporation. Lawrence told me that you were
accepting applications for a product manager. From Lawrence's report,
your company sounds very attractive to me. I would be interested in
talking with you to learn more about your company and the position.

For the past four years, I have been at Quile Investment Products, Inc.
Before that, I was at Laramy Products, Inc. The work I've done at these
companies has given me a wide range of experience and an opportunity to
develop skills that would be beneficial to a product manager.

I would welcome the opportunity to talk with you or to answer any
questions about my background and career that you might have. You can
reach me during the day at 343-5555.

Thank you for your consideration.

Sincerely,

Gladys T. Namelock

enc.

Sample Letter 11.5 was written to thank a prospective employer for a job interview.
He thanks the letter reader, goes on to express his pleasure at having met the
addressee and others at the company, and mentions the fact that he would welcome
the opportunity to work at the company.

SAMPLE LETTER 11.5.   Letter thanking prospective employer for job
interview (full-block format).

May 26, 19X2

Mr. George Penelope
Assistant Personnel Officer
Boonton Life Insurance Trust
34 Old Boonton Road
Boonton, New Jersey 98765

Dear Mr. Penelope:

Thank you very much for the opportunity to talk with you on May 25. It
was a very enjoyable experience, and I also learned a great deal about the
responsibilities your job opening entails.

My conversation with you, along with my conversations with Mr. Hoelsch
and Ms. Sivad, reinforced my opinion that Boonton Life Insurance Trust is
a first-rate company, for which I would like to work. I feel that Boonton
Life Insurance Trust offers an opportunity for professional as well as
personal growth. For these reasons, I would very much like to be a part of
the personnel division.

Thank you again for your time. I am looking forward to hearing from you
soon.

Sincerely,

David A. Inacca

Résumé-Accompanying Letters

Sample Letters 11.6 and 11.7 were both written to accompany résumés sent to a
prospective employer.

Sample Letter 11.6 was sent to follow up a meeting with the addressee. The
letter writer reminds the reader where they met, goes on to give some information
about his professional and academic background, and closes by asking that he and
the letter reader meet to discuss employment prospects.

Sample Letter 11.7 was written to accompany a résumé. Here, the writer's
purpose is to introduce himself to a prospective employer. He mentions some
information about his personality and his professional experience. He expresses an
interest in meeting with the addressee at his earliest convenience.

SAMPLE LETTER 11.6.   Letter accompanying résumé from recent graduate (block format).

August 19, 19X2

Mr. King L. Smythe
Boonton Life Insurance Trust
34 Old Boonton Road
Boonton, New Jersey 98765

Dear Mr. Smythe:

Several weeks ago, I stopped into your department to apply for a position with Boonton Life Insurance Trust. On my way out, I had the opportunity to speak with you for a few minutes on the elevator. You mentioned at the time that there were no openings available to match my interests, but that you would keep me in mind for any openings in the future. As I told you when we spoke, I am a recent graduate of the New Jersey State University with a Bachelor of Science degree in finance and I am interested in an entry-level position in life insurance sales.

Throughout my four years in college, I maintained consistently high grades in my business courses as well as in my elective courses. I feel that the courses I have taken have strengthened my analytical skills and provided me with a sound background in the financial system.

In addition to my academic work, I have also held various jobs in the past six years to help finance my education. Through my work experience and my involvement in extracurricular activities at school, I have developed a sense of responsibility and a deeper understanding of dealing with people. I feel that these qualities, along with my sincere interest in insurance as a career, will make me an asset to Boonton Life Insurance Trust.

At your convenience, I would like to get together with you to learn more about career opportunities at Boonton Life Insurance Trust and also to discuss my career interests in greater detail. Will you please get in touch with me so that we can arrange an interview?

Thank you for your consideration.

Sincerely,

Ned Lared

Enclosure

SAMPLE LETTER 11.7.   Letter accompanying résumé from a person
seeking to change jobs (semiblock format).

July 1, 19X2

Mr. Sidney T. Fairview
Data Center Manager
Arlington Products, Inc.
43 West Main Street
Boonton, New Jersey 07005

Dear Mr. Fairview:

 I am a young, aggressive data processing manager in the market for a
new, more challenging position in a data processing environment that is
conducive to career advancement and personal growth.

 I have gained my experience at JLS, Inc., of Levittown, Pennsylvania.
JLS, Inc., is a service bureau providing financial institutions in the United
States and Canada with automated trust management systems including
on-line data access, daily file updates, and periodic report generation. JLS,
Inc., maintains one of the largest data center operations in this region of
the country, and is supported by more than 45 Prime computers, more
than 200 "310 megabyte" disc drives, 100 tape units, and more than 100
access terminals.

 I enclose my résumé for your review and consideration. I have also
included an expanded version of my résumé to highlight some of the
responsibilities and some results of my work in the positions I have held.
If you would like further details or clarification of my experience, I would
be more than happy to supply anything further I can. I am anxious to
meet with you to discuss possible career opportunities at Arlington
Products, Inc., at your earliest convenience.

 Thank you for taking the time to review my résumé. I look forward to
the possibility of discussing my professional career with you in the near
future.

Cordially,

Larry E. Mahaffey

Enclosures

Letters Responding to Job Applications

Sample Letters 11.8 through 11.22 are designed to be used in a variety of circumstances to respond to job applicants.

Sample Letter 11.8 is an example of a standard acknowledgement of a job application that was written to a recent applicant. The letter writer courteously acknowledges the reader's application and assures him that his application will be reviewed. She concludes by expressing her appreciation that the letter reader applied for the position. This letter may easily be used as a model letter for any applicant search in which acknowledgments must be sent out.

Sample Letter 11.9 is an example of an acknowledgment sent to an applicant qualified for a position. The letter writer thanks the applicant, informs him that there were many qualified applicants, and asks him to feel free to inquire about his status once a certain date has passed.

Sample Letter 11.10 may also be sent as an acknowledgment to a qualified applicant, but here the letter writer asks the applicant to call his office to arrange for a second interview. He expresses the fact that he was impressed with the applicant and that he would like to have him meet more members of the firm.

Sample Letter 11.11 was written to inform a qualified applicant about the status of a job search to fill a position for which the letter reader has applied. The letter writer clearly spells out the status of the job search to date and lets the letter reader know exactly what procedure the search committee will be taking to make its decision.

SAMPLE LETTER 11.8.   Letter acknowledging application for position (full-block format).

May 10, 19X8

Mr. Maxwell L. Topor
988 Boston Avenue
Huntington, Maine 34321

Subject: Writing Instructor Position

Dear Mr. Topor:

Thank you very much for applying for the writing instructor position at Boonton Community College. Please be assured that your application will be reviewed along with others that have been received. If your qualifications are considered appropriate for this position, you will be contacted again for the purpose of setting an appointment date.

In any event, please accept the appreciation of Boonton Community College for wishing to include us in your future professional plans.

Sincerely yours,

Elizabeth R. Jennifer
Director of Personnel

erj:jls

SAMPLE LETTER 11.9.   Letter responding to qualified applicant (semiblock format).

May 23, 19X8

Mr. Brian Aberbroom
3 Forrester Place
Bethany, Ohio 54567

Dear Mr. Aberbroom:

Thank you for your application for the position of clerical supervisor.

We have had an overwhelming response to our ad for this position and expect to select a qualified applicant by June 5. If you have not heard from us by then, please feel free to call and inquire about the status of the position.

Thank you for your interest in the company. Best wishes for the future.

Cordially,

Blaise T. Rendeler
Personnel Director

btr/nls

SAMPLE LETTER 11.10.   Letter inviting applicant in for second interview
(block format).

October 16, 19X7

Mr. Peter Jensen
34 Eckerd Drive
Fontaine, Nebraska 32253

Dear Peter:

Thank you very much for having taken the time to meet with me during
my recruiting trip to Fontaine. I was most favorably impressed with you,
and our recruiting committee has concurred in my recommendation that
we invite you to meet more members of our company.

If you continue to be interested in our company, I would appreciate it if
you would call our recruiting coordinator, Bill Cryer, to arrange a
mutually convenient time to visit us.

We look forward to hearing from you. Again, thank you for your interest in
our organization and for having taken the time to talk with me.

Best regards,

Gary A. Tieszen

GAT:jls

SAMPLE LETTER 11.11.   Letter giving applicant status report on search for
employee (semiblock format).

August 5, 19X3

Mr. Trevor L. Kemper
56 Bethany Road
Belvedere, Washington 43456

Dear Trevor:

   I wanted to send you a short note to tell you where we are in the
search for an alumni director for Boonton Community College. As of

August 1, we had received 34 applications. A selection committee composed of members of the alumni council, faculty, and staff has been appointed and will review résumés by mid-August. The committee will select four or five applicants who seem to be best prepared to do the job and will invite them to Boonton for an interview later in the month. Following those interviews, the committee will recommend to the president its first three choices in order of its preference. The president will decide from among the three the person he thinks can best do the job. He will announce the appointment on or about September 1.

Please note that we will not be reporting on the progress of the search until an appointment is announced. Should you have any questions, however, please do not hesitate to telephone me.

Trevor, let me tell you again how much we appreciate your willingness to be considered for this important position. You are well qualified for the position, and I know that the committee will be very interested in your candidacy. It is going to be a difficult task for the selection committee, and I know you will bear with it whatever the outcome.

Thank you for all you have and will do for Boonton Community College.

Sincerely,

David R. Xenadnas
Vice President

drx/ras

Sample Letter 11.12 was written to an applicant who did not qualify for a position. The letter writer thanks the applicant for his interest and regretfully informs him that he does not have the qualifications to fill the position. She then wishes him her best in his job search.

SAMPLE LETTER 11.12. Letter to applicant who did not qualify for position (semiblock format).

May 21, 19X8

Mr. Adam Beazle
67 Yorkway Plaza, Apt. 4
York, New Jersey 56432

Dear Mr. Beazle:

Thank you for your interest in the position of production manager for the Belmont Sheet Metal Company. I have carefully reviewed your application and regret to tell you that I do not feel you have the qualifications necessary to fulfill the responsibilities of this job.

Good luck in your job search. I feel certain that you will find a position where you can use your talents and experience to good advantage.

Sincerely,

Gwendolyn T. Quackenbush
Personnel Director

gtq:nls

Sample Letter 11.13 was written to respond to a qualified applicant to inform him that no position was open. The letter writer makes it clear that he thinks the applicant is well qualified but that there were simply more applicants than the company had positions to offer.

SAMPLE LETTER 11.13.   Letter responding to qualified applicant
informing him that no position is available (full-block format).

January 11, 19X8

Mr. Stanley R. Pixell
32 Roskanokov Drive, Apt. 3A
Endicott, Wisconsin 95456

Dear Mr. Pixell:

We want to thank you for interviewing with our company during our
recruiting trip to Brighton. You have an outstanding academic background,
and you made a very favorable impression.

We have delayed making final determinations about employment offers
until we had been able to interview the majority of potential candidates,
including those whose schedules did not permit them to interview until
the Christmas holidays. It is unfortunate that we have fewer available
spaces than we do qualified candidates. Accordingly, we regret that we will
not be able to make an offer to you at this time.

Thank you again for your interest.

Cordially,

FISKE, TRUSOME, SCADABOUT & YIELDS, P.C.

Craig D. Creyton III

CDC:GAD

Sample Letter 11.14 was written to a qualified applicant who did not match
exactly the qualifications that were being sought for an open position. The letter
writer thanks the applicant for his interest, explains that because there were so many
applicants from which to choose, they chose the applicant who was an exact fit. The
letter writer then suggests that perhaps in the future there will be a more suitable
position open. She closes by wishing the applicant well in his search.

SAMPLE LETTER 11.14.   Letter to qualified candidate who did not match position exactly (simplified format).

January 13, 19X8

Mr. Martin L. Preston
43 Lorraine Terrace
Punxatawney, Pennsylvania 43456

FACULTY POSITION AT PUNXATAWNEY COALITION COLLEGE

Mr. Preston, thank you for your interest in a faculty position at Punxatawney Coalition College. We received many responses from very highly qualified candidates like you.

With so many superbly qualified candidates, we looked finally for the one whose background and qualifications gave us just the right "fit" for our exact needs this semester. I'm sorry to have to say that the position is being offered to one of the other candidates.

This does not mean, however, that we were unimpressed with the credentials of the other candidates. Perhaps in the future we will have another opening that will better fit your qualifications. I wish you well in your pursuit of the right position.

DR. HELEN L. DAVIDS
CHAIR, HUMANITIES

jls

Sample Letter 11.15 was written to inform an applicant that a different applicant who was deemed more appropriate was chosen to fill an open position. The letter writer clearly explains the situation and closes by thanking the applicant for his interest.

SAMPLE LETTER 11.15.   Letter informing applicant that someone else got the job (full-block format).

June 15, 19X8

Mr. Harold M. Peeking
543 Houghton Place
New Britain, Connecticut 32345

Dear Mr. Peeking:

Thank you for the time you took to come in and talk with us about the quality control engineer position. We cannot place you now because we have chosen another candidate whose background, we feel, is more closely suited to our current needs. We will keep your résumé in our active file, however, should a more suitable position open up.

Thank you again for your interest in Ainsworth Sheet Metal Company. Best wishes for success in your career endeavors.

Cordially,

Letitia T. Hall
Personnel Officer

LTH:mln

    Sample Letter 11.16 was written to an applicant who was partially qualified for a position. The letter writer thanks the applicant for her application and explains that the job requires someone with more experience. The writer closes with best wishes.

SAMPLE LETTER 11.16.   Letter responding to applicant who is partially qualified (semiblock format).

May 20, 19X8

Ms. Alice Graybar
36 Festoon Boulevard, Apt. 6W
Georgia, Kentucky 43456

Dear Ms. Graybar:

    Thank you for your application and for your interest in Harmony Electronics, Inc.

We had a very large number of applicants for the position of product designer and gave all the applications serious consideration. Although we were impressed with your application, we feel that the job requires someone with more experience than you currently have. With your qualifications, however, I am sure you will find a suitable position very soon.

I wish you the best for your future success.

Best regards,

Lindley H. McCaw
Personnel Director

lhm/nls

Sample Letter 11.17 was written to an applicant explaining that no positions were open that matched her training or experience. The letter writer acknowledges the employment inquiry, explains that the company has no positions open currently to match her credentials, but asks that she be allowed to keep a record of the applicant's qualifications on file should a suitable future opening come about.

SAMPLE LETTER 11.17.   Letter informing applicant that there are no positions matching her training or experience (semiblock format).

September 20, 19X9

Ms. Pauline R. Yeltar
34 Douglass Road
Far Hills, Vermont 76543

Dear Ms. Yeltar:

Thank you for inquiring about employment possibilities at Farmington & Gray. We appreciated the opportunity to review your qualifications in relation to our current job openings.

At this time, however, we do not have a position open that would properly use your training and experience. We would like to keep a record of your qualifications in our active file, however, so we may consider you for any appropriate future openings.

Although we are currently unable to offer you a position, we do wish you success in your career.

Cordially,

Linda B. Blaisdale
Personnel Officer

lbb/dls

Sample Letter 11.18 was written to reject an application that came as a result of a newspaper advertisement. The letter writer thanks the applicant, informs him that he did not get the job, assures him that a record of his application will be kept on file, and closes by wishing the applicant well in his search for employment.

SAMPLE LETTER 11.18.   Letter rejecting a newspaper advertisement applicant (block format).

December 26, 19X0

Mr. Jacob L. McGuffie
5 Merrimac Trail
Trailblaze, Idaho 23245

Dear Mr. McGuffie:

Thank you for your letter responding to our advertisement for an executive secretary. As you can guess, the response was overwhelming. Although your résumé was impressive, we had only one opening.

Even though we were unable to place you in this job, we will keep your résumé on file for future reference in the event that a suitable position becomes available.

Thank you for your interest in Vladmir, Tilling & Underquist. Best wishes in your search for employment.

Sincerely,

David Marshall
Personnel Officer

mn

Sample Letter 11.19 was written to reject a summer job applicant. The letter writer keeps the letter short and to the point, thanking the applicant for her inquiry, but explaining that no summer jobs were open. She assures the applicant that her name will be kept on file and thanks her for her interest.

SAMPLE LETTER 11.19.   Letter rejecting applicant for summer job (semiblock format).

December 23, 19X5

Ms. Tricia Levon
34 Rightone Road
Greenfreer, West Virginia 32345

Dear Ms. Levon:

Thank you for your inquiry about the possibility of summer employment at our company. While we do not anticipate any summer openings currently, we will be glad to keep your name on file in the event that the situation should change.

Thank you again for your interest.

Sincerely,

Francis K. Cheff
Personnel Officer

fkc/jls

Sample Letter 11.20 was written to reject an applicant who was recommended for the job. The letter writer thanks the applicant and acknowledges the recommender, but explains that the response to the opening was overwhelming and he is unable to offer the applicant a job.

Sample Letter 11.21 was written to the recommender of a person who was not hired to fill a position. The letter writer thanks him for the recommendation, but explains that since the company is cutting back, few jobs are being offered. The writer offers to keep an eye out for other jobs in the field, but is not overly encouraging that anything will change at his company.

SAMPLE LETTER 11.20.   Letter rejecting person recommended for job
(full-block format).

August 5, 19X4

Mr. Wilson Davidson
P.O. Box 704
Sparta Community College
Sparta, West Virginia 26032

Dear Mr. Davidson:

Thank you for applying for the position of editorial assistant at our
organization. While you were recommended by Professor Gary E. Limes,
and your education and experience appear to be exceptional, the response
that we received from the few inquiries that we made was overwhelming. I
regret to inform you that a candidate was chosen shortly before your letter
of interest arrived.

Best wishes for success in your career search.

Best regards,

David Marshall
Personnel Director

DM:ll

cc: Gary E. Limes

SAMPLE LETTER 11.21.   Letter to recommender of person who could not be hired (semiblock format).

May 18, 19X8

Mr. Frederick T. Jones
Jones, Jones & Gary
43 Edgar Drive
Humanity, South Carolina 32345

Dear Fred:

Thank you for sending me Eugene Balk's résumé.

Arlington Products, Inc., is in the midst of a severe staff reduction program, which, it appears, will continue throughout the summer. As a result, a hiring freeze is in effect.

There is some growth in the computer industry. I wonder whether Eugene has looked into the possibility of working with one of the city's many computer firms. He has impressive credentials in programming support.

I will keep my eyes open for other possible jobs available in artificial intelligence, both at our company and elsewhere. But in view of the current situation here, I would not want to get Mr. Balk's hopes up.

Cordially,

Hope T. McCormick
Personnel Director

HTM:lmn

Sample Letter 11.22 was sent as a letter of rejection to a person who had been asked to apply for the job. The letter writer thanks the applicant for applying, but explains that after reviewing the applicant's work samples and experience, he does not feel the job would be appropriate for the applicant.

SAMPLE LETTER 11.22.   Letter rejecting solicited employment application
(semiblock format).

March 3, 19X8

Mr. Mark Perkins
95 Belltoll Road
Ketchum, Idaho 00005

Dear Mr. Perkins:

Thank you for sending your work samples and discussing your views
about the editor's position we have open. I've reviewed your work and
reflected at length on our last conversation, particularly your hesitancy to
take on an assignment to demonstrate your editorial approach to
analytical topics. Since we talked I've interviewed several other candidates
with substantial editorial credentials and have become convinced that
proven analytical skills or technical knowledge of the investments area is
an important prerequisite for the job.

My conclusion is that your background is not appropriate for the
position and, frankly, that you would not enjoy the job during a necessary
period of training. If, however, you are interested in establishing a free-
lance relationship with our publication, I'd be happy to consider using
you.

Thanks again, Mark, for your interest in the job.

Cordially,

Florence Hoagland
Publisher

FH/ec

Letters Thanking Recommenders

Sample Letters 11.23 and 11.24 were written to thank people who recommended
applicants for jobs. Sample Letter 11.23 was written to thank a person who had
recommended someone who was offered the job but decided to take a job elsewhere.
The letter writer explains that he really would have liked to hire the applicant. He
asks that the recommender keep in mind other potential applicants.

Sample Letter 11.24 was written by an applicant to thank someone for recommending him for the job he got. The letter writer is direct and sincere in expressing his gratitude.

SAMPLE LETTER 11.23. Letter thanking someone for referral of prospective employee (block format).

July 24, 19X7

Dr. Lisa L. Ekorb
Brikton Management Services, Inc.
43 Clark Street
Bayonne, West Virginia 23234

Dear Lisa:

Thank you so much for referring Carla Sorel and Donna Asconia. Your assessment of each was right on the mark. Both are superior candidates at their respective professional levels.

I offered the assistant's job to Carla. She, however, decided to take a position with another public relations firm in town, Vladmir & Associates. Donna and I were interested in each other, but we both agreed that someone with her credentials was overqualified for the position I was seeking to fill.

I am still looking for someone. It's very hard finding candidates as good as Carla and Donna. Carla was the person I wanted.

Please keep me in mind if you have any other suggestions. I would very much like to take you to breakfast or lunch at your convenience. It would give me a better chance to understand what Brikton Management Services does.

I look forward to hearing from you.

Cordially,

Maryanne L. Niltes

mln/mfr

SAMPLE LETTER 11.24.   Letter thanking reference (semiblock format).

December 26, 19X6

Mr. Martin Heady
Raphel Design Inc.
312 West Main Street
Boonton, New Jersey 07005

Dear Mr. Heady:

Graphcon Tittle Inc. has offered me a position as a graphic designer beginning January 15, 19X7. I realize you are probably just finishing up with the holiday madness, but I'd like to stop by and see you before I head down to start work.

Thanks so much for the kind words you had to say about me to Al Newport, the managing director at Graphcon Tittle. The designer's position promises to be grueling, but the internship I had at Raphel Design was good training ground for anything they plan to throw my way.

Thanks again. I look forward to seeing you soon.

Sincerely,

Brad T. Zeiber

Job-Offer Letters

Sample Letters 11.25 through 11.30 are job-offer related letters.

Sample Letter 11.25 is an example of a straightforward job-offer letter. The letter writer expresses pleasure at offering the position, lists the various benefits the prospective employee will receive, specifies the date by which she hopes to receive acceptance, and offers to answer any questions.

Sample Letter 11.26 confirms an offer that had already been verbally accepted. The writer clearly confirms the offer by naming the position and salary offered. He then explains some of the benefits that will be offered and the regular hours of employment expected of employees. He closes by stating the date on which he expects the reader to report for duty.

Sample Letter 11.27 was written to offer an executive position to an applicant. The letter writer makes the offer, briefly recounting the responsibilities and compensation, then closes by asking for confirmation by a specific date.

Sample Letter 11.28 was written as an acceptance of a job offer. The letter writer confirms when he will start and to whom he will report.

Sample Letter 11.29 was written to turn down a job offer. The applicant expresses appreciation for the offer but explains that he thinks it is best for him to stay at his current job.

Sample Letter 11.30 was written to an applicant who has accepted a job offer. The letter writer expresses pleasure at the applicant's decision, confirms his starting salary, and states the date on which he'd like the applicant to begin work.

SAMPLE LETTER 11.25.   Letter making a job offer (full-block format).

May 18, 19X9

Ms. Joan B. Delan
3045 Triston Road
Blarneysville, Illinois 09876

Dear Ms. Delan:

We at Hinsdale-Reed Construction Company are pleased to offer you the position of Assistant Controller at the annual salary of $32,000. In addition, you will be paid cash in lieu of profit sharing until you are eligible for the normal profit sharing plan, and you will receive two weeks' paid vacation in 19X9 if you start on or before May 31, 19X9. Hinsdale-Reed will also reimburse you for family medical insurance coverage until you are picked up on our plan. I hope this letter will assist you in making your decision.

Hinsdale-Reed hopes you will be able to join its family. We look forward to hearing from you on or before Monday, May 22, 19X9.

If you have any questions about Hinsdale-Reed, please call me.

Sincerely,

Tracey Hunt
Assistant Personnel Officer

TH/LG

enc.

cc: Jack Reed
      Personnel File

SAMPLE LETTER 11.26.   Letter confirming job offer (semiblock format).

December 17, 19X5

Mr. Ambrose L. Mason
323 Alewife Brook Parkway
Hyde Park, New Hampshire 32345

Dear Ambrose:

It gives me great pleasure to confirm our verbal offer and your acceptance to join Parrisish Accounting as an auditor.

Your compensation will include your monthly salary of $2,416.67 (which is equivalent to $29,000.04 annually) plus the benefits outlined in the enclosed summary. After three months of employment, you will be eligible for nine days of vacation in the calendar year 19X6. According to the terms of our current policy, your salary and performance will be reviewed in October 19X6.

Our regular working hours are from 9 A.M. to 5 P.M., Monday through Friday. On your first day, please report directly to Carl Josephs in the Personnel Department to arrange orientation and to initiate the administrative procedures. We believe that you will make a significant contribution to Parrisish and, at the same time, will realize both the personal and professional growth you seek.

As soon as possible, please acknowledge your acceptance of this job offer by signing the enclosed copy of this letter and returning it to me. We very much look forward to your joining the company on Monday, January 27, 19X6.

Best regards,

Roy E. Early
Employment Supervisor

ree:jls

Enclosures

cc: John Taylor
      Personnel File

SAMPLE LETTER 11.27.   Letter offering executive position (semiblock format).

April 25, 19X9

Mr. Kent L. Bornard
56 Savin Hill Avenue
Beacon, Colorado 34345

Dear Kent:

It was a pleasure to meet with you in Houston last week. I'm glad we had the time to have lunch and talk.

I was very impressed with your ideas about architectural design and your suggestions for growth for our company. After discussing you and your application with the Board of Directors for Gagnon Architectural Company, I am pleased to offer you the position of Design Director of our Commercial Design Division.

In this position, you would report directly to me. You would be responsible for strategic planning and budgeting for the Commercial Design Division.

We spoke briefly about benefits, but a brief rundown might be helpful for you. The salary is $72,000 a year. You will be eligible for 4 weeks vacation, master medical coverage for you and your family, a daycare subsidy of $50 a week, a retirement plan, and stock options in the company. We can discuss these benefits in more detail if you are interested in accepting the position.

I hope you will give this offer your serious consideration. I would like to receive an acknowledgment by May 9. I hope it will be an enthusiastic yes.

Best regards,

Joanna Murray
Principal

jm/ns

SAMPLE LETTER 11.28.   Letter accepting job offer (block format).

November 20, 19X4

Mr. Mark L. Weyton
Dynoplast Plastics, Inc.
12 West Main Street
Brigton, New Jersey 07005

Dear Mr. Weyton:

I was overjoyed to receive your job offer. I am pleased to accept your offer
of the position of associate quality control director at Dynoplast Plastics,
Inc.

On Tuesday, December 1, 19X4, I will report to the personnel office to fill
out the necessary forms and to arrange for an orientation session.

After meeting you and the others at Dynoplast, I knew it would be a place
where I would enjoy working. Thank you for giving me this opportunity.

Sincerely,

Alan R. Rabsen

SAMPLE LETTER 11.29.   Letter turning down job offer (semiblock format).

May 25, 19X8

Ms. Mary Matin
Blast Management Consulting
312 Main Street
Alenton, New Jersey 07005

Dear Ms. Matin:

Thank you for offering me the associate's position at Blast
Management Consulting.

I am sorry that I will have to decline your generous offer. The
prospect of working at Blast is an exciting one. But right now, I think
there is much I can learn at my current position at Houston & Fretter.

That, coupled with the big move from Denver to Alenton that the job would entail, convinces me that it's just not the right time for me to accept your offer.

Thanks again for the kind offer. I enjoyed meeting you and all the people at Blast Management and wish you well.

Best regards,

Simon T. Blasder

SAMPLE LETTER 11.30. Letter to applicant who has accepted offer (semiblock format).

July 15, 19X8

Mr. Edward J. Cole
301 Morlan Street
Bethany, North Carolina 23215

Dear Edward:

We are very pleased that you have accepted the position of Assistant Communications Director at the annual salary of $28,500, with one week's paid vacation in 19X8. We hope that this will be a mutually rewarding and long-lasting relationship.

I hope that you can start work on August 1, 19X8 at 8:30 A.M., at which time you can sign up for our benefits plan and I can orient you to our company. Once again, it is a pleasure to have you in the Petuchnkik Brothers family.

If you have any questions, please call me.

Best regards,

Joanne L. Berrigan
Personnel Director

JLB:KAT

cc: John Crimen
      Personnel File

Letter Welcoming New Employee

Sample Letter 11.31 was written to welcome a new employee. The letter writer expresses his enthusiasm for the new employee's arrival and offers any help in making his transition easy.

SAMPLE LETTER 11.31.   Letter welcoming new employee (full-block format).

May 25, 19X8

Mr. Alan Drake
15 River Road
Bagdad, Vermont 45455

Dear Mr. Drake:

We are looking forward to your arrival here in Maine and having you as part of the Allagash Cane Company. We were very pleased when you accepted our offer of employment, and are sure that you will be a valuable employee.

As you know, the company has plans for growth in many areas. In your new position as controller, your experience and knowledge will help fuel that growth.

Please let me know if there is anything I can do to make your move easier. We are looking forward to having you in the office on June 15, 19X8.

Sincerely,

Martha Granaloff
Personnel Director

MG:ns

Recommendation Letters

Sample Letters 11.32 through 11.34 are examples of letters related to recommendations.

Sample Letter 11.32 is an example of an unqualified letter of recommendation. The letter writer explains that he has been privileged to know the applicant and that he found her to be an invaluable employee. He goes on to enthusiastically support the applicant.

SAMPLE LETTER 11.32.   Letter of recommendation (semiblock format).

August 12, 19X0

Mr. Thomas Stout
Personnel Officer
Riderim Manufacturing Company
12 Western Street
Bont, New Jersey 07005

Subject: Allison K. Sullivan

Dear Mr. Stout:

I have been privileged to know Ms. Sullivan for three years in my role as Managing Supervisor at Perceval, McKormick Manufacturing. I am currently director of business products.

While Ms. Sullivan reported to me at Perceval, McKormick, I found her management abilities to be invaluable in helping me to establish Perceval, McKormick as a leader in the office products market. Her conscientious effort and cooperation in doing professional, high-quality work were appreciated.

As a group supervisor, Allison was efficient, innovative, and responsive. She motivates her people with challenge and the opportunity for personal growth.

If you find that Allison's career objectives match your position description, I know of no reason you would be disappointed by her employment performance or personal habits. Please let me know if you require further information.

Sincerely,

Edward R. Erante

ere/mjm

Sample Letter 11.33 is an example of a qualified letter of recommendation. Here the letter writer explains that he is not qualified to comment on the applicant's ability for the type of job for which he is applying. He does comment that the applicant was an average employee who seemed enthusiastic. Such an underwhelming recommendation is qualified without being slanderous.

SAMPLE LETTER 11.33.   Qualified letter of recommendation (simplified format).

May 18, 19X8

Ms. Stacey R. Zeno
Personnel Director
Elevated Buildings, Inc.
66 High Street
Directed, Texas 09876

RECOMMENDATION FOR WILLIAM B. TROMBOND

Ms. Zeno, I am writing to you in response to your request for a recommendation of Mr. William B. Trombond, who worked for me in the bookkeeping department of Big Buildings Corp. He was not a clerk when he worked for me, however, but rather a bookkeeper. I am not qualified to comment on his capabilities as a clerk.

Bill was an average bookkeeper. He is a pleasant person who got along well with his fellow employees.

He also seemed enthusiastic about his job in the bookkeeping department. His attitude toward his work and his cooperation were above average.

If you need any further information from me, please let me know.

JENNIFER R. TRUDESCAH
CONTROLLER

JRT:mrm

Sample Letter 11.34 was written to request a recommendation from a reference who was listed on an applicant's résumé. The letter writer clearly explains the position for which the applicant is applying and asks that the letter reader send a verification of the applicant's employment and his performance record.

SAMPLE LETTER 11.34.   Letter asking for employee reference (full-block format).

May 29, 19X4

Ms. Alison T. Lewis
Personnel Manager
Andoris Products Company
312 West Main Street
Pontoon, New Jersey 07005

Dear Ms. Lewis:

Zed Phlange has applied for the position of marketing supervisor at our company. On his résumé, Mr. Phlange has listed your company as a former employer.

Could you please send us verification of Mr. Phlange's employment, including his job description, dates of employment, performance rating, and the reason for his departure? We will, of course, consider this information to be confidential.

Thank you for your assistance.

Sincerely,

Farley T. Zummerzalt
Personnel Manager

ftz/jls

Commendation Letters

Sample Letters 11.35 through 11.40 are examples of commendation letters. All of these letters are positive greetings to employees who have done well on the job.

Sample Letter 11.35 was written to commend an employee for her job performance over the year. The letter writer mentions some specific accomplishments and asks that the letter reader join her for dinner at an awards banquet.

SAMPLE LETTER 11.35.   Letter commending employee on job well done
(semiblock format).

December 3, 19X0

Ms. Katherine T. Hardsdale
Sales Representative
Better Copier Than Yours, Inc.
43 Hemingway Drive
Bullard, Wisconsin 43456

Dear Katherine:

Congratulations on your outstanding performance during 19X0. Adding 10 new clients with an average gross profit of $150,000 each is truly commendable.

Please plan to join my husband and me at the annual awards dinner slated for January 29, 19X1. I hope that Jeffrey will be able to accompany you.

Please accept my sincerest congratulations on a job well done.

Very truly yours,

Kate McGuffie
President

KM/js

cc: KTH Personnel file

Sample Letter 11.36 was written to an employee to announce that he has won a cash award for his excellent performance over the year. The letter writer announces the award, mentions the specific amount plus the fact that a certificate will be awarded at an awards luncheon. The writer concludes by informing the applicant that a copy of the award notification will be placed in his personnel file, and congratulates him on a job well done.

SAMPLE LETTER 11.36.   Letter announcing cash award for job well done
(semiblock format).

November 24, 19X7

Mr. Rhett L. Newbury
District Manager
USCSD Engineering Corp.
3234 Jagged Maple Way
Oneonta, Maryland 34345

Dear Rhett:

I am pleased to announce that a cash award has been approved for
you for your exceptional work performance during fiscal year 19X7.

For your special service you will receive a certificate of merit and a
cash award for $500 less withholding tax. The certificate will be presented
at the annual awards luncheon. The check will be forthcoming as soon as
it is processed by the Washington office.

A copy of this letter will be placed in your official personnel folder.

Congratulations on a job well done.

Sincerely,

Lars G. Pendleton
Group Manager

mrm

cc: RLN Personnel File

Sample Letter 11.37 was written to congratulate an employee on an outstanding
report. The letter writer acknowledges the good work the employee has done and
expresses pride that the employee is on his staff.

SAMPLE LETTER 11.37.   Letter congratulating employee on outstanding
report (semiblock format).

May 20, 19X8

Ms. Dorothy R. Levine
67 Granscome Road
Clifton, Pennsylvania 32345

Dear Dorothy:

    I wanted to let you know how much I appreciate the efforts you made
to prepare the monthly report for the meeting of the division heads. The
report was comprehensive and well organized. It was simply an
outstanding job.

    I am certainly proud to have you on my staff, and to have the benefit
of your careful, conscientious approach to any project you are assigned.
Congratulations on a job well done.

Best regards,

John Kerrigan
Group Manager

jk/ns

cc: DL Personnel File

    Sample Letter 11.38 was written to commend an employee for a large sale she
had made.

SAMPLE LETTER 11.38.   Letter congratulating employee on large sale
(block format).

June 15, 19X8

Ms. Susan Shmansky
56 Yourite Road
Tripoli, Pennsylvania 34345

Dear Susan:

Congratulations on your sale of 130 cases of Zinnia Styling Mousse to
Jovan Salons in Philadelphia. Yours was the largest sale of Zinnia Mousse
since the product was developed in 19X7.

I know that Jovan Salons has been a difficult franchise to sell to. Yet, with
its international distribution network, it should be worth all the extra
hours you put in.

Your willingness to learn your market and your creative ideas will take
you far in the Zinnia Corporation.

Again, thank you and congratulations.

Sincerely,

Zweno Shalk
Sales Manager

ZS:LG

     Sample Letter 11.39 was sent to congratulate an employee on community
recognition. The letter writer commends the employee for the recognition and offers
support for the group in which the employee has become involved.

SAMPLE LETTER 11.39.   Letter congratulating employee for community
recognition (semiblock format).

May 21, 19X8

Ms. Joan R. Linster
56 Yorkaway Terrace
Resnick, North Dakota 34345

Dear Joan:

I learned last week that you had been elected to the Board of Directors
of the Spruce Shelter. The Spruce Shelter has provided food to more than
1,000 battered women and their children in the past two years. The
shelter's support groups for women and their children are exemplary in
the field. The format for these groups has been duplicated throughout
North Dakota.

Endeavor Apprise Company has supported the shelter movement over
the years. I will make sure we provide particular financial and volunteer
support to the Spruce Shelter because of your initiative and good work.

Sincerely,

Donald T. Barter
Executive Vice President

dtb:ltg

Sample Letter 11.40 was written to congratulate an employee on a new idea.
The letter writer goes on to explain how others have commented on her good work,
and extends an offer of help should it be needed.

SAMPLE LETTER 11.40. Letter congratulating employee on new idea (semiblock format).

May 21, 19X8

Ms. Sally Devine, LICSW
Westland Community Services, Inc.
176 North Pine Street
Detroit, Michigan 34321

Dear Sally:

It was a pleasure to join you and your staff for your workshop at the regional meeting last week.

Your outreach and education program in the Detroit public schools focusing on adolescents and sex is truly exemplary. I was most impressed by your education program and the openness and availability of your staff.

The handbook you have developed, including topics from contraception to AIDS, was clear, with examples the teens could understand. Since your staff has its own experiences as inner-city adolescents it is particularly empathic and sensitive to the population. The staff seemed so open that I felt that almost anyone could talk with them.

Your work is being recognized throughout the agency. I talked with Andrew Brown in San Francisco, who will be calling you to talk about starting a similar program out there.

Call me any time you need to. Meeting with your staff was invigorating and informative. Keep up the good work.

Sincerely,

Wil Denehy, LICSW
Director

wd/lg

New Employee Announcement

In Sample Letter 11.41, the letter writer expresses his pleasure at announcing the arrival of two new employees. He goes on to give a brief background on both of the

newcomers, and closes by adding what he thinks the two new employees will bring
to the company.

SAMPLE LETTER 11.41.   Letter announcing new person added to the
business (full-block format).

January 5, 19X8

David R. Slater
Financial Products Marketing, Inc.
312 Silver Place
Running Woods, Missouri 32345

Dear Mr. Slater:

The Review is pleased to officially announce the appointment of Larry T.
Letz as Southwest Sales Manager and Sally Phenon as Managing Editor.

Larry has worked for the past two years with financial advertisers to our
publication in the southwest. He brings a keen understanding of the
financial services industry and is anxious to work with each of you to
define and meet your marketing objectives.

Sally comes to The Review from The Journal of Financial Services
Marketing where she covered the financial industry as a news editor. Sally
has also been a staff writer for both United Press International and
Associated Press.

These new appointments bring additional strength to The Review. I
encourage you to call Larry at 232-323-4432 for your advertising needs or
Sally at 322-545-6543 for editorial assistance.

Sincerely,

Martin L. Noten
Publisher

jls

No-Longer-With-Us Letters

Sample Letters 11.42 and 11.43 are examples of letters that were written to inform people that specific employees were no longer with the company. Sample Letter 11.42 simply states that a particular employee was no longer with the firm and that all information formerly directed to her should be directed to a different, specified employee.

Sample Letter 11.43 was written to inform someone that the employee in question had left the company years ago. The letter writer asks that the letter reader remove her name from any future correspondence to the company. He then gives a forwarding address for the former employee.

SAMPLE LETTER 11.42.   Letter informing that employee is no longer with the company (semiblock format).

March 20, 19X5

Mr. Quinn T. Renege, Vice President
Renege and Company, Inc.
23 Franklin Drive
Liberty Corner, California 23456

Dear Mr. Renege:

Ms. Lesley W. Hamilton is no longer with our company. All future correspondence about service and sales should be directed to Larry R. Wireblade, who is the sales representative for your area.

Thank you for noting this change.

Sincerely,

Fred Williamson
Personnel Director

fw/ap

SAMPLE LETTER 11.43. Letter giving forwarding address for former employee (block format).

July 8, 19X2

Mr. John S. Tucker
Tucker Systems Corporation
13 April Stsreet
Gary, Illinois 23245

Dear Mr. Tucker:

Jane L. Berrigan, Vice President of Personnel, left Andore Products Company five years ago. Please remove her name from any correspondence you direct to Andore Products.

Ms. Berrigan can be written to at Bixley Products Ltd., 62 Recognition Road, Porzio, Utah 19614.

Sincerely,

Ralph E. Jersey
Vice President

rej/jls

Retirement Letters

Sample Letters 11.44 and 11.45 are examples of letters written to an employee upon his or her retirement.

Sample Letter 11.44 is a joyful letter written to congratulate an employee on his retirement. The letter writer reminisces about the employee and wishes him well in retirement plans.

Sample Letter 11.45 was written to an employee retiring for health reasons. The letter expresses regret over losing the employee but wishes her the best on her retirement plans. The letter is sympathetic without being maudlin.

SAMPLE LETTER 11.44.   Letter congratulating employee on retirement (semiblock format).

June 15, 19X8

Mr. Robert E. Lang
345 West Hartford Street
Trumball, Vermont 23234

Dear Bob:

After I gave that small talk at your retirement dinner, I was struck with how quickly the 15 years have passed since you first came to Andoris Publishing Company. It seems like only yesterday when you heeded my call for a well-seasoned chief financial officer to come in and put financial controls in place at a haphazardly growing publishing company.

Looking back on the 15 years, it's safe to say that you've surpassed my wildest dreams in helping Andoris to grow to where it is today -- a $10 million company. No small feat considering we barely broke a million when you first arrived.

You'll be missed here, Bob. But our loss is somewhat tempered by the fact that you and Gwen will be chasing another dream down in Kokamo. I'm not sure that buying into that Triple-A baseball team was what I would consider a relaxing retirement, but for someone who is determined to live out a baseball dream, it seems perfect.

Zoe and I wish you the best in your retirement and in your new adventures. We hope you will still find time to visit us up in the Northeast whenever you're in town.

Sincerely,

Martin L. Nathan
President

MLN:jls

SAMPLE LETTER 11.45.   Letter to employee retiring for health reasons (semiblock format).

May 20, 19X8

Mrs. Jeanette Long
45 Twinscomb Place
Transit, California 45456

Dear Jeanette:

When we met last week, I told you how distressed I am at the prospect of your leaving Los Angeles and Pet World. It is our loss, and we all regret the development of your allergies to the Los Angeles smog.

Your work has been outstanding, particularly in your supervision of staff. I also appreciate your loving attention to our pets.

I wish you the best as you move to the Sierras. Any time you need a letter of recommendation, please let me know.

Sincerely,

Barbara Cole

bc/lg

Termination Letters

Termination letters are one type of correspondence that is almost invariably difficult to write. Few people want to sit down to write a letter firing an employee. Unfortunately, it is a task that must be handled from time to time. When termination must be faced, it is best to be well equipped to deal with the situation.

A standard dismissal letter does not exist. Since every job termination has particular circumstances, each termination letter must be written to fit the situation at hand. Each termination letter is a very personal matter. Each employee has a different relationship to a company. As a result, he or she will have to be informed about the procedures to take upon termination on everything from severance pay to collecting accumulating pension benefits.

As such, the sample termination letters included here are meant to serve as a starting point upon which to build. Using these letters as basic samples, you can develop your own termination letters to fit the particular circumstances you face.

Before a termination letter is written, however, many companies follow a procedure that is known as progressive discipline. Some also refer to this process as building a case against an employee. The process involves an oral warning, followed by a written warning that clearly spells out the consequences of an employee's further actions, followed by some sort of disciplinary action such as a suspension, and ultimately termination. Each step of the process should be noted in the employee's personnel file.

The need for disciplinary action will often show up during employee performance evaluations. Rather than write a separate warning letter, managers doing the evaluation will indicate on a performance appraisal form where job performance has been unsatisfactory. These evaluations serve as warnings to employees about poor job performance. They also serve as a good record of the employee's performance in his or her personnel file.

As far as following a set procedure for terminating an employee, one personnel director of a major business recommends that you should:

- Send termination letters registered or certified mail, return receipt requested. Such action gives the employer proof of sending a letter and puts a damper on claims that a letter was never received.
- Clearly state the reason for the termination.
- Write termination letters in a brief but understanding tone.

Sample Letters 11.46 through 11.48 are examples of termination letters. Sample Letter 11.46 was sent as a warning to an employee. The letter writer clearly states the violation the employee has made and warns that if he does not hear from the employee by a specific date he will face possible termination.

SAMPLE LETTER 11.46.   Letter warning employee of possible termination (full-block format).

April 1, 19X0

Mr. Eliot R. Davids
28 Laurel Avenue, Apt. 3
Somerville, New York 32345

Dear Mr. Davids:

We have not heard from you about your absence since Wednesday, March 22, 19X0. At that time I informed you of the problems we have been having with your performance as a sales representative for our organization. Before you left the office, I reminded you that your performance -- documented in your biannual performance appraisals -- simply was not acceptable by company standards. I tried to present you with possible solutions to the problems you are facing.

Now, in light of the fact that you have broken company policy by not reporting to work for the last 8 days without notifying anyone here, I am concerned that you have compounded your problems.

Please get in touch with me before April 8, 19X0, or you will face the possibility of termination from Pandora Engineering. Our company policy states that employees who are unable to report to work must notify their supervisor within the first half hour of the working day. An absence is considered excused only when an employee has notified his or her supervisor and has obtained approval.

We would like to work with you to solve this problem, Eliot, but you must comply with company policy and work with us to successfully find a solution.

Cordially,

David Penny
Personnel Director

DP/jh

     Sample Letter 11.47 was sent to an employee who broke company policy and refused to respond to a warning letter. The letter is brief, but clearly points out why the employee is being terminated.

SAMPLE LETTER 11.47.   Letter terminating employee. Follow-up to no response to Sample Letter 11.46 (full-block format).

April 11, 19X0

Mr. Eliot R. Davids
28 Laurel Avenue, Apt. 3
Somerville, New York 32345

Dear Mr. Davids:

Your employment with Pandora Engineering has been terminated effective April 8, 19X0, because of your failure to comply with Personnel Policy #34-Z, and your failure to respond to my letter of April 1, 19X0.

Please contact Muriel Wilson in the personnel department to discuss severance pay and pension plan disbursements.

Cordially,

David Penny
Personnel Director

dp/js

Sample Letter 11.48 was written to an employee who had broken company policy, informing her that she has been terminated. The letter writer clearly explains the violation of company policy and informs the employee that she has been terminated.

SAMPLE LETTER 11.48.   Letter terminating an employee who has broken company policy (semiblock format).

May 23, 19X8

Ms. Karen T. Woot
32 Restpark Place
Feldtown, Nevada 23234

Dear Karen:

On Wednesday morning, May 16, 19X8, you and I had a meeting with David Marshall in his office. When the conversation was over, you went back to your area and then left the building without telling anyone where you were going.

According to Davis Construction Company's policy on absences, employees who will be absent must notify their superior during the first half-hour of each working day.

Because we have not heard from you for the last seven days, and have been unable to reach you, your employment at Davis Construction Company is considered terminated.

You will receive one month's severance pay. All of the stock you have purchased through the employee stock ownership plan will be disbursed to you. Please contact Muriel Viewton in the personnel department to make arrangements.

Sincerely,

Vanessa K. Jewett
Vice President

vkj/ahh

CHAPTER 12
Transmittal Letters

Letters that accompany enclosed material are frequently referred to as transmittal letters. Their chief function is to identify the material that is enclosed. This chapter features many of the more common forms of transmittal letters that you may have to write.

Letters Transmitting Payment

Sample Letters 12.1 through 12.5 are examples of transmittal letters that were written to accompany payment.

Sample Letter 12.1 is a standard transmittal of payment on account letter. The letter writer clearly identifies the amount enclosed and the purpose of the payment. He closes by thanking the letter reader for her services.

SAMPLE LETTER 12.1.   Transmittal of payment on account (semiblock format).

May 20, 19X8

Ms. Alice D. Edwards
Tisk-a-Disk Office Supplies
76 Tuscon Drive
Lake Forest, Kentucky 23234

Dear Ms. Edwards:

My check for $75.42 is enclosed. This is my final payment on my order number 73A2 for office supplies for Kearney Public Relations, Inc. placed on March 30, 19X8.

Thank you for extending us the credit. We appreciate the service you provided us.

Sincerely,

Allen T. Quagmire
Office Manager

atq/fwd

enc.

238

Sample Letter 12.2 was sent to transmit payment that was different from the total on an invoice. Here the letter writer indicates the amount he is transmitting, explains the discrepancy, and asks that the letter reader call if there is any confusion about the account.

SAMPLE LETTER 12.2.   Letter transmitting payment totaling different amount from invoice (full-block format).

May 29, 19X1

Mr. Brandt Henry
Quimby Office Supplies, Inc.
312 Respite Way
Santiago, Idaho 43456

Dear Mr. Henry:

Enclosed is my check for $27.22 to cover payment of stationery supplies I purchased from your company. You'll notice that the amount does not jibe with the amount stated on the invoice dated April 30, 19X1. This is undoubtedly because my check of May 5, 19X1, was not credited to my account.

Please call me if there is any problem with my account. If I do not hear from you I will assume that my account has been paid in full.

Sincerely,

Zachary T. LeBoeuf

ztl/pcd

enc.

Sample Letter 12.3 was sent to transmit payment to a speaker whom the letter writer found to be outstanding. The letter writer announces in the first paragraph that the payment is enclosed, but goes on to praise the speaker for playing such an integral role in the success of the convention at which he spoke. The letter writer clearly is pleased with the speaker's performance.

Sample Letter 12.4 was written to a speaker who was not particularly outstanding. The letter writer indicates that she is transmitting payment and thanks the speaker for his participation. Nowhere does she complain about the speaker's performance. She simply does not lay on as much praise as the letter writer did in

Sample Letter 12.3. Sample Letter 12.4 is a courteous letter used to transmit payment.

SAMPLE LETTER 12.3.   Letter transmitting payment to outstanding speaker (semiblock format).

March 20, 19X7

Mr. James Lewis
Funny for Money, Inc.
228 West 78th Street
Manhattan, Kansas 43456

Dear Mr. Lewis:

Enclosed is a check covering your speaking fee for the luncheon speech you delivered at our group's annual convention.

Once again, the annual convention of the Association of Internal Auditors (AIA) met with the resounding approval of its membership. On their evaluation forms, our members rated your talk as one of the top speeches given during the four-day convention.

Thank you for helping to make our convention a success. We hope to call on you again to enlighten our group.

Sincerely,

Oscar D. Terradect
Convention Director

ODT:jls

enc.

SAMPLE LETTER 12.4.   Letter transmitting payment to not-so-great
speaker (block format).

May 9, 19X6

Mr. Martin Laramy
Modifier Parries Company
312 West Main Street
Boonton, New Jersey 07005

Dear Mr. Laramy:

Enclosed is a check for your appearance as a speaker at our weekend
retreat in Chatham. Thank you for agreeing to speak to our group of
brokers.

Once again, our brokers found the retreat to be a useful time to gather and
share knowledge with fellow professionals.

Thank you again.

Sincerely,

Sheila T. Picksups

stp/fwd

enc.

Sample Letter 12.5 was written to transmit payment to a reviewer of a
manuscript. The letter is brief but clear. The letter writer states the amount enclosed
and thanks the letter reader for his services.

SAMPLE LETTER 12.5. Transmitting payment to reviewer (semiblock format).

December 12, 19X5

Professor Adam R. Ecuamen
Holiday University
67 Right Venere Hall
Holiday, New Mexico 32345

Dear Professor Ecuamen:

Enclosed please find your check for $250 for the recent review you did for me. I appreciate the time and effort you put into it.

I hope to be able to call on you again.

Sincerely,

Edward Colen
Program Director

EC/jh

enc.

Letter Transmitting Contracts

Sample Letter 12.6 is an example of a letter that was written to transmit contracts. It was sent to transmit a representation agreement. The letter writer indicates in the first paragraph what she is enclosing and what the letter reader must do. The letter writer offers to furnish any explanation if it is needed, and closes by expressing delight over the prospect of working with the letter reader.

SAMPLE LETTER 12.6.   Transmittal of representation agreement (semiblock format).

October 29, 19X7

Ms. Adrienne D. Storm
54 Cadillac Road
Water Hills, California 34323

Dear Adrienne:

Enclosed are two copies of a representation agreement. Please countersign one copy and return it to me. Of course if you have any questions, feel free to call.

I'm delighted that we'll be working together, Adrienne. I look forward to a long and productive relationship.

Best regards,

Vanessa J. Jewett

vjj/jjm

Enclosures

Letters Transmitting Requested Materials

Sample Letters 12.7 and 12.8 were written to accompany material that had been requested. Both letters are short and do nothing more than confirm what is being transmitted.

SAMPLE LETTER 12.7.   Transmitting requested materials (semiblock format).

March 16, 19X8

Robert E. Black
51 Trevor Avenue
Dorfleck, New Jersey 42810

Dear Bob:

Enclosed are printouts of the results of the calculations you requested for insurance rate of return if you were to buy term insurance instead of whole life and invest the difference in cost. I used our new five-year renewable and convertible term rates, which include a $40 policy fee.

Please feel free to call me if you have any questions.

Best regards,

Mary T. Amock

mta/mld

encl.

SAMPLE LETTER 12.8.   Transmitting supplies (simplified format).

January 18, 19X8

Mr. Lawrence R. Effredge
Effredge and St. Paul, Inc.
186-A Savin Road
Rontclen, New Hampshire 43468

TRANSMITTAL OF STATIONERY

Larry, enclosed are approximately 500 sheets of stationery and 500 envelopes for your project. We hope you like them, and that they will bring good luck to the project.

Please call me if you need any further assistance.

LEONARD D. DELB
ADMINISTRATIVE ASSISTANT

LDD:pt

ENC.

Letter Transmitting Manuscript

Sample Letter 12.9 was written to an author from an editor to accompany a copy-edited manuscript for an article he had written. The editor instructs the author what he is to do with the copy-edited manuscript.

SAMPLE LETTER 12.9.   Transmittal of edited copy (semiblock format).

December 22, 19X7

Mr. Allen T. Price
Price & Price Company, Inc.
17 Metro Drive
Horticulture, Alaska 45456

Dear Allen:

Enclosed for your review is an edited copy of your article, which will appear in an upcoming issue of Guam City Magazine. Please look it over and telephone me in the copy-editing department within 72 hours. Alert us to any factual inaccuracies. We will not be able to accept substantive editorial changes at this time, owing to the time constraints of our production schedule.

Your immediate attention to this matter will expedite our production process. You need not mail back the enclosed copy.

Thank you for your cooperation.

Sincerely,

Lauren J. Palay
Copy-Editing Supervisor

ljp/kka

enc.

Letter Transmitting Manuscript to Reviewer

Sample Letter 12.10 is an example of a letter written to accompany manuscript that was being transmitted to a reviewer. This transmittal letter is an excellent model to use when sending out a manuscript for review to a first-time reviewer.

SAMPLE LETTER 12.10.   Transmittal of instructions to reviewer (simplified format).

January 31, 19X5

Mr. Jeffrey L. Jacobs
Rice & Hall, Inc.
4567 Yourow Place
Falstaff, New Jersey 32345

SIX POINTS TO COVER IN A REVIEW

Mr. Jacobs, thank you for agreeing to review Electronmagnetics Today. You will find the manuscript enclosed.

In looking over the manual, would you comment on the following:

1. Is the material well organized, up-to-date, and accurate? If not, please include a sample of specific criticisms.

2. Has the author placed too much emphasis upon certain topics? Should any be excluded? Added? Transposed? Please feel free to suggest changes.

3. Are the vocabulary and information suited to the target market for which the manuscript is intended?

4. What are the current trends in this area? Does this manuscript reflect them? In your opinion, will it be up-to-date three years from now?

5. If this text were now available in published form, would you use it, or recommend its use?

6. In your review, would you please make any definite suggestions for improving the manuscript you have?

Page 2
Mr. Jeffrey L. Jacobs
January 31, 19X5

We do not identify the reviewer to the author, so please do not let your name appear anywhere on your review.

If possible, we would like to have two copies of your review within three weeks. If you cannot complete it by then, please let me know. We will be happy to send you an honorarium of $225 for your assistance with this project.

Could you please return the material with your review so that we can process your honorarium? We will, of course, reimburse you for the postage fee.

Thank you for your efforts. If you should have any questions, please call me at 343-545-6754.

MAXWELL L. NICHOLAS
EXECUTIVE EDITOR

mln/jls

enc.

Letter Transmitting Final Invoice

Sample Letter 12.11 was written to accompany a final invoice that was being transmitted to a customer. The letter writer expresses pleasure at having been able to serve the customer. He then indicates that a final invoice is enclosed.

SAMPLE LETTER 12.11.   Transmittal of final invoice (semiblock format).

January 23, 19X6

Ms. Annmarie L. Long
186 Grampian Street
Alexander, Wisconsin 34321

Dear Annmarie:

It was a great pleasure having your reception/luncheon/dance in the London Room. We do hope that you and your guests were pleased with all of the services provided.

Enclosed you will find the completed invoice for your function. Should you have any questions about it, please do not hesitate to call us.

We look forward to the opportunity to be of service to you again in the near future.

Sincerely,

R. David Lawrence
Director of Marketing

RDL/jls

encl.

CHAPTER 13
Confirmation Letters

When a professional receives information or material from someone, most often the courteous thing to do is to write a confirmation letter. Sometimes it simply makes sense to write one to make sure that you understood the information you discussed with someone. The letters in this chapter are examples of some basic confirmation letters that a professional might have to write.

Letter Confirming Supplier's Oral Instructions

Sample Letter 13.1 was written as a follow-up to a supplier's oral instructions. By writing this type of confirmation letter, the writer makes sure that she has understood the supplier's instructions correctly. The letter writer clearly reiterates the discussion she had with the supplier, asks that she call to discuss the instructions, and expresses interest in her feedback.

SAMPLE LETTER 13.1. Letter confirming a supplier's oral instructions (semiblock format).

May 23, 19X8

Ms. Joan Whitener
Bright & Shining Shirt Service
150 Western Street
New York, New Jersey 34345

Dear Joan:

As we discussed at the area meeting last week, I am revising the schedule of shirt deliveries for New York. The deliveries should take place between 6:30 A.M. and 3:30 P.M., Monday through Friday. Those loyal customers with a long-standing relationship with Bright & Shining should be surveyed and given priority for day and time of delivery each week.

Please call me in the next week to discuss this plan. I would appreciate your thoughts on the feasibility of reworking the schedule.

Again, it was good to talk with you last week and hear of your high volume. Your feedback on this new plan is appreciated.

Sincerely,

Eliza Rodriquez

er/lg

Letter Confirming Prices and Quantity Discounts

Sample Letter 13.2 was written to confirm prices and quantity discounts that were quoted to the letter reader by the letter writer. The writer clearly recounts the price discount and lists the prices he quoted. As a result, he can reduce the risk of a misunderstanding.

SAMPLE LETTER 13.2. Letter confirming prices and quantity discounts (block format).

October 19, 19X5

Mr. Mario Dumas, Owner
Mercado Mexicano
114 West Webster Street
Chicago, Kansas 43456

Dear Mario:

As we discussed on the telephone on October 15, Enrico's Enchiladas is planning a special enchilada festival to begin on December 1. From December 1 through December 31, all of our enchiladas will be available at a 25% discount. All phone and mail orders placed during this period will receive the discount. Special freezer displays and complimentary aprons will be sent with each order.

The discount applies to those enchiladas listed on our spring order sheets, page 3, in boxes of 12. These include:

Order #	Type	Regular Price	Discount Price
#1062	Cheese Enchiladas	$24	$18
#1063	Bean Enchiladas	$20	$15
#1064	Beef Enchiladas	$28	$21
#1065	Chicken Enchiladas	$32	$24

We will ship your order within 24 hours of receipt. Unless you specify otherwise, we will deliver on our freezer truck, which will arrive three days from the time we ship your order. Each order will be charged an additional 5% for regular delivery.

I look forward to our December Enchilada Festival and to hearing from you soon. I will be glad to handle your shipment with special care.

Sincerely,

Enrico Sanchez

es/js

Letter Confirming Arrangements for Speakers

Sample Letter 13.3 was written to a person who had commited to speak at a conference. The letter writer confirms the agreement and gives the speaker information on the luncheon he is to attend.

SAMPLE LETTER 13.3.   Confirming arrangements for a speaker (semiblock format).

October 28, 19X7

Mr. Mario L. Rodriguez
312 West Main Street
Boonton, New Jersey 07005

Dear Mr. Rodriguez:

Thank you for agreeing to speak at the IAFPAA Conference luncheon on Friday, November 7. Here are the final details of the event.

The luncheon will start at noon at the City Club, 12 State Street, Morriston (see the enclosed map for directions). If you wish a vegetarian menu, please call me at 632-567-8706 before Wednesday, November 5.

The luncheon should last about one hour, after which you will address the attendees. We have arranged for a microphone and lectern for your speech. If you need other equipment or have any questions about the luncheon, please call me.

We look forward to hearing your speech.

Sincerely,

Samuel D. Nead
Program Coordinator

sdn/mls

enc.

Letter Confirming Appointment

Sample Letter 13.4 was written to confirm an appointment. The letter writer briefly confirms the date and time when she is to meet the reader. She mentions that she will be bringing two people to the meeting.

SAMPLE LETTER 13.4.   Letter confirming an appointment (block format).

September 3, 19X7

Mr. John Egnald
Managing Director
Association Widgets, Inc.
5775 Peachtree Road
Quantico, Alaska 45456

Dear Mr. Egnald:

I look forward to meeting you on Monday, September 21, to further discuss the North Widget Project, which Legyern Associates will be designing. I will plan to see you around noon.

Both Mack MacIntyre and Bethany Cole are planning to meet with you as well. We are extremely excited about this project and the prospect of your participation.

Cordially,

Martha Long
Executive Editor

ml/kw

cc: Mack MacIntyre
     Bethany Cole

Letter Confirming Telephone Conversation

Sample Letter 13.5 was written to confirm the facts discussed in a telephone conversation. The letter writer briefly confirms the information she had given the letter reader over the phone and asks that he call should he have further questions.

SAMPLE LETTER 13.5.   Letter confirming a telephone conversation (block format).

November 5, 19X4

Mr. Mack MacIntyre
Mandate and Associates
45 Winck Road
Pechee, Arizona 43454

Dear Mr. MacIntyre:

As we discussed in our phone conversation earlier this week, I have sent letters to the 15 project advisory board members for the North Widget Project. As you can see from the enclosed copies, the letters welcome each member to the board and ask them to enclose a biographical profile.

A file has been set up for each advisory board member.

If you need further information or assistance, feel free to call on me.

Cordially,

Ellen Short
Assistant Coordinator

es/kw

cc: Bethany Cole

Letter Confirming Telegram

Sample Letter 13.6 was sent to confirm a telegram the letter writer had sent to the letter reader. Such a letter serves as a backup in case there was a foul-up with the telegram that was to be sent.

SAMPLE LETTER 13.6.   Letter confirming a telegram (semiblock format).

May 14, 19X8

Sarah Miles
Strawberry Fields Forever
Ludlow, Vermont 45435

Dear Sarah:

I sent you the following telegram today:

Send 45 quarts of strawberries to Sweet Dreams Inn as soon as possible. Pack in flats. Cover with mesh, not plastic wrap. I need them by May 25 for the Lenox Spring Festival.

Please send us your spring and summer prices and delivery costs. Your strawberries are consistently great. We look forward to continuing to work together.

Sincerely,

Sue Frank

SF:lg

Letters Confirming Receipt of Materials

Sample Letters 13.7 and 13.8 were sent to confirm receipt of materials. Sample Letter 13.7 confirms that the material has been received and that the letter writer will send it out for review. Sample Letter 13.8 also confirms receipt of the material, but here the writer explains that the person to whom it was sent is away and that he will turn his attention to it when he returns.

SAMPLE LETTER 13.7.   Letter confirming receipt of material (semiblock format).

March 20, 19X7

Dr. Alice T. Cooperburg
Department of Mathematics
Fortified College
Westernite, Connecticut 45456

Dear Dr. Cooperburg:

This letter will acknowledge receipt of the outline and 12 chapters of your manuscript on mathematic modeling. We are very pleased to receive your material and welcome the opportunity to review it.

Your material has been referred to several critics for their comments. I should have their recommendations within three to four weeks and will be glad to send you their reactions at that time.

Thank you for sending this material to me. I will be in touch with you soon.

Cordially,

Maxwell L. Nicholas
Executive Editor

mln/jls

SAMPLE LETTER 13.8.   Letter confirming receipt of material (full-block format).

May 9, 19X6

Dr. Lionel T. Aramet
Department of Economics
Transit University
43 Alban Hall West
Transit, New York 45355

Dear Dr. Aramet:

I'm writing this letter to acknowledge receipt of the outline and 5 chapters of your manuscript on econometrics.

Mr. Nicholas is currently away on business. I will bring your material to his attention immediately upon his return. He will be in touch with you as soon as your material has been reviewed.

Sincerely,

Chauncy D. Tortoise
Secretary to Maxwell Nicholas

cdt

Letter Confirming Assignment

Sample Letter 13.9 was sent to confirm an assignment accepted by the letter writer. The letter writer briefly but clearly indicates what she believes she has agreed to do: in this case, contribute an article to a professional journal. She lists the agreed-upon length and due date.

SAMPLE LETTER 13.9.   Letter confirming assignment (semiblock format).

October 26, 19X4

Mr. Martin L. Rodney
The Armchair Reader's Review
327 Merrimac Trail
Boonton, New Jersey 07005

Dear Mr. Rodney:

I want to confirm that I have accepted the assignment of writing an article on the breakdown of the Glass-Steagall Act for The Armchair Reader's Review. I have obtained the approval of my supervisor for this undertaking. A copy of my vita is enclosed.

I will deliver the draft of the 1,500-word article to you no later than November 30, 19X4.

If you need any more information from me in the meantime, please call.

Sincerely,

Dr. Nalia G. Hinzt

ngh/wos

enc.

CHAPTER 14
Request Letters

The letters in this chapter fall into the broad category of request letters. These are commonly written by professionals to request everything from information and assistance to reprints of articles.

Information Request Letters

Sample Letters 14.1 and 14.2 were written to request some type of information. Sample Letter 14.1 was written to request information about accommodations that were to be provided to a speaker. The speaker writes to request information about the room he will be speaking in and the equipment he has requested. He opens by saying that he is looking forward to the meeting, then asks a series of questions about the accommodations that will be provided. The letter is clear and to the point, and should get the letter writer the results he needs.

SAMPLE LETTER 14.1. Letter requesting information about accommodations (semiblock format).

November 11, 19X7

Mr. James B. Dreyfus
Assistant Seminar Director
Business Writers Association
23 Floriador Street
Ausley, New York 39495

Dear Mr. Dreyfus:

I am looking forward to speaking at your upcoming seminar. I've completed and enclosed the form you sent me. I've also checked off the audiovisual services I will need for my talk.

At your earliest convenience, please let me know how many people will attend my two seminar sessions, "Public Relations Primer." There are a few other questions I hope you can answer for me as soon as possible:

Will I be able to see the room where I'll be speaking before my first
    session on Tuesday at 9:00 A.M.?
Will I be able to check the handouts to ensure they are all there?
Will I be able to check the audiovisual equipment I requested?
Should I plan to meet you or someone on Monday or should I just
    show up for my sessions?

Can you also correct the name of my company to Napier Public
Relations, Inc., not Napier Communications as you refer to it in your
outline? I would also appreciate the initials APR (Accredited Public
Relations) being used after my name. I've enclosed a business card for
your reference. Thanks very much.

I look forward to speaking with you.

                              Best regards,

                              Max Napier, APR

mn/pb

Enclosures

Sample Letter 14.2 was written to request information about seminars available
in the letter writer's area of interest. The writer wastes no time; he gets right to the
point in the first paragraph, thanks the recipient in the second, and closes the letter.

SAMPLE LETTER 14.2.   Letter requesting information on seminars offered
(semiblock format).

                          May 16, 19X8

Ms. Carla Moore
Wholesaler Carpeters Association
One Park Avenue
Westport, Nebraska 23432

Dear Ms. Moore:

Please advise me of any seminars you might have that focus on
training wholesale carpet distributors on effective management skills.

Thanks for your assistance.

                              Best regards,

                              Lin O. Leehum

lol/jls

Letter Requesting Assistance

Sample Letter 14.3 was written to request the assistance of a former life insurance policy holder by asking him to fill out a questionnaire about the company's services. The letter writer clearly states why she is asking the reader for the information, is cordial, and does not attempt to sell anything in the process.

SAMPLE LETTER 14.3.   Letter requesting assistance by filling out questionnaire (full-block format).

December 1, 19X7

Mr. Timothy Marshall
Dean, Haskell, Marshall & Quiksilber
65 Basil Place
Attic, Montana 34235

Dear Mr. Marshall:

New Day Life Insurance Company is committed to providing the small employer with the best service and group insurance products. Although your group health insurance policy is no longer in effect, it is important to us that we obtain your feedback about the quality of service and products.

By completing the enclosed questionnaire you will provide us with the ideas and suggestions necessary to better serve small employers like you. Your opinions and comments are especially important to us.

Please take a few minutes to complete the questionnaire as accurately and honestly as possible. It is important that the person in your company who has the most influence and decision-making authority over group insurance coverage fill out the survey. All responses are for planning purposes and will be used only in combination with other responses.

We would appreciate your response by December 28, 19X7. Simply fold this questionnaire and place it in the postage paid envelope provided. If you have any questions, please call Mr. Alan Suez, market research and product development administrator, at 534-675-0987.

Thanks for your consideration in this important matter.

Very truly yours,

Joanne Tufts
President

jt/mn

Enc.

Letters Requesting Return of Material

Sample Letters 14.4 through 14.6 request the return of materials of one sort or another.

Sample Letter 14.4 is a short letter requesting the return of a proposal. The letter writer makes her request simply and to the point.

Sample Letter 14.5 requests the reader to fill out a form that the writer needs to have on file. The writer makes the request, briefly explains why she needs the form, and closes.

Sample Letter 14.6 is a short letter written to request that materials be returned. The writer is courteous and explains why he has to have the materials.

SAMPLE LETTER 14.4.   Letter requesting return of material (block format).

November 4, 19X7

Mr. Alan Tromaine
Teraracen Northwest
453 Triple Street
New Brunswick, Pennsylvania 32456

Dear Alan:

Can you please return to me the Markup Project materials I sent to you as well as the product specifications for our new piece of hardware.

Many thanks. I hope all is well with you.

Best regards,

Priscilla Lahsram

pl/em

SAMPLE LETTER 14.5.   Letter requesting completion of required form
(semiblock format).

October 30, 19X7
TTT-456-789-3542

Mrs. Roberta Cupelman
Cupelman Contractors
139 Station Place
Rutineo, Illinois 32456

Dear Mrs. Cupelman:

The purpose of this letter is to request your organization to assist Coleridge Ship, Inc. in fulfilling its obligation to the Department of Defense by completing the enclosed Representation and Certification Form.

As prime contractor for the U.S. Government, Coleridge Ship, Inc., requires that this information be obtained on an annual basis. Failure to respond may be detrimental to the future business between our companies.

Please forward the completed form to the above address. If you have any questions or desire additional information, please feel free to call me.

Sincerely,

COLERIDGE SHIP, INC.

(Miss) Roxane Trustman
Manager of Contracts

rt/mn

enc.

SAMPLE LETTER 14.6.   Letter requesting that materials be returned since too much time has passed (semiblock format).

August 12, 19X5

Mr. John Blank
Fortified Developers
45 Rineland Drive
Hasquath, New Mexico 23456

Dear Mr. Blank:

Thank you for consenting to review the architectural plans for our downtown shopping mall project. Since there was a time element involved in having these plans reviewed, we have had to make other arrangements concerning the project.

Please return the material to us at your earliest convenience.

We appreciate your willingness to review this plan, Mr. Blank, and hope that we may call upon you for future critical reviews.

Sincerely,

Fran Lison
President

ls

Letter Requesting Material from Speaker

Sample Letter 14.7 was written to request material from a speaker. The letter writer explains that he needs the material, offers to help the speaker if he needs assistance filling out the forms requested, and stresses the importance of the reader sending in the information.

SAMPLE LETTER 14.7.   Letter requesting that speaker supply material
(full-block format).

January 31, 19X4

Mr. Larry C. Rebekkah
Emline Products Inc.
34 Richardson Drive
Farnsworth, Kentucky 23456

Dear Mr. Rebekkah:

I have been looking daily for the speaker's suggestion form that was
mailed to you on December 1, 19X3.

If you are having difficulty or if you have any questions about what
information we want, please write to me or call me at the Boonton office. I
will be glad to answer any questions that you might have.

It is important that we have this information. I would appreciate it if you
would return the forms at your earliest convenience.

Sincerely,

Mack Leges
Program Coordinator

ml/ms

Letter Requesting Correction of Charge Account

Sample Letter 14.8 was sent to a credit service asking that a correction be made on
an account. The letter writer clearly states her case in the opening paragraph,
mentioning that she is enclosing copies of documents to verify her claim. Rather
than go off on a tirade, she clearly states her problem and asks for a solution.

SAMPLE LETTER 14.8.   Letter requesting that correction be made on charge account (semiblock format).

November 10, 19X7

Mr. Lawrence Brians
Customer Service Representative
Cabot Credit Company
56 Frithy Drive
Lanscome, Idaho 32456

Dear Mr. Brians:

Enclosed is a copy of my cancelled check #161 for $20.95. This amount was not credited to my account, and this month's statement shows a past due balance. I neglected to write my account number on the check. Whoever at Cabot Credit wrote the number on the check put the incorrect number on the face of the check.

I am enclosing a check for $44.93, which takes into account all new charges through November 1. I hope that this will settle the account balance.

Please let me know that this matter has been resolved.

Sincerely,

Lisa L. Long

encs.

Letter Requesting Reprint of Article

Sample Letter 14.9 was written to request a reprint of an article that was published in a magazine. The letter writer clearly states his request, leaving little doubt what he is after.

SAMPLE LETTER 14.9.   Letter requesting reprint of article (block format).

December 26, 19X6

Mr. Marl Simons, Editor
Options Trading Review
312 West Main Street
Boonton, New Jersey 07005

Dear Mr. Simons:

I would like to purchase a reprint of the article you published on options trading on pages 23 through 30 in your March 19X6 issue. Please send the reprint and any invoice to me at: 456 Frunton Street, Denville, Pennsylvania 12321.

Thank you for your assistance.

Sincerely,

Giles K. Julian
Vice President

gkj/jls

CHAPTER 15
Replies

On many occasions, professionals find it necessary to write reply letters. The letters included in this chapter serve as models that professionals can use in a variety of commonly faced situations.

Letter Acknowledging Order

Sample Letter 15.1 was written to acknowledge an order for a product. The letter writer explains that more information is needed before shipment can be made, and clearly explains the procedure the reader should take to ensure timely delivery of his order.

SAMPLE LETTER 15.1. Letter acknowledging order (semiblock format).

May 9, 19X3

Mr. Blake Brinne
Hanley Hascomb & Doyle
327 Merrimac Trail, Suite 4B
Williamstown, Missouri 32345

Dear Mr. Brinne:

Thank you for your order for 250 executive desk calendars. We will ship your calendars as soon as possible.

Before we ship, however, we need to know how you would like us to ship the calendars. You failed to indicate on your order whether you wanted overnight delivery, first-class mail, or parcel post. If you will check off your preference on the enclosed postage-paid card and return it to us, or call us toll-free at 800-122-6563, we will ship you your calendars immediately.

Our executive desk calendar is practically designed to help the busy executive keep business appointments organized. We are sure you will be among those who find it to be an indispensable tool.

Thanks again for your order. We look forward to filling it as soon as we receive your instructions.

Sincerely,

Jeffrey L. Oscar

jlo/jls

Letter Acknowledging Registration to Conference

Sample Letter 15.2 was written to a person who had registered for a conference. In the first paragraph, the letter writer thanks the letter reader for his registration. Not only does this suggest politeness, the writer also lets it be known right off that his letter confirms the registration. He continues by explaining some specifics about the conference and closes by offering any help the reader might need.

SAMPLE LETTER 15.2.   Letter following up on registration to conference (semiblock format).

April 20, 19X6

Mr. Mark Holden
Pover Products, Inc.
45 Savin Avenue
Boonton, New Jersey 07005

Dear Mr. Holden:

Thank you for your recent registration to the Independent Wholesalers Trade Exposition at the Elmira Inn. This letter will confirm our receipt of your registration form and fee.

The Wholesalers Trade Society registration desk will open at 10:00 A.M. on Thurdsay, April 28, followed by the opening general session. The national exposition will conclude at 5:30 P.M. on Saturday, April 30, 19X8. Please note the enclosed general information.

We look forward to welcoming you to Elmira and to this innovative national conference. Should you have any questions, please call me.

Cordially,

Simon Lexington
Education Coordinator

sl/pp

encl.

Remittance Letter

Sample Letter 15.3 is a remittance letter that was written to accompany payment for a product. It is brief and clearly states what is included with it. By writing such a letter, the writer ensures that the chances of making a mistake with his payment are minimized. Sample Letter 15.3 could also be used as a guide for transmittal letters (see Chapter 12).

SAMPLE LETTER 15.3.   Remittance letter (full-block format).

August 8, 19X5

Mr. Oscar T. Rodman
Rodman and Sons Stationery, Inc.
5432 Red Bank Drive
Chelmsford, Massachusetts 34345

Dear Mr. Rodman:

I have enclosed a check for $119 for the stationery and envelopes I ordered from you for our business. Also enclosed is a copy of your invoice number 3352217. Please credit the $119 to my account number 12-26-5631.

Sincerely,

Loudon P. Schlenger

lps/kpc

encs.

Response to Request for Clarification

Sample Letter 15.4 was written as a reply to a request for clarification on an account. The letter writer clearly explains what he is enclosing with the letter and offers an explanation for the discrepancy in the account. He closes by apologizing for the discrepancy.

SAMPLE LETTER 15.4.   Letter responding to a request for clarification (full-block format).

January 20, 19X7

Mr. Alan Lahsram
The Lahsram Literary Agency, Inc.
55 Nosidam Street
Los Angeles, California 12023

Dear Mr. Lahsram:

Enclosed is a copy of the original royalty statement for the period January–June 19X6, and corrected copies for July–December 19X5. An error in our computations caused the problems you cited in your letter to me.

The prepublication sales that you refer to in your letter were not as great as we originally thought. Those are also reflected in the corrected royalty statements.

I'm sorry for the delay and the error in royalty statements.

Sincerely,

Phlange R. Lunk
Controller

prl/ajh

encls.

Response to Request for Information About Member of Organization

Sample Letter 15.5 was written to respond to a request for information about a member of a professional organization. The letter writer indicates in her opening paragraph that the professional in question is no longer a member of the organization, but provides the letter reader with what information she can about the former member. She closes by thanking the letter reader for his letter.

SAMPLE LETTER 15.5.   Letter responding to request for information about member of a society (block format).

May 29, 19X6

Mr. Jacob L. Irons
Investigative Management
25 Huntington Avenue, Suite 408
Boonton, New Jersey 07005

Subject: Membership of Bill Senyl

Dear Mr. Irons:

As we feared, Mr. Senyl is no longer a member of the Investment Managers Society of America. He was a member for just one year from May 19X4 through May 19X5, at which point he allowed his membership to lapse.

In his application, he indicated licenses and registrations in accounting, life insurance, law, real estate, and securities. He also indicated he was a registered investment advisor with the Securities and Exchange Commission. He indicated his highest level of education was a Ph.D., not a Masters degree as you mention he suggested to you. He also stated that he had memberships in the American Bar Association, American Society of Certified Life Underwriters, and the Million Dollar Round Table.

We certainly appreciate your interest and assistance. Your information will be lodged with the membership department of the Investment Managers Society of America.

Sincerely,

Lisa Antolini
General Counsel

la/js

Letter Responding to Request for Information from a Government Agency

Sample Letter 15.6 was written in response to a request for information from the Internal Revenue Service. The taxpayer who wrote the letter acknowledges the request and carefully points out the procedure he took that led the I.R.S. to query him. The letter writer encloses support documentation that backs up his explanation. The result of this well thought-out response was resolution of the problem and the I.R.S. notifying the letter writer that it was satisfied with his response.

SAMPLE LETTER 15.6.   Letter responding to inquiry from Internal Revenue Service (full-block format).

December 22, 19X6

Ms. Ellen Rolwaren
Department of the Treasury
Internal Revenue Service
Box 505
Andover, Massachusetts 04054

Dear Ms. Rolwaren:

I received a notice from your office asking about a 1099-B dividend declaration that was issued by Backyard Investments. The amount was said to be $869 for an account numbered 020752345. Your letter asked for me to indicate where the $869 was accounted for on my 19X4 tax return.

I checked through my records and have found what I believe to be the source of the confusion. I am enclosing copies of two Backyard Investment receipts from November 19X4 to corroborate my findings.

In 19X4, I established my first IRA account with a total of $2,000. I asked Backyard Investments to form the IRA from funds I had in its Winged Stock Fund, and another $1,130 I had in its money market fund. I then made an exchange of all proceeds into the money market fund to keep the IRA liquid until I made a decision about where to invest it. The money is now part of my IRA, which is divided evenly between Backyard Investment's Lockness Stock Fund and its government securities fund.

It is my understanding that switching from one fund to another within an IRA is a nontaxable event. Therefore, my understanding was that the switch from Winged Stock Fund to the money market fund was done within the parameters of an IRA switch. This was the intended action and the instructions I gave to Backyard Investments when I set up the IRA. If

Page 2
Ms. Ellen Rolwaren
December 22, 19X6

Backyard Investments issued a 1099-B for 19X4, I believe it was a clerical error on its part. I acted with the full belief that the switch was a permissible IRA transaction.

Therefore, the $869 you asked about, as I told an Internal Revenue Service representative on the phone this morning, was part of my overall $2,000 deductible IRA contribution, which appears on my 19X4 tax return. The I.R.S. representative suggested that I spell this out for you and that you would understand the confusion.

Please call me if you have any questions. Thanks for giving your attention to this matter.

Sincerely,

Max Pearson

encls.: copy of I.R.S. notification
        Backyard Investment statements

Letters Responding to Requests for Materials

Sample Letters 15.7 through 15.9 were written to respond to requests for material.

Sample Letter 15.7 responds to a request for an article to be submitted for a publication. The letter writer expresses an interest, but first wants to know more about the publication. She clearly spells out her questions in a numbered list in the letter.

Sample Letter 15.8 was written to respond to a request for background information on a particular investment vehicle. The letter writer writes a brief cover letter to accompany a publication that discusses the investment the reader wants to know about.

Sample Letter 15.9 responds to the recipient's request for materials. The letter writer briefly explains what he has enclosed with the letter and mentions that some of the material may change as a result of the gathering of more information.

SAMPLE LETTER 15.7.   Letter responding to request for material—asking
for more information (block format).

October 8, 19X4

Mr. Marvin Hopping
The Armchair Reader's Review
350 Bixley Hall Drive
Boonton, New Jersey 07005

Dear Mr. Hopping:

Thank you for inquiring about my interest in submitting an article for The
Armchair Reader's Review. I am interested in this opportunity to put my
ideas about deposit insurance reform before an audience of financial
services marketing professionals. Before committing myself, however, I
would like to know more about the Review and its editorial policies:

1. Is this a new publication or have you published one or more
   issues? A recent copy of the publication would be appreciated, if it
   exists.

2. Will the published articles be subject to peer review, in-house
   editorial review, or both?

3. What is your objective for my article in terms of style and technical
   complexity? An example of a "typical" article would be a good
   response to this inquiry.

4. Do you offer an honorarium for solicited articles?

Again, many thanks for thinking of me. I hope we can find a way to work
together.

Yours truly,

Eleanor Elypdiva

ee/dp

SAMPLE LETTER 15.8.   Letter responding to inquiry about a potential
industry's investment potential (semiblock format).

December 29, 19X7

Dr. Samuel Johnson
Vice President, Planning & Acquisition
Dynamite Electronics Corporation
P.O. Box 5465
Alistair, Wisconsin 65437

Dear Sam:

I have enclosed a copy of our Analyst's Viewpoint publication, which
includes our economics perspective on page one and a number of industry
viewpoints in the pages following. Although the specific industry piece on
the electronics industry may not directly speak to your interest in
investment potential, it may have some relevance.

I hope you find this piece interesting. I will talk to you soon.

Sincerely,

Mary E. Elkots
Vice President

MEE:hfg

Enc.

SAMPLE LETTER 15.9.   Letter sending materials requested (full-block format).

August 1, 19X6

Mr. Evan Efferen, Editor
The Reader's Review
25 Huntington Avenue, Suite 408
Boonton, New Jersey 07005

Dear Evan:

Enclosed is the media kit you requested. As I told you this morning, we will be updating this kit with more specific information about ratings and demographics. We are currently gathering the information from WLEE-TV, channel 37 in Bayonne.

I hope all is going well for you and that you might find our show an interesting story for your publication. If I can be of further assistance, please call.

Sincerely,

Lee Iname
Sales Coordinator

LI/mn

enc.

CHAPTER 16
Permissions Letters

The letters in this chapter were written to seek permission of one sort or another. In most cases the letters seek permission to reprint or use copyrighted material. When a professional uses parts of an article or book it is crucial that he or she receive the permission of the owner of the copyright on the material, not only to protect himself, but also to appropriately acknowledge the person whose work is being used.

Letters Seeking Permission to Reprint

Sample Letters 16.1 through 16.4 were all written to seek permission to reprint material. Sample Letter 16.1 was written by an editor to an author to seek permission. Sample Letter 16.2 was written by an author to a publishing company seeking permission to reprint. Sample Letter 16.3 was written by the permissions editor of a publication seeking permission to reprint material. And Sample Letter 16.4 was written by an editor to a reviewer seeking permission to use part of his review in the advertising copy for a book.

SAMPLE LETTER 16.1.   Letter from editor requesting permission to reprint material (semiblock format).

May 17, 19X8

Mr. Mark Nies
45 Productive Row
Northcross, Wisconsin 23245

Dear Mr. Nies:

I am editing a book tentatively titled <u>Basic Marketing Research</u> and wish to include a reprint of your writing entitled "Everything You Ever Wanted to Know About Market Research." The material intended for use will extend from November 19X8 through November 19X3. I have already acquired permission to use the material from <u>The Reader's Review</u> with the understanding that I will meet the regular requirements governing such use.

Any comments you wish to make would be most welcome. I am enclosing a postage-paid card, which I ask you to return to me to acknowledge this notification.

                         Cordially,

                         Christina Dinah
                         Editor

cd/js

enc.

SAMPLE LETTER 16.2.   Letter from author requesting permission to include material in book (full-block format).

May 9, 19X6

Ms. Zoe Long
Permissions Editor
Andoris Publishing Company
86 Grampian Way
Plattsburgh, New York 12323

Dear Ms. Long:

In my book on marketing, which is designed for use as a hardcover textbook priced at approximately $50, and is scheduled for publication by Business Textbook Publishing Company, Inc. in June 19X7, I would like to include the material found in Basic Marketing by John Struddelson, published by your company in 19X5.

May I have your permission to include this material in my forthcoming book and in all future editions and revisions, covering nonexclusive world rights in all languages? These rights will in no way restrict republication of your material in any other form by you or others authorized by you. Should you not control these rights in their entirety, would you tell me who does?

A release form is provided below and a copy of this letter is enclosed for your files. Your prompt consideration of this request will be appreciated.

Sincerely,

Jeffrey Palay

mp

I grant the permission on the terms stated in this letter.

CREDIT LINE TO BE
USED: _____
_____
_____

Date: _____

     By_____

                        _____
                        _____

_____

SAMPLE LETTER 16.3.   Letter from publication's permission editor seeking permission from author to reprint material (block format).

July 22, 19X7

Mr. Max Kemper
45 Troublesome Road
Boston, New Jersey 09876

Dear Mr. Kemper:

We are considering the item attached for possible use in Home Life.

May we have your permission to use this material in every edition of Home Life worldwide? Such use will be limited to one-time publication in each edition. Should this item be used in a foreign edition, it may be translated and the wording may vary to conform to local idiom.

Payment of $120 will be issued upon first publication of your item in an edition of Home Life.

You warrant that you have the authority to grant the above rights. We have already received permission from Boonton magazine, where your work first appeared.

If you are in agreement with these terms, we would appreciate your signing and returning one copy of this letter at your earliest convenience.

Sincerely,

Jacob L. Alan
Permissions Editor

PERMISSION GRANTED
BY: _____

If additional permission is required, name and address: _____
_____

Date: _____

SAMPLE LETTER 16.4. Letter requesting permission to quote from critic's review (semiblock format).

June 14, 19X1

Professor Larry E. Duerr
Campbell College
13 Bethany Hall
Campbell, West Virginia 23456

Dear Professor Duerr:

I would like to take this opportunity to thank you again for reviewing the <u>Business Communications</u> manuscript for us.

We are now working on the advertising copy for the book and would very much appreciate it if we might have your permission to quote you in our advertising copy. The quotation we'd like to use from your review is enclosed with the letter.

If we may have your permission to quote you, would you kindly sign both copies of this letter, return the original to us, and retain the carbon for your personal files? I have enclosed a stamped, self-addressed envelope for your convenience.

Sincerely yours,

Marvin Norts

mn/br

encls.

Signature of Professor Larry E. Duerr

Letters Indicating More Information Needed for Permission

Sample Letters 16.5 and 16.6 both instruct people on the appropriate procedure to take for getting permission to reprint. Sample Letter 16.5 informs the letter reader that she must get in touch with the author of the material to secure permission and gives her his address.

SAMPLE LETTER 16.5.   Letter referring permission request to author (full-block format).

November 9, 19X7

Professor Carlton Long
Sathceko University
45 Kit Clark Lane
Dorchester, Massachusetts 32345

Dear Professor Long:

We have your letter of October 25, 19X7, requesting permission to reproduce material on pages 134 and 135 from Labor Negotiations Handbook in your forthcoming publication by Important Management Books Corp.

I am sorry but I am unable to grant you this permission since the copyright has been assigned to the author and it is to him you must direct your request. The latest address we have for him in our files is: Professor Simon Nemplar, University of the Upper Midwest, 56 Cochran Hall, Grand Forks, North Dakota 58201.

I am sorry I could not be of more help.

Sincerely,

Serge Bukoski
Permissions Editor

mn

Sample Letter 16.6 acknowledges receipt of a request for permission to reprint but asks for more information before permission can be granted.

SAMPLE LETTER 16.6.   Letter asking for more information before permission can be granted to reprint (semiblock).

November 6, 19X8

Mrs. Rita Margolis
23 Point Breeze Drive
Allentown, Michigan 23245

Dear Mrs. Margolis:

We have your letter of October 20, 19X8, requesting permission to reprint from page 435 of <u>Introduction to Management.</u>

I am sorry, but I cannot consider your request until I know exactly what material from that page you wish to reproduce, and in what context the material will appear. Would you kindly resubmit this request, quoting the beginning and ending words of the passage? I will then be happy to consider your request.

I would also like to know the approximate size of the printing of your book, the tentative publication price and date, and the name of your publisher.

I look forward to hearing from you.

Cordially,

Serge Bukoski
Permissions Editor

sb/js

Letters Granting Permission

Sample Letters 16.7 and 16.8 grant permission to reprint material. Sample Letter 16.7 grants permission to reprint in a specified, limited quantity, and indicates how the permission line should read in the book holding the reproduced material. Sample Letter 16.8 is a letter from a publisher to an author granting him permission to republish specific portions of a book he had published with the publisher's company.

SAMPLE LETTER 16.7.   Letter granting permission to reproduce in specified, limited quantity from a book still in print (block format).

June 14, 19X9

Ms. Joan W. Sherman
45 Heritage Drive
Dictionary, Pennsylvania 23234

Dear Ms. Sherman:

We have your letter of May 29, 19X9, requesting permission to reproduce material from page 345 of Professor Janice McNurty's Basic Marketing.

We are pleased to be able to grant you permission for use of this material. The fee is $50 and is payable upon publication of the reprints. We ask that your credit line appear on the first page or on an acknowledgments page of every copy as follows:

> from Basic Marketing by Janice McNurty, Copyright 19X8 by Andoris Publishing Company, Boonton, New Jersey. Reprinted with permission.

Thank you again for your interest in this title.

Best regards,

Serge Bukoski
Permissions Editor

sb/mn

SAMPLE LETTER 16.8.   Letter from publisher to author granting rights (semiblock format).

October 22, 19X5

Mr. John L. Neorn
34 Sout Street
Massasoit, New Jersey 32345

Dear John:

You have our permission to use any and all information that appears in sections one and three of your book, Business Writing Handbook, in any

and all books that you write on any subject so long as the book(s) that you
write does not compete with the sale of the above-mentioned book. We
would consider a book to be competitive if it were sold to the same
audience and was on the same subject.

I wish you the best of luck with your future writing efforts.

Sincerely,

Adam R. Quartermain, Jr.
Executive Editor

ARQ:jls

Letters Denying Permission

Sample Letters 16.9 and 16.10 were written to deny permission to reprint material.
Both letters clearly state reasons why the permission is being denied. Sample Letter
16.9 explains that allowing the requested material to be used might hurt sales of the
existing book. Sample Letter 16.10 explains that the volume of material requested is
too large for permission to be granted.

SAMPLE LETTER 16.9.   Letter denying permission to reprint because of
potentially hurt sales (full-block format).

August 8, 19X9

Mr. Webster Berrigan
24 Watershed Drive
Maui, Hawaii 21234

Dear Mr. Berrigan:

We have your letter of July 15, 19X9 requesting permission to reprint from
pages 345 to 365 of America's New Breed of Entrepreneurs by Jeffrey L.
Seglin.

After careful consideration, our editorial board has advised me that,
although permitting sections of America's New Breed of Entrepreneurs to
be reprinted freely in magazines throughout the country might publicize
the book to some extent, it could seriously curtail its sale.

We are extremely sorry not to be able to give you permission to use this material. We are compelled to take this position because we have had previous requests of a similar nature and are likely to have many more.

Cordially,

Serge Bukoski
Permissions Editor

sb/mn

SAMPLE LETTER 16.10.   Letter denying permission to reprint because of volume of material asked to be reproduced (semiblock format).

March 20, 19X0

Ms. Patrice Rhodese
56 Trainway Parkway
Montclair, Pennsylvania 23456

Dear Ms. Rhodese:

We have your letter of March 1, 19X0 requesting permission to reproduce material on pages 233 to 253 of Acting Techniques by Dr. Edmond Jonson for use by you in a book you are writing for Andoris Publishing Company.

After careful consideration, our editorial board has advised me that they do not feel justified in allowing this material to be reproduced. While it has been our policy to be as accommodating as we possibly can be in the matter of granting permission to use material from our books, we feel that, in all fairness to our authors and to ourselves, we should not give permission for such an amount of material to be reproduced or reprinted.

I am very sorry not be able to grant your request.

Sincerely,

Serge Bukoski
Permissions Editor

mn

Cover Letter for Contract

Sample Letter 16.11 was sent as the cover letter to accompany a contract being offered an author. The letter writer cordially welcomes the author, explains that the company will support the author, introduces the author's in-house editor, and requests that the author fill out enclosed material. Though Sample Letter 16.11 is not a clear-cut permissions letter, it serves ideally as an example in covering another aspect of the discussion of this chapter.

SAMPLE LETTER 16.11.   Letter used as cover letter for contract (semiblock format).

August 4, 19X9

Mrs. Venita Applebaum
34 Lucrese Drive
Winchester, Pennsylvania 56455

Dear Mrs. Applebaum:

Our entire staff joins with me in extending our best wishes to you as a future Andoris Publishing Company author. Your decision to work with Andoris is appreciated. I am confident that your textbook on macroeconomics will make a unique contribution to the field of economics. A copy of our agreement is enclosed for your personal records.

Andoris is ready to assist you in every way possible. Our editorial facilities are at your disposal, and we want you to call upon us for any guidance or help that we can give.

We look forward to working with you for many years to come. With this in mind, let me take this opportunity to remind you of the importance of timely revisions of successful textbooks. Your editor, Nan Long, will remain in close contact with you throughout your association with Andoris, and she will work with you on plans for future editions.

Please complete and return the enclosed copyright card. Again, welcome to Andoris.

Sincerely,

Kate Allen
Executive Editor

ka/mn

encls.

Letter Requesting Reversion of Rights

Sample Letter 16.12 was sent by an agent to a publisher requesting the reversion of rights on a book his client has written. Such a letter would be written when a book has had slow sales or a publisher had decided to take the book out of print. The letter writer introduces himself, makes his request, and closes.

SAMPLE LETTER 16.12.   Letter requesting reversion of rights (block format).

September 2, 19X7

Mr. Mark More
Andoris Publishing Company
23 Lathrop Avenue
Boonton, New Jersey 07005

Dear Mark:

As the agent for Loren Gray, I am writing to request reversion of rights to two of his books, Fun on a Shoestring and Fun with More Shoestring, which he wrote for Andoris under the pseudonym Bud Genry. I believe that these two titles are both out of print.

Please include the original certificate of copyright for both of these titles when you acknowledge reversion.

Thanks for calling our attention to this matter.

Cordially,

Ephrain Noldercan

mj

CHAPTER 17
Social, Personal, and Miscellaneous Letters

Every professional knows that some occasions that call for a letter have little to do with specific business matters, like closing a big sale or acquiring a small company. Often, the professional must write letters for a variety of social and personal occasions. At such times, the rules of effective letter writing should apply as much as they do in more business-related letters.

The sample letters in this chapter consist of the types professionals may often find themselves needing to write. The letters here were written by professionals for a diverse range of social and personal occasions. The letters can serve as ideal models on which to base your own social and personal letters.

Thank-You Letters

Sample Letters 17.1 through 17.12 are all examples of thank-you letters that were written for a variety of reasons. Thanking someone for something is not only courteous, it also builds goodwill with the person you are thanking. Forget what you see on the big screen about corporate megalomaniacs seizing fortunes and building fiefdoms. In the professional world, manners never hurt.

Sample Letter 17.1 was written to thank someone for a personal favor. The letter writer clearly expresses gratitude to the letter reader without getting schmaltzy. She thanks him, wishes him well, and closes.

Sample Letter 17.2 was written to thank someone for her hospitality. Here too the letter writer expresses gratitude, specifically mentioning what he is thanking the reader for.

Sample Letter 17.3 was written to thank a contributor for a charitable contribution. The letter writer thanks the letter reader for the gift, briefly recaps what it was for, mentions how the letter reader's donation will help, and closes.

Sample Letter 17.4 thanks someone for a public service. Here the letter writer expresses his appreciation and gratitude to the letter reader. He closes by reiterating his thanks.

Sample Letter 17.5 was written to thank a professional who had appeared on a television panel show. The letter writer thanks the letter reader, expresses appreciation, lets him know that he was a good guest, and closes.

SAMPLE LETTER 17.1.   Letter thanking someone for a personal favor (semiblock format).

May 25, 19X8

Dr. Ralph Junot
Key Vineyards
43 Rensit Chateau
Tours, Oregon 34345

Dear Dr. Junot:

I can't tell you how much Ward and I appreciate the loan of your automobile when we were in Tours. The rental car was completely demolished; fortunately it was insured!

I hope the new wine wins critical acclaim in the contest next month. We've already placed our personal order for a case.

Best regards,

Jaqline Shopenhauer

JS:lh

SAMPLE LETTER 17.2.   Letter thanking someone for hospitality (semiblock format).

December 26, 19X6

Ms. Eileen Durga
Seminole College of Engineering
32 Rajpoor Drive
Jaipur, India 48113

Dear Eileen:

Once again you've treated us to an enjoyable annual meeting. India was breathtaking. We've just gotten our photographs developed and they're smashing. Our slides will be ready any day. We'll send you duplicates of any that feature you and Prakash.

Anna and I have decided to return to India in December. It looks like we'll be touring Rajashthan. We'd love to meet you in Jaipur for dinner.

Let us know when you are planning a trip back to the States.

Sincerely,

Nils Loflin

SAMPLE LETTER 17.3.   Letter thanking contributor for contribution (semiblock format).

March 6, 19X7

Mr. Loren "Bud" Terrece
56 Yorkway Place
Eufala, Arkansas 34321

Dear Mr. Terrece:

Thank you for your generous gift to the Ellen Y. Timmons Scholarship Fund. The award is intended to provide an annual full-tuition scholarship to a deserving journalism senior or master's candidate at Highlands University.

Your gift will help future generations of students receive an outstanding education. Thank you for this tribute to the memory of Ellen Timmons.

Sincerely,

John T. Dalnor
Development Officer

JTD/JLS

SAMPLE LETTER 17.4.   Letter thanking someone for public service (block format).

October 19, 19X2

Mr. Maxwell Y. Samson
Andover Company
312 West Street
Bonton, New Jersey 07005

Dear Maxwell:

I appreciate your service to alma mater, Max, and the variety of forms it takes. Your most recent contribution, as part of the professionals' seminar, was quite valuable to our students.

With alumni like you who are willing to pitch in and lend their help when we need it, it is truly a joy to be in my position as alumni director.

Thanks again.

Sincerely,

Sam C. Leigh
Alumni Director

SCL:fcl

SAMPLE LETTER 17.5.   Letter thanking panelist on talk show (semiblock format).

February 18, 19X6

Mr. Jacob Trust
Byers Public Relations
312 West Main Street
Astoria, New Jersey 07005

Dear Mr. Trust:

　　Thank you so much for joining us on Cyclorama. We appreciate your taking time from your busy schedule to be with us. Your discussion with our host, Jimmy Lewis, was both interesting and informative.

It was a pleasure having you on the show. We wish you continued success and happiness.

Sincerely,

Claire B. Janeway
Executive Producer

CBJ:eel

Sample Letter 17.6 thanks a writer for mentioning a professional in an article. The letter writer thanks the writer for mentioning her in his magazine column and tells him that she admires his work.

Sample Letter 17.7 was written to thank a book reviewer for his comments. The writer thanks the columnist for reviewing his book positively and expresses his gratitude.

SAMPLE LETTER 17.6.   Letter thanking writer for mentioning person in article (semiblock format).

December 31, 19X7

Ms. Etsuko Chin
The Armchair Reader's Review
34 Eliot Boulevard
Piscataway, Texas 02103

Dear Etsuko:

I didn't want to let 19X7 slip away without extending my thanks for including Women's Issues magazine and me in your marketing column last month. The article was terrific. It pulled together all the pertinent statistics and showed why women need and want to plan, without making us look like weak-kneed ninnies. A delicate balance indeed!

Here's hoping that 19X8 brings you much health and prosperity.

Sincerely,

Ellen T. Cincinnati

etc/jls

SAMPLE LETTER 17.7.   Letter thanking reviewer for comments (full-block format).

June 1, 19X7

Ms. Alice Longworth
Professional's Magazine
287 Merrimac Trail
Boonton, New Jersey 07005

Dear Ms. Longworth:

Thank you very much for your insightful and kind review of my book: How to Manage Your Way to the Top in the May issue of Professional's Magazine.

When the book was published, I told the publisher that there were two publications whose review would be critical to its success: Global Management, for the international manager, and Professional's Magazine. I really had my heart in my mouth when I picked up the May issue. It was a terrific kick for me to read your review.

I wish that there was a way for me to return the favor. Suffice it to say that I am grateful to you and the magazine for the kind words you have to say about my book.

Sincerely,

Arnold T. Yarrum
President

aty:caf

cc: RTS, Publisher

    Sample Letter 17.8 was written to thank the letter reader for an outing that the letter writer had attended. The writer thanks the reader, follows up by mentioning he is enclosing an article that the two had discussed at the outing, and closes by offering assistance to the reader if he should need it in the future.

SAMPLE LETTER 17.8.   Thank-you letter for outing (block format).

January 27, 19X8

Mr. Alan Marshal
Tillinghurst & Partners
423 West Watchung Road
Ordeal City, Illinois 34345

Dear Alan:

It was good seeing you and meeting your wife at the Tillinghurts' annual
bash. Maggie and I had a great time. It's always nice to see familiar faces
and to catch up on our hectic lives.

As promised, I'm enclosing an article on public relations activities relating
to the law profession that appeared in a recent issue of <u>Lawyer's and
Professional Practice</u>.

Again, it was great to see you at the outing. If I can ever be of service to
you, please call on me.

Best regards,

Julius Norton

jn/js

Enc.

    Sample Letter 17.9 was written to thank the recipient for dinner. The letter
writer briefly expresses his thanks, mentions that he is enclosing an article he
thought the letter reader might find interesting, and closes by suggesting they meet
soon.

SAMPLE LETTER 17.9.   Thank-you letter for dinner (full-block format).

November 2, 19X7

Mrs. Minerva T. Uronim
Executive Director
The Brain Trust of New Jersey
54 General Road, Suite 600
Circle City, Vermont 54345

Dear Minerva:

Maggie and I want to thank you for the lovely dinner we had at your home last week. We enjoyed both the cuisine and the company of the other invited guests.

Enclosed is an article from one of the publications to which I contribute. I thought you'd find this article of particular interest.

I'll call your secretary next week to check your schedule for lunch.

Best regards,

Ambrose Kinton

ak:js

Sample Letter 17.10 was written to thank the recipient for the kind words he had to say about the writer's newspaper column. The letter writer expresses her thanks, suggests that the reader stop by if he is ever in the area, and closes by expressing her best wishes.

SAMPLE LETTER 17.10.   Thank-you letter for compliments on article
(semiblock format).

December 21, 19X6

Mr. Jacob L. Prentice
Prentice Public Relations, Inc.
312 West Main Street
Boonton, New Jersey 07005

Dear Mr. Prentice:

Thank you for your kind words about my newspaper column and for the thoughtful gift of <u>Marketing Financial Advisory Services</u>. It is always a pleasure for me to hear that my column is read, and even more that it is appreciated. I have found it to be a great outlet for creativity with many of the matters that I deal with in my insurance business.

If you are ever in the Denville area, please stop by my office, which is located at the Morris County Village Center, across the street from the Powerville Inn. It would be my pleasure to meet you and thank you in person for making my day.

My best wishes to you during this holiday season.

Sincerely,

Anne L. Krauss, C.L.U.

ALK:JLS

Sample Letter 17.11 was written to thank someone for his professional services. While the letter writer had hired the recipient to do a job, she took the time to write a letter expressing her thanks for such a good job.

SAMPLE LETTER 17.11. Letter thanking professional for help with services rendered (semiblock format).

October 13, 19X7

Mr. Jacob L. Prentice
Prentice Public Relations, Inc.
312 West Main Street
Boonton, New Jersey 07005

Dear Jacob:

Thank you for your assistance in making the visit of our national director to the Boonton area a highly successful one. Your hard work on publicity and press arrangements was most appreciated.

I feel that Dr. Helen Louise McGuffie's tour went quite well. By traveling to such historic sites as Jockey Hollow and touring New Hope she was able to experience firsthand a bit of New Jersey and Pennsylvania history. The weather for the weekend was not ideal, of course, but it certainly could have been worse. Both days we were fortunate enough to miss the worst of it, with rain coming before or after, but never actually during any of the events. We must have been doing something right to be blessed with cooperative weather.

Again, my sincere thanks to you and your staff. I look forward to seeing you again.

Very truly yours,

Mrs. Minerva T. Uronim
Executive Director

MTU:mln

Sample Letter 17.12 was sent to thank someone who had nominated a professional for recognition. The letter writer thanks the recipient, acknowledges that the nominee will be considered, and closes by thanking the letter reader again.

SAMPLE LETTER 17.12.   Letter acknowledging nomination (full-block format).

March 28, 19X8

Ms. Anne L. Krauss, C.L.U.
Morris County Village Center, Suite 3542
Denville, New Jersey 09876

Dear Ms. Krauss:

Thank you for your nomination of Dr. Roscoe T. Miller, LIA, CLU, ChFC for the 19X8 Rebecca A. Grimes Award for Excellence in the Industry. We will be glad to include his name in the book of biographies we will consider at our meeting on May 25.

Thank you again.

Cordially,

Geoffrey Spaulding
Director of Awards

GS/wb

Invitations

Sample Letters 17.13 through 17.16 are examples of invitations. Sample Letter 17.13 was written to invite the letter reader to dinner. The letter writer clearly explains who is making the invitation and spells out the details in the letter. She closes by asking the letter reader to call her office to confirm her attendance.

SAMPLE LETTER 17.13.   Letter making invitation for dinner (official-style format).

June 15, 19X9

Dear Lois:

Mark Nilton, the president of Andoris Products, Inc., joins with me in inviting you and Jacob to cocktails and dinner at 6 P.M. on Wednesday, June 30, 19X9 at the House of Fine Foods Inn, 23 Berkely Street, Boston, Massachusetts.

While the evening will be principally social, I do expect that Mark will have some informal remarks to make after dinner on a topic of interest to the gathering. We anticipate about 30 good friends of the company joining us for the evening.

I hope you will be able to attend. Please call my office to indicate if you plan to join us. I look forward to seeing you that evening.

Yours truly,

Lisa T. Gray
Editor

Ms. Lois T. Kemper
Kemper Lifestyles, Inc.
232 Scituate Road
Brookline, New Hampshire 21234

LTG:WLG

Sample Letter 17.14 was written to invite the letter reader to an open house. The letter writer makes a brief invitation by clearly spelling out the date and the event. She closes with a personal note to the letter reader.

SAMPLE LETTER 17.14.   Letter inviting someone to an open house
(semiblock format).

May 14, 19X8

Max G. Growne
5A Stomping Hill Lane
Tretorne, Nebraska 45432

Dear Max:

    Oz and I are having an open house to celebrate our move to Westwood. The date is June 6. We're hoping that it will be warm enough for people to use the swimming pool. Do bring your suit.

    I've heard things have been crazy in your work at the archives. I hope things quiet down soon.

Best regards,

Tenia Lapadoor

    Sample Letter 17.15 was written to invite the letter reader to a special event. The writer describes the seminar, then asks that the reader call to confirm whether or not he can attend.
    Sample Letter 17.16 was written to invite a speaker to speak at an event. The letter writer invites the speaker, gives the dates, and asks that the speaker respond by a specific date.

SAMPLE LETTER 17.15.   Letter inviting someone to special event (full-block format).

October 23, 19X6

Mr. Jeffrey R. Kemper, Editor
Weekly Business Chronicle
8 Lorraine Terrace
Santiago, Pennsylvania 07654

Dear Jeff:

I thought you might be interested in a tax seminar we are putting on next Thursday, October 30. It will be the first seminar available after the new tax bill gets passed. I've enclosed a brochure on the topics that will be covered at the seminar.

Let me know if you or one of your reporters would like to attend. I look forward to hearing from you.

Sincerely,

R. Kyle Yennik

jls

enc.

SAMPLE LETTER 17.16.   Letter inviting speaker (semiblock format).

May 23, 19X0

Mr. Terrence Derand
Derand Management Systems, Inc.
65 Follansbee Road
Wellsburg, Ohio 98764

Dear Mr. Derand:

During the May meeting of our products division, we voted unanimously to invite you to be our speaker at next year's annual meeting in Brasilia. We would enjoy hearing about your new research on distribution improvements in Lithuania.

The dates set for the meeting are July 2-5, 19X1. Travel arrangements are being handled by the company agency.

Because we are trying to finalize our arrangements in time for our regional meeting, I hope you will be able to respond to this invitation by August 1.

Sincerely,

Roxanna Hughes
Program Coordinator

rh/lh

Responses to Invitations

Sample Letters 17.17 through 17.23 are examples of responses to invitations. Sample Letter 17.17 was written to accept an informal invitation from the letter reader. The letter writer accepts, confirms the date, and closes.

SAMPLE LETTER 17.17.   Letter accepting informal invitation (semiblock format).

May 23, 19X9

Dr. Marston P. Farqhuad
65 Runabout Road
New London, South Carolina 43456

Dear Marston:

Wilma and I are delighted to accept your invitation to accompany you and Sylvia to a Red Sox game and to come to your benefit buffet dinner afterwards.

It's been a long time since we've seen you. The twins must be so grown up by now.

We'll see you on June 16.

Best regards,

Claude Sylvia

Sample Letter 17.18 was written to express regrets that the letter writer could not accept an invitation. The letter writer makes it clear that he cannot accept by explaining he will be out of town, and closes by saying he will get in touch with the letter reader when he returns.

Sample Letter 17.19 was written to accept an invitation to speak at a workshop. The letter writer encloses the material and information the letter reader had requested, and closes by asking that the letter reader inform him if there is any other information she needs.

SAMPLE LETTER 17.18.   Letter expressing regrets about turning down invitation (semiblock format).

May 20, 19X8

Ms. Sue Ellen Nojjen
6789 Puscadora Drive
Trogladite, Utah 56543

Dear Sue Ellen:

    I am so sorry to tell you that Sierra and I will be out of town during the dates of your weekend getaway bash. How we wish we could come.

    I'll phone when we get back and press you for a full report on the weekend's parties, which will no doubt be the hit of the season.

            Sincerely,

            Georgio Costovez

SAMPLE LETTER 17.19.   Letter accepting invitation to speak (semiblock format).

June 6, 19X7

Mrs. Katherine R. Kicker
Wonderful Writers of the South Club
432 South Beauty Drive
Eufala, Alabama 34321

Dear Kate:

    Thanks very much for your letter of May 28. I would be delighted to take part in the workshops you asked me to speak at at your convention. As you requested, I'm enclosing two photographs.

    As for the biographical sketch: I am the president of The Lawrence R. Lamatin Agency, which represents authors of general adult and young-adult fiction and nonfiction. Previously, I was an agent with Global Agents of America. Before becoming an agent, I was a senior book editor with Andoris Publishing Company, Fun Books, and Wonderful Reader, Inc. I'm the author of a nonfiction book, <u>How to Read Your Way to Fortune</u>, as well as a number of articles on writing and publishing for various magazines. I live in Wisconsin with my wife, Coral Phlange, an actress, and our daughter, Penelope.

I have enclosed a brief summary of my workshop speeches.

Please let me know if there's anything else I can provide. I very much look forward to meeting you and to attending the conference.

Sincerely,

Lawrence R. Lamatin

lrl/gmf

enc.

Sample Letter 17.20 was written to decline an invitation to speak. The letter writer keeps it brief and simple. He informs the reader that he will be unable to attend the conference. He expresses his appreciation at having been asked and wishes the letter reader luck with the conference.

SAMPLE LETTER 17.20.   Letter declining invitation to speak (semiblock format).

September 30, 19X7

Ms. Deborah C. Acesa, Director
AGIE Conferences
54 Westwood Terrace
North Blixi, Michigan 03234

Dear Ms. Acesa:

Many thanks for your letter of September 20, and your kind invitation to participate in your conference in February. Unfortunately, I will be unable to attend.

I do appreciate your having thought of me. I hope the conference is a great success.

Sincerely,

O. C. Dillock

ocd/jls

Sample Letter 17.21 declines an invitation to contribute an article to a publication. The letter writer states that he will be unable to contribute, expresses his appreciation, and closes.

Sample Letter 17.22 was written to decline an invitation to serve on an editorial board. The letter writer expresses his appreciation for the invitation but declines the offer because of a conflict.

SAMPLE LETTER 17.21.   Letter declining invitation to contribute article (full-block format).

November 1, 19X4

Mr. Martin L. Armont
The Reader's Journal
327 Merrimac Trail
Boonton, New Jersey 07005

Dear Mr. Armont:

You flatter me by asking my participation as an author in your forthcoming journal. I regret, however, that I will be unable to accept.

I wish you well with the venture.

Yours very truly,

A. T. Redmont
Senior Vice President — Marketing

ATR:nwp

SAMPLE LETTER 17.22.   Letter declining invitation to serve on editorial board because of conflict (block format).

October 24, 19X4

Mr. Martin L. Armont
The Reader's Journal
327 Merrimac Trail
Boonton, New Jersey 07005

Dear Mr. Armont:

Pardon the delay in responding to your letter of September 21, but I have been in the process of negotiating the sale of our Financial Services Marketing Review to Hungadunga Publications of Beloit, England. A copy of the most recent issue is enclosed.

I appreciate your invitation to serve as a member of the editorial advisory board for your forthcoming journal, but I believe it would be in conflict with our role with the Financial Services Marketing Review.

Best regards,

Alan C. Idomeck
Executive Director

aci/jls

encl.

        Sample Letter 17.23 was written to accept an invitation to contribute an article to a publication. The letter writer clearly states that the invitation has been accepted, gives the letter reader a number where he can be reached, and closes by thanking the letter reader for his interest.

SAMPLE LETTER 17.23.   Letter accepting invitation to contribute article (semiblock format).

October 12, 19X4

Mr. Martin L. Armont
The Reader's Journal
327 Merrimac Trail
Boonton, New Jersey 07005

Dear Mr. Armont:

Mr. Revonock has asked me to respond to your letter of September 28 asking him to submit an article on the benefits of deregulation to bank customers. The article would be used in your quarterly Journal of Financial Services Marketing.

Mr. Revonock would be pleased to submit such an article. Please call me directly about your deadlines and any other information he will need to prepare the article. I can be reached at 434-706-6050.

Thank you for your interest in the views of the Deregulation Regulatory Agency's Office. I look forward to hearing from you.

Sincerely,

Aaron S. Sorce
Communications Director

ASS:jls

cc: TR

Letter Expressing Interest in Speaking

Sample Letter 17.24 was written to express an interest in speaking. The letter writer follows up a conversation he had with the letter reader by sending her background information on him and spelling out the different topics he can speak on. He closes by expressing his enthusiasm at the prospect of speaking.

SAMPLE LETTER 17.24.   Letter expressing interest in speaking (block format).

September 8, 19X7

Professor Christine Franklin
Georgian Hotel School
Edwardus Jacobus University
543 South Michigan Drive
Holstice, Kentucky 34321

Dear Christine:

It was good to hear from you. Your new job certainly sounds exciting and challenging. I wish you the best of luck.

I've enclosed my press kit. It will give the university an idea of my credentials to qualify for a guest lecture appearance. I was recently asked to speak at the January 19X8 Hotels and Motels Association of America Annual Meeting in Key West, Florida. I will be delivering a speech titled, "How to Make Your Money in an Independent Inn."

As you know, I can discuss myriad aspects of marketing, including advertising, direct mail, publicity, promotions, or special events. Just let me know what would be the most interesting for your students and I'll focus my presentation in that direction.

I am very excited about the possibility of speaking at the Georgian Hotel School of Edwardus Jacobus University. I look forward to hearing from you.

Best regards,

Maxwell R. Levine

jls

encls.

Follow-Up Letter to Speech Attendees

Sample Letter 17.25 was written by someone who had given a speech to a group that had included the reader. The letter writer expresses the pleasure he had in addressing the group and follows up by reiterating some of the thoughts he had expressed in his speech. He closes by offering to answer any questions the letter reader might have.

SAMPLE LETTER 17.25.   Letter writen as follow-up to attendees of a speech (full-block format).

November 10, 19X7

Dr. Anne T. Laos
Whirling Computer Corporation
34 Reindollar Road
Statehood, New Jersey 23234

Dear Dr. Laos:

I was very pleased to have the opportunity recently to make a presentation on behalf of the Statehood Foundation to your Breakfast Group. Maxwell Nil has kindly given me a list of the members and I will see to it that you are added to our mailing list. In the meantime, I thought you would find the attached case statement for the Statehood Foundation of some interest.

As the Statehood community's foundation and the largest grant issuer in New Jersey, the Statehood Foundation is in the position to have a major role in supporting programs that serve a broad sector of the Statehood community. As a public charity, we are also charged with increasing our permanent endowment (currently at $125 million) so that our efforts can continue to benefit the citizens of Statehood. For many individuals and corporations, the Statehood Foundation is a unique vehicle for carrying out charitable activities.

Please know that I would be happy to answer any questions that you might have about opportunities for giving through the Statehood Foundation.

Yours truly,

Oscar R. Atner
Donor Relations Officer

ORA:jls

enc.

Compliments on Article

Sample Letter 17.26 was written to compliment a writer on an article he had written. The letter writer offers his commendation of the writer's work and closes by offering his services should the author need them in the future.

SAMPLE LETTER 17.26.   Letter complimenting author on article (full-block format).

February 29, 19X0

Mr. Ambrose T. Kemper
The Armchair Reader's Review
34 Eliot Boulevard
Piscataway, Texas 02103

Dear Mr. Kemper:

I would like to commend you on your fine article on financial planning in the January issue of The Armchair Reader's Review. Your article hit on the fundamentals of prudent money management in a forthright and easy to understand manner. The complexities of today's economy necessitate careful evaluation about one's personal finances, and I have witnessed greater awareness by the public about the benefits provided by financial planning. Should your research in the future require my assistance, I would be more than happy to discuss my thoughts with you.

I would also like to suggest that The Armchair Reader's Review consider a monthly column that addresses money management concerns. It is evident that the publication is targeted to individuals who have achieved a certain level of financial success, and who would be interested in securing future financial security.

Congratulations again on a job well done. Please feel free to call on me in the future should the need arise.

Sincerely,

Manny N. Depocet, CFP

mnd/jls

cc: MLN, editor

Birthday Greetings

Sample Letter 17.27 was written as a brief note to wish the letter reader well on his birthday.

SAMPLE LETTER 17.27.   Letter wishing someone a happy birthday (semiblock format).

June 15, 19X8

Mr. Poindexter T. Spaulding
Lockridge and Lockridge
7654 Roundabout Plaza
Osaka, Montana 34234

Dear Poindexter:

Happy birthday! Everyone here at the Piscataqua office sends their best and hopes for a wonderful year for you.

We hear you are enjoying your new position in the Osaka branch. Come visit us when you're in our area.

Yours truly,

Marvin Samantha

ms/lh

Birth Congratulations

Sample Letter 17.28 was written as a brief note to congratulate the parents of a new baby.

SAMPLE LETTER 17.28.   Letter congratulating someone on new baby
(semiblock format).

December 26, 19X7

Gladys and Girard Grady
65 Matrix Court
New Haven, California 32345

Dear Gladys and Girard:

All of us here in the spirits division want to send you our
congratulations on the birth of your child. We know how much you wanted
a little girl. You must be thrilled.

We're sending along a small gift that we hope will keep your daughter
Belinda amused.

Best regards,

Lindsey Hurlbut

enc.

Public Service and Fund-Raising Letters

From time to time most professionals are called on to perform some public
service. Sample Letters 17.29 through 17.31 are examples of public service and
fund-raising letters.

Sample Letter 17.29 was written by a class agent to his classmates seeking to
raise funds for their alma mater. The letter is anecdotal and makes a solid plea for
funds.

SAMPLE LETTER 17.29.   Letter written to raise funds (semiblock format).

March 24, 19X9

Mr. James Lewis
186-A Savin Hill Avenue
Bethany, North Carolina 23234

Dear Jim:

There's a story told about a conversation between F. Scott Fitzgerald and Ernest Hemingway. Fitzgerald remarks to Hemingway: "The rich are different from you and me." To which Hemingway responds: "Yes, they have more money." The encounter came to mind when I heard a talk given by John Templeton, one of the beacons of light in the investment world. When he came to the part of his speech where he was to tell the audience what he thought the best investment would be for the future, he had the entire audience on the edge of their seats in anticipation. And then he hit them with it: "The best investment for the future," he said, "is tithing 10% of your annual income." It seems Templeton had followed this philosophy for years and felt it had paid off handsomely.

Now, I'm not suggesting that you "tithe" 10% of your income to Clarkson Community College. But I think there is a lot of merit in what Templeton says. If you want to see tangible results from your money, if you want to see your dollars at work, then investing in the future of Clarkson Community College is a sure bet. When the stock market languishes, Clarkson Community College continues to flourish doing what it does best—educating students.

The outlook for the future of Clarkson Community College is good. The college is blessed with a growing number of entering students each year. Academically, the college continues to challenge students. Athletically, the teams of Clarkson continue to tough it out on the playing field (or courts or pools). Student publications and productions continue to provide experiential opportunities. All the trappings needed to educate graduates who go out and find success are there.

Please try to give what you can to Clarkson. Make sure to see if your company has a matching contribution plan.

Think of what you give not so much as a charitable donation, but as an investment, one that you will know is at work every time you visit Clarkson, talk to a Clarksonian, or hear from a recent graduate nervously

Page 2
Mr. James Lewis
March 24, 19X9

encountering the world outside of college for the first time—just like we
did when we graduated.

                                            Sincerely,

                                            Maxene Right
                                            Class Agent

mr:js

enc.

        Sample Letter 17.30 is also an example of a fund-raising letter, but this one is
sent as a follow-up to a previous contributor.
        Sample Letter 17.31 was written requesting that the recipient perform a public
service. The letter writer is clear in his request and lays out the details of what he is
asking.

SAMPLE LETTER 17.30.   Letter attempting to raise funds—sent to
previous contributor (full-block format).

April 1, 19X8

Mrs. Ann L. Kemper
23 Deerfield Avenue
Rather, Michigan 43456

Dear Ann:

Three years ago this month, our friend and colleague, The Chronicle
reporter Ellen Yalter, was killed in a drunk driving accident. This is a
somber time for us and for Ellen's family. Even though Ellen is gone, she is
not forgotten. Thanks to your overwhelming support and generosity, we've
raised $75,000 for the newly established Ellen Yalter Memorial
Scholarship at Highlands University. As you know, this will provide a full
tuition scholarship to a deserving graduate student in print journalism at
the School of Journalism. It is a wonderful tribute to Ellen and her
memory.

Page 2
Mrs. Ann L. Kemper
April 1, 19X8

On June 15, 19X8, we will award the first annual Yalter Scholarship during a special event planned at the Lewis & Carey Inn in Boonton. We will also be doing something else to further honor Ellen's achievements. On that night we will announce the recipient of the first annual Ellen Yalter Memorial Excellence in Reporting Award. This honor will go to a metropolitan area print journalist who has demonstrated outstanding ability during the previous year. A Lifetime Achievement Award will also be made to a nationally known news broadcaster. It should be an exciting night.

Last June, more than 500 of you paid tribute to Ellen at the Morris County Courthouse reception. This summer, we can all get together again on a happier note, with the knowledge that Ellen will continue to be remembered and honored in a variety of ways. Now we can pay tribute to those among us who are striving for the same standard of excellence that Ellen did.

We'll have a buffet style meal, music, and a brief awards ceremony. Mostly, I hope we'll all have fun and share in the kind of camaraderie we all felt the last time around. Tickets will be $75 per person to help raise the additional $75,000 needed to meet our fund-raising goal for the scholarship. If you make your contribution to the scholarship now, you'll receive your tickets in the mail by early May. Please be as generous as you can. I look forward to seeing you June 15.

Very truly yours,

Carl B. Combsen
Committee Chairman

cbc/jls

enc.

SAMPLE LETTER 17.31. Letter requesting public service (block format).

December 18, 19X7

Mr. Alan T. Pine
45 Trusty Road
Barnstable, Georgia 45432

Dear Alan:

If you're like me at this time of year, you're searching for the perfect holiday gift and for the bulb that makes the Christmas tree lights stop blinking. And you're not sure when you'll find time to assemble that new bicycle or bake cookies for the neighbors.

With all the joys and hassles of the holiday season, I would like to ask you to add one more item to your Christmas list: to continue your good work as a Preston Community College Class Agent.

We would like to mail the Class Agent letter in January, which is why we are approaching you during the holiday season. Believe it or not, January is one of the best times of the year for direct mail solicitations, something I learned in my direct mail class at Preston Community College.

As always, you are welcome to write your own letter to your class. As an encouragement, I am enclosing a copy of an excellent article on letter writing by Jeffrey L. Seglin, author of The AMA Handbook of Business Letters.

I encourage you to write your Class Agent letter just as you would write a letter to a friend. After all, you share two years of special memories with your classmates. Your letter should bring out the bonds that tie your class.

Let people know what's happening at Preston now. Let them know what's changed and what hasn't. If you've visited the campus recently, describe what you saw. Along the same lines, let people know what other classmates are doing. Encourage people to send you news about what's new in their lives—it'll be great material for your spring letter.

If you just can't put pen to paper (and believe me, I know how that feels) I'm also enclosing a "ghost" letter that you can adapt as your own. Write your own, change mine, or use mine without any changes. But please have your letter to the Development Office by January 5, 19X8. Also, complete the enclosed card and send it with the letter so the office will know how it is to be mailed.

Page 2
Mr. Alan T. Pine
December 18, 19X7

This year we have an incentive for our Class Agents: a signed, limited edition watercolor of Old Preston Hall will be given to the Class Agent who has the largest percentage increase in the number of donors from his or her class and to the Class Agent who has the largest percentage increase in the total amount given by his or her class. A copy of the Preston Community College Report describing the limited edition print is enclosed.

I encourage you to be innovative in your appeals to your class. Don't be limited by the two required letters. I'm open to your suggestions, ideas, and spurts of creativity—anything that will help improve the Class Agent program.

Many thanks for your help. Your work as a Class Agent is a year-round gift to Preston.

Sincerely,

Rhett L. Retson
Class Agent Coordinator

rlr:jls

Congratulations on New Position

Sample Letters 17.32 and 17.33 were written to congratulate people on new positions. Sample Letter 17.32 was written to congratulate the letter reader on her new position and to take the opportunity to introduce the letter writer's services to the reader. The writer encloses material for the reader to review.

Sample Letter 17.33 is a short letter of congratulations to the letter reader on his new position. There is no attempt to sell anything here.

SAMPLE LETTER 17.32.   Letter congratulating someone on new position, using opportunity to promote services (full-block format).

November 17, 19X7

Ms. Connie S. Ebergen, President
Smokehouse Restaurants, Inc.
56 Stone Street
Nottingham, Massachusetts 34321

Dear Ms. Ebergen:

Congratulations! I read of your recent appointment to president of Smokehouse Restaurants, Inc. in November's issue of National Dining Out Newsalerts.

As specialists in the restaurant industry, Naidu Public Relations, Inc. provides a full range of marketing services. For publicity, we have great press contacts, locally and nationally. To serve as an informal introduction to Naidu Public Relations, Inc., I have enclosed our press kit. It contains marketing articles we've written for Eating Out Often and Restaurants of the World, a client list, my biography, and other relevant materials.

We would truly welcome an opportunity to meet with you and your marketing team at Smokehouse Restaurants, Inc. to discuss how we might contribute to your expansion plans. I'll call your office next week to arrange an appointment at your convenience.

Thank you, in advance, for taking the time to review these materials, Ms. Ebergen. I look forward to speaking with you.

Sincerely,

Leo J. Naidu
President

LJN:JLS

Enc.

SAMPLE LETTER 17.33.   Letter congratulating someone on new position (official-style format).

December 1, 19X6

Dear William:

I had the pleasure of learning that you recently became the president of Kismick Department Stores. Congratulations on your new position.

I hope I will have a chance to stop in and see you next time I'm in Guam City. In the meantime, good luck with your new responsibilities.

Best regards,

Pearl Pendleton

Mr. William Martin, President
Kismick Department Stores
One Symphony Place
Guam City, Arizona 73812

PP:js

Letters to Sick Employees, Acquaintances

Sample Letter 17.34 was written to express concern for an employee who has been ill. Sample Letter 17.35 was written to an employee who is in the hospital. Sample Letter 17.36 was written to a business acquaintance who is hospitalized. All three letters are brief, but show genuine concern for the letter reader.

SAMPLE LETTER 17.34.   Letter expressing concern for ill employee
(semiblock format).

July 26, 19X8

Mr. Edward T. Landsale
45 Beaumont Place
Rose, Texas 90876

Dear Ed:

Everyone here at Furomont Building & Engineering joins me in wishing
you a speedy recovery from your bout with pneumonia. We hope you take
care of yourself so that you can be back on the job soon.

Please accept our best wishes.

Sincerely,

Alan T. Ransdade
Project Supervisor

atr/jls

SAMPLE LETTER 17.35.   Letter to employee in the hospital (semiblock
format).

October 6, 19X7

Ms. Patrice R. Chin
Room 756
Medical Hospital
Medino, California 45467

Dear Patrice:

Please accept my best wishes for a speedy recovery from your surgery. I
hope that the doctors and nurses over at Medical Hospital take good care
of you so that you are healthy and back on the job as soon as you feel up to
it.

We miss you here at Altmont Minerals and hope that you are back on your feet just as soon as possible.

Sincerely,

John U. Uxbridge
Personnel Director

juu/jls

SAMPLE LETTER 17.36.   Letter to hospitalized business associate (full-block format).

June 5, 19X5

Mr. Jack Wagner
Room 4545
Doctor's Hospital
Newburgh, Connecticut 43456

Dear Jack:

I learned from your office that you had been hospitalized. I wish you the speediest recovery and hope that you will be home and healthy soon.

Regards,

Alice R. Treat
Sales Representative

art/jjj

Condolences

Sample Letter 17.37 is an example of a brief, tactful letter of condolence written to the letter reader on the occasion of his mother's death. Such letters are difficult to write, but are appreciated by the person being written.

SAMPLE LETTER 17.37.   Letter expressing condolences (semiblock format).

May 19, 19X8

Mr. Joshua T. Leopard
Fulton, Carlton & Leopard, P.C.
One Blazen Avenue
Fort Utah, Nevada 23234

Dear Joshua:

I was sorry to learn of the death of your mother. I hope you will accept the sincere condolences of your friends at Andover Parris Publishing Company.

If I or anyone else here can be of help to you, please let us know. I look forward to meeting with you as soon as you get back into the swing of things.

Sincerely,

Maxwell L. Shorter
Publisher

jls

PART III
APPENDIXES

Rule #1: Remember *to never split* an infinitive.
Rule #2: Prepositions are something you should
never end a sentence *with*.
Rule #3: Dangling a participle at the end of a
sentence is uncouth
and requires *changing*.
Rule #4: Your spelling will improve if you consult
your dictionary *alot*.

Larry E. Grimes
from "Rules of the Writing Game"

Appendixes I, II, III, and IV feature many items that can make your letter writing a more pleasant and less arduous task. All four appendixes are arranged alphabetically for easy reference.

Appendix I is by no means an all-inclusive list of every word ever used incorrectly. It does, however, include some words that are either tricky to use or often are used incorrectly. If you have a question about how a word or phrase should be used, check Appendix I. If it is not included in the Appendix, you will find a good reference to consult listed in the Bibliography.

Appendix II lists several rules of punctuation that cause confusion or problems in correspondence. For a more extensive discussion of the proper use of punctuation, there are several good references available. I recommend: *The Chicago Manual of Style, Thirteenth Edition.* Chicago: The University of Chicago Press, 1982.

Appendix III is divided into two categories. The first gives a list of two-letter state abbreviations. The second lists common abbreviations. Abbreviations should be used sparingly in your correspondence. Occasionally you will receive a letter or memorandum that contains an abbreviation. The list in Appendix III will help you decipher some common abbreviations.

Appendix IV, The Grammar Hotline Directory, consists of names of various universities, colleges, and services across the country that offer help with grammar problems to people who call. The list is categorized alphabetically by state. The information given consists of: the city in which the hotline is located as well as a zip code; the college, university, or individual sponsoring the hotline; the phone number and name of the hotline; the hours of operation; and the contact at the hotline. If you are faced with grammar problems, consider turning to one of these hotlines.

323

APPENDIX I
Words to Watch

The words listed in this appendix are often used incorrectly in correspondence.

acknowledge with thanks or **acknowledge receipt of**   Using the words "thank you" is a more direct way of expressing gratitude after receiving something.

affect vs. **effect**   When used as verbs, "affect" means "to influence"; "effect" means "to accomplish." Both words can also be used as nouns. "Affect," as a noun, is usually used only in a psychological context. When the construction calls for a noun, and you are not using the word in a psychological sense, you will almost always use "effect."

aforesaid   Write "named" or "mentioned earlier."

after the conclusion of   Write "after."

along these lines   Another trite expression to avoid.

all right   Always written as two words.

allude vs. **elude**   You allude to a piece of literature. You elude someone who is chasing you.

a lot   Always written as two words. (Avoid the common mistake italicized in the epigraph to Part III.)

alternative   Means the choice between two possibilities. In constructions such as "no other alternative," the word "other" is unnecessary.

amounting to or **in the amount of**   Write "for" or "of" or "totalling."

and/or   Avoid the use of "and/or" unless it is absolutely necessary as a legal term. It destroys the flow of a sentence and causes confusion or ambiguity.

anybody   An indefinite pronoun meaning "any person." Should be written as one word. as should "somebody," "nobody," and "everybody." If you are writing about a body that was looked for but not found, you could write: "The investigators did not find any body." In most businesses such usage would be rare.

anyone   Best written as one word unless meaning, "any one of them," as in the sentence: "He didn't like any one of them."

arrived enclosing   Write "enclosed with."

as of even date herewith   Unclear. Merely give the date.

as per copy   Instead of writing, "We wrote you last Friday as per copy enclosed," it is clearer to write, "We have enclosed a copy," or "Enclosed you will find a copy . . . ."

as requested   It is a little more personal to write "you requested," "you described," or "you mentioned."

as soon as possible   Give a specific date whenever possible.

as to   Write "about."

as to whether   Write "whether."

as yet   Write "yet."

at   Do not use after the word "where."

attached hereto   Forget the "hereto"; write "attached."

at the present time or **at this time** or **at this writing**   Write "now" whenever possible instead of these words.

attorney vs. **lawyer**   A lawyer who has a client is an attorney.

bad or **badly**   The adjective "bad" is used after verbs of the sense—smell, sound, feel, look, taste. For example: "He looks bad." Or: "It tastes bad." "Badly" indicates manner. For example: "He was hurt badly in the accident."

beside or **besides**   "Beside" means at the side of. "Besides" means in addition to or other than. Sometimes the use of "besides" can result in an ambiguous sentence such as: "Something besides the bad credit rating caused us to sever business ties." It would be best to clarify by writing, "in addition to the bad credit rating," or "other than the bad credit rating."

between vs. **among**   Where the number exceeds two, use "among" for both persons and things. "Between" is a preposition that takes the objective pronoun. See Chapter 5 for a complete discussion of objective pronouns.

bimonthly   Every two months.

biweekly   Every two weeks. (Sometimes "bimonthly" is used to mean "twice a month" and "biweekly" to mean, "twice a week." The preferred usages, however, are the ones given here.)

both alike   "Both" is superfluous. Write "alike."

by means of   Write "by."

calling for   Often used needlessly. In a sentence such as, "A proposal calling for 70 shares," the word "calling" can be omitted.

communication   Avoid using to mean a letter, telegram, or conversation. Use the specific reference. See section on jargon in Chapter 5.

contact   Use more specific words such as "talk to," "write," or "call."

data vs. **datum**   The plural form "data" is generally used and it takes a plural verb. The singular reference is "datum."

different from vs. **different than**   Things differ *from* one another. Write "different from."

direct vs. **directly**   "Direct" is both an adjective and an adverb. "The man was sent direct (or directly) to Chicago." The sentence: "The professional made a direct trip to Chicago," takes the adjective "direct." "Directly" is always an adverb, as in the sentence: "We remit directly to a beneficiary if there is no intermediary."

disinterested   Means impartial. Do not confuse with the word "uninterested."

drop in or **drop a line**   Avoid using these colloquialisms in your letters.

due to the fact that   Write "because."

earliest convenience   Encourages delay. Whenever possible, be more specific.

enclosed herewith   Forget the "herewith"; write "enclosed."

enclosed please find   Write "enclosed is."

etc.   Don't use unless the omitted context is understood. Because the meaning of *et cetera* is "and so forth," you would never write "and etc." or "etc. etc."

equally as well   Write "equally well."

factor   Overused. Instead of writing: "Good salesmanship is an important factor in account management," write: "Good salesmanship is important to account management."

farther vs. **further**   "Farther" refers to distance. "Further" refers to discourse or to something additional. The distinction between these two words is blurred by many writers who also use "further" to refer to distance. Eventually, this usage may become acceptable.

for your information   Usually superfluous.

go over   Write "examine," "look over," or "read."

hopefully   An adverb meaning "with hope" or "in a hopeful manner." It is used incorrectly by many writers to mean "I hope."

however   Best used in the middle of a sentence. When "however" is used at the beginning of a sentence, it usually means "to whatever extent."

i.e. vs. e.g.   "I.e." is an abbreviation for *id est*, which means "that is." The abbreviation is set off by commas in a sentence. "E.g." is an abbreviation for *exempli grata*, which means "for example." It too is set off by commas in a sentence.

in position   Implies "at attention," or "standing around." Write "prepared," "ready," "willing," or "available."

in receipt of   Write "We (I) have received" or "We (I) have."

in reference to or **in regard to** or **in reply to**   Write "concerning," "proposing," "inquiring about," or "suggesting."

in the last analysis   Trite expression. Don't use it.

in which you enclosed   Write "with which you enclosed." Information is given *in* a letter. You receive an enclosure *with* a letter.

irregardless   Not a word. The proper word is "regardless."

its vs. it's   "Its" shows possession. "It's" is a contraction for "it is."

like vs. as   "Like" is a preposition that introduces a prepositional phrase and is used to compare things: "He looks like his mother." "As" is usually used as a conjunction and introduces a subordinate clause (clauses have a subject and a verb): "He acts as his mother did."

matter   Too general a term. Use the specific word: "problem," "request," "subject," "question," or whatever you may be writing about.

most   Don't substitute for "almost." Write "almost everyone," instead of "most everyone."

myself, ourselves, himself, herself, yourself (pronouns ending in -self)   Avoid using as the subject in a sentence. Write "Max and I are approving the purchase," instead of "Max and myself. . . ." Pronouns ending in -self are used for reference and emphasis in a sentence. In the sentence, "I approved the purchase myself," "myself" emphasizes "I."

neither, nor and **either, or**   These correlatives should be kept together.

party vs. **person**   Use "party" as a legal reference. "Person" should be used in ordinary reference.

people vs. **persons**   Use "people" when referring to large groups; "persons" for small groups.

per   Use of "per" is acceptable in an economic context, such as "20 shares per dollar." Although it has been said to avoid mixing Latin and English ("per" is Latin), if the construction is made less awkward by using it, use it. Avoid writing "per your letter" or "per my last letter," however, because this does nothing to simplify your letter.

please be advised that   Avoid this wordy construction.

previous experience   Write, "Our experience with this person," instead of "Our previous experience . . . ."

principal vs. **principle**   "Principle" refers to basic truths. "Principal," as an adjective, means "leading" or "chief." As a noun, "principal" means either a person in charge or, in finance, capital.

shall vs. **will**   The rule to use "shall" as the future indicative of "to be" in the first person and "will" in the second and third person, and that to express determination the forms are reversed, is no longer followed by most people in the United States. "Shall" sounds too lofty to many people and is avoided. Most educated people use "will" instead of "shall" in their writing.

taking this opportunity   Instead of writing, "We are taking this opportunity to thank you," write, "We thank you."

than vs. **then**   "Than" is used for comparison. "Then" is used to indicate time.

that vs. **which**   A simple rule is to use the pronoun "which" if the clause it modifies can be separated from the rest of the sentence with commas. Otherwise use "that."

thereafter   Too lofty. Use "after that" when possible.

this will acknowledge receipt of your letter   An answer to a person's letter will let him or her know it was received.

transpire   Means "to become known." Used incorrectly to mean "occur" or "happen."

try and vs. **try to**   Write "try to."

under date of   Write "on," "dated," or "of."

under separate cover   Write "We are sending separately," or "You will receive."

unique   There are no degrees of uniqueness. "Very unique," "most unique," or "extremely unique" are incorrect. It's just "unique."

utilize   Inflated language for "use."

via   Means "by way of" (geographically) and is properly used as a railroad, airline, or steamship term. Write "by express" or "by parcel post."

we ask you to kindly   Write "please."

we wish to thank you   Write "thank you."

writer   Write "I" or "me."

APPENDIX II
Punctuation

Punctuation is a worrisome thing, not the least because experts differ in their interpretation of its rules. Here I present the system I believe is most useful in business writing. You may encounter other opinions of what is "correct." No matter. Be consistent with your own usage, and remember the cardinal rule: the purpose of punctuation is to help readers follow your meaning.

apostrophe (')

The apostrophe indicates omission, possession, and sometimes the plural of certain letters, nouns, numbers, and abbreviations.

1. The possessive pronouns—its, hers, his, ours, yours, theirs—do not use an apostrophe.
2. The possessive of singular nouns that end in "s" is formed by adding an apostrophe: Miss Jones' loan.
3. The possessive of plural nouns ending in "s" is formed by adding an apostrophe: 10 days' trial.
4. Joint possession is indicated by adding an apostrophe and an "s" to the last noun only: Ben and Jerry's Ice Cream. To indicate separate possession, add the apostrophe and an "s" to each noun: Ben's and Jerry's ice cream cones.
5. Add an "s" with no apostrophe to form the plurals of letters, nouns, numbers, and abbreviations, if it is possible to do so without causing confusion: several YWCAs and YMHAs; in the 1960s; in fours and fives.
6. Add an apostrophe and an "s" to form the plurals of lowercase letters used as nouns, abbreviations using periods, and capital letters that would otherwise be confusing: C.P.A.'s; a's and b's; I's, A's, U's.

colon (:)

The colon warns the reader that what follows will complete what was promised in the preceding words.

The colon is used:

1. After the salutation of a letter
2. To indicate that pertinent information follows
3. Preceding a formal or extended quotation
4. To introduce a list

The words "as follows" and "the following" should be eliminated if possible in your letters. If it is necessary to use either phrase, it should be followed by a colon.

After such expressions as "for instance" or "for example," a colon may be used when the example is tabulated or consists of more than one sentence.

A colon is always placed outside of quotation marks.

comma (,)

Use the comma:

1. To separate distinct, independent statements in a compound sentence.
2. To separate a series of words or phrases having equal value and not connected by conjunctions. In a series, do not omit the comma before the word "and."
3. To separate a series of adjectives or adverbs that are equal in value and are not connected by conjunctions.
4. To set off a long dependent clause preceding its principal clause.
5. To precede nonrestrictive relative clauses introduced by "who," "which," and similar pronouns. The pronoun "that" is frequently used in a restrictive sense and does not require a comma preceding it.
6. To set apart a parenthetical expression. Do not isolate by parenthetical commas a phrase essential to the meaning of the sentence.
7. To separate the year in a complete date from the continuation of the sentence: June 14, 1981, was his graduation.
8. To separate the name of the state, following mention of the city located within its borders, from the rest of the sentence.
9. When the thought is broken by a connective, such as "however," "obviously," or "namely."
10. To avoid a confused reading of a sentence.

Do not use a comma at the end of a subject when that subject is formed by a series of words.

dash (—)

The dash indicates an abrupt change in thought. Dashes are generally preferable to parentheses. Use dashes to:

1. Set off expressions foreign to the sentence.
2. Set off explanations and repetitions.

elipsis (. . .)

When letters or words are omitted in a quotation, use an elipsis (three periods on the typewriter: " . . . ") to indicate the omission. If the omission ends on a period, use an elipsis, plus a period (four periods on the typewriter: " . . . .").

exclamation point (!)

An exclamation point should not be overused or it will lose its effectiveness. It should be used:

1. To indicate surprise
2. To indicate a strong command
3. To indicate sarcasm
4. To follow a strong interjection, such as "Ouch!" or "Hurray!"

hyphen (-)

Avoid hyphenation. Excessive use of the hyphen tends to distract from a letter's message and does not add to its appearance. Consult a dictionary on the proper hyphenation of words when you must hyphenate.

1. Insert a hyphen in compound adjectives preceding a noun: absent-minded office manager.
2. Insert a hyphen in compound numerals: twenty-one through ninety-nine.
3. Avoid using a hyphen at the end of the first line or the last full line of a paragraph.

parentheses (( ))

Parentheses may be used:

1. To set apart explanatory detail that can be omitted without changing the grammatical structure of a sentence
2. To enclose a word or clause that is independent of the sentence in which it is inserted

Punctuation should be placed outside of the closing parenthesis unless it is a part of the parenthetical expression.

period (.)

In addition to the traditional uses of the period, use one after a question of courtesy, which is really a request, and when a reply of action is expected.

question mark (?)

Use after every direct question. After a question of courtesy and when a reply or action is expected, use a period.

quotation marks (" ")

Any material quoted within a sentence or a paragraph should be set off with quotation marks.

Use single quotation marks to enclose a quotation within a quotation.

Titles of books, magazines, and plays should be underscored. Titles of poems, articles, television programs, or chapters in a book are enclosed in quotation marks.

Lengthy quotations should be set off by indentation—blocking—in which case quotation marks are unnecessary.

If quotation marks are used and the text is continued into two or more paragraphs, use quotation marks at the beginning of each paragraph, but at the end of only the last paragraph of the quotation.

Periods and commas are always placed inside quotation marks, colons always outside. Other punctuation marks go inside quotation marks if they relate to the quoted segment, and otherwise outside.

semicolon (;)

The semicolon is used:

1. To separate the clauses of a compound sentence when the conjunction is omitted
2. Between the clauses of a compound sentence that are joined by one of the conjunctive adverbs: accordingly, also, besides, consequently, further, hence, furthermore, however, moreover, nevertheless, otherwise, still, then, thus, yet, or therefore
3. To separate units in a series when they are long and complicated or internally punctuated
4. Between clauses of a compound sentence that are connected by a conjunction when those clauses are somewhat long, or when a more decided pause is desirable

word division

Avoid

1. Dividing a one-syllable word
2. Dividing a word of four letters
3. Dividing a word on the first or last syllable unless that syllable has three or more letters
4. Dividing proper names, abbreviations, figures, addresses, or dates
5. Dividing a word before a syllable containing a vowel that is not pronounced
6. Separating the initials or the first name from the surname
7. Separating qualifying letters or signs from the figures to which they belong

Always divide a compound word on its own hyphen.

APPENDIX III
Abbreviations

Two-Letter State Abbreviations

AL	Alabama	MT	Montana
AK	Alaska	NE	Nebraska
AZ	Arizona	NV	Nevada
AR	Arkansas	NH	New Hampshire
CA	California	NJ	New Jersey
CZ	Canal Zone	NM	New Mexico
CO	Colorado	NY	New York
CT	Connecticut	NC	North Carolina
DE	Delaware	ND	North Dakota
DC	District of Columbia	OH	Ohio
FL	Florida	OK	Oklahoma
GA	Georgia	OR	Oregon
GU	Guam	PA	Pennsylvania
HI	Hawaii	PR	Puerto Rico
ID	Idaho	RI	Rhode Island
IL	Illinois	SC	South Carolina
IN	Indiana	SD	South Dakota
IA	Iowa	TN	Tennessee
KS	Kansas	TX	Texas
KY	Kentucky	UT	Utah
LA	Louisiana	VT	Vermont
ME	Maine	VA	Virginia
MD	Maryland	VI	Virgin Islands
MA	Massachusetts	WA	Washington
MI	Michigan	WV	West Virginia
MN	Minnesota	WI	Wisconsin
MS	Mississippi	WY	Wyoming
MO	Missouri		

Common Abbreviations

Accountant	ACCT	Affiliate	AFF
Administrator	ADMIN	Affiliated Company	ACO
Administrators	ADMINS	Agency	AGCY

Also known as	AKA	Colonel	COL
Ambassador	AMB	Commission	COMMN
Annex	ANX	Committee	CTE
Annuitant	ANT	Common-tenancy	CTN
Apartment	APT	Commonwealth	COMM
Archbishop	ABP	Company	CO
Associate	ASSOC	Construction	CONST
Association	ASSN	Consultant	CONS
Attorney	ATTY	Corporation	CORP
Authorized Officer	ATO	Court	CT
Auxiliary	AUX	Cove	CV
Avenue	AVE	Creek	CRK
Beneficiary	BENEF	Crescent	CRES
Beneficiaries	BENEFS	Custodial	CUST
Bend	BND	Custodian	CUSTOD
Board of Directors	DIR	Custodians	CUSTODS
Boulevard	BLVD	Dealer	DLR
Branch	BR	Department	DEPT
Branch Manager	BRM	Deputy	DPY
Brother	BRO	Development	DVLPMNT
Brothers	BROS	Director	DIR
Building	BLDG	Distributor	DISTRIB
Bureau	BUR	Division	DIV
Business	BUS	Doctor	DR
Bypass	BYP	Doctor of Dental	
Causeway	CSWY	Sciences	DDS
Center	CTR	Doctor of Divinity	DD
Certified Employee		Doctor of Education	EdD
Benefits Specialist	CEBS	Doctor of Medicine	MD
Certified Financial		Doctor of Philosophy	PhD
Manager	CFM	Doing business as	DBA
Certified Financial		Dominion	DOM
Planner	CFP	Drive	DR
Certified Life		East	E
Underwriter	CLU	Electric	ELEC
Certified Management		Endorser	END
Consultant	CMC	Ensign	ENS
Certified Public		Equipment	EQUIP
Accountant	CPA	Escrow account	ESC
Chartered Financial		Establishment	ESTAB
Analyst	CFA	Estate	EST
Chartered Financial		Executive Vice	
Consultant	ChFC	President	EVP
Chartered Property		Executor	EXEC
and Casualty		Executors	EXECS
Underwriter	CPCU	Expressway	EXPY
Circle	CIR	Extended/Extension	EXT
Comaker	COM	Father	FTHR
Cosigner	COS	Federal	FED

Fifth	V	Miss	MISS/MS
Finance	FIN	Mister	MR
First-name	F-N	Mrs.	MRS/MS
Floor	FLR	North	N
Foundation	FNDTN	Northeast	NE
Fourth	IV	Northwest	NW
Freeway	FWY	Not sufficient funds	NSF
Fund	FND	Organization	ORGN
Gardens	GDNS	Park	PK
Garage	GRGE	Parkway	PKY
Gateway	GTWY	Participant	PTP
Government	GOVT	Partner	PTR
Group	GRP	Pharmacy	PHAR
Grove	GR	Place	PL
Guarantor	GTR	Plaza	PLZ
Guardian	GDN	Post office	PO
Guild	GLD	Power-of-attorney	POA
Heights	HTS	Primary	PRI
Highway	HWY	Products	PRODS
Honorable	HON	Professor	PROF
Hospital	HOSP	Profit-sharing	PRS
Husband	HUS	Realtor	RLTR
Incorporated	INC	Redevelopment	REDVLPM
Indirect liability	ILB	Registered Health	
Industries	INDS	Underwriter	RHU
Institute	INST	Registered Nurse	RN
Insurance	INS	Rental account	REN
Joint	JNT	Restaurant	REST
Joint venture	JNV	Retired	RETD
Judge	JDGE	Reverend	REV
Junction	JCT	Ridge	RDG
Junior	JR	River	RV
Laboratory	LAB	Road	RD
Lake	LK	Roadway	RDWY
Landing	LNDG	Room	RM
Lane	LN	Route	RT
League	LGE	Rural	R
Legal	LEG	School	SCH
Legal name	LEGN	Science	SCI
Legal title	LGT	Second	II
Limited	LTD	Secondary	SEC
Manager	MGR	Secretary	SECT
Master	MST	Senior	SR
Manor	MNR	Senior Vice President	SVP
Manufacturing	MFG	Service	SV
Market	MRKT	Signatory	STR
Meadows	MDWS	Sister	SR
Minor	MIN	Society	SOC
Minors	MINS	South	S

Southeast	SE	Trustee	TTEE
Square	SQ	Trustees	TTEES
Station	STA	Turnpike	TPKE
Store	STR	Union	UN
Street	ST	United	UTD
Subdivision	SUBDIV	Vice President	VP
Subsidiary	SUB	View	VW
Terrace	TER	Village	VLG
Third	III	Warrant Officer	WO
Trading as	T/A	West	W
Trail	TRL	Wholesale	WHSLE
Treasurer	TREAS	Wife	WIF
Trucking	TR		

Grammar Hotline Directory©

Because most of the services listed in this Appendix are staffed by colleges and universities, many close or have reduced hours during college breaks. Only those that indicate they accept collect calls do.

You can use any of the services listed in this directory by calling the hotline and asking your grammar questions. The universities, colleges, organizations, or people sponsoring the hotlines, the contact people, and the phone numbers are all provided for your convenience.

The zip codes following the city locations of each hotline are given in case you wish to ask your question in writing. Address your correspondence to the director of the hotline, whose name is given at the end of the entry.

Alabama

Auburn 36830
Auburn University
205-826-5749
Writing Center Hotline
Monday through Thursday, 9 A.M. to noon and 1 P.M. to 4 P.M.; Friday, 9 A.M. to
    noon; reduced hours during the summer
Peter Huggins

Tuscaloosa 35487
University of Alabama
205-348-5049
Grammar Hotline
Monday through Thursday, 9 A.M. to 4 P.M.; Tuesday and Wednesday, 6 P.M. to 8
    P.M.; Friday, 9 A.M. to 1 P.M.; summer hours vary
Carol Howell

Arkansas

Little Rock 72204
University of Arkansas at Little Rock
501-569-3162
The Writer's Hotline
Monday through Friday, 8 A.M. to noon
Marilynn Keys

California

Moorpark 93021
Moorpark College
805-529-2321
National Grammar Hotline
Monday through Friday, 8 A.M. to noon, September through June
Michael Strumpf

Colorado

Pueblo 81001
University of Southern Colorado
303-549-2787
USC Grammar Hotline
Monday through Friday, 9:30 A.M. to 3:30 P.M.; reduced hours May 15 through
    August 25
Margaret Senatore and Ralph Dille

Florida

Ft. Lauderdale 33314
University School of Nova University
305-475-7697
Grammar Hotline
Monday through Thursday, 8 A.M. to 4 P.M.; Friday, 8 A.M. to 1 P.M.
Dr. S. Solomon

Pensacola 32514
University of West Florida
904-474-2129
Writing Lab and Grammar Hotline
Monday through Thursday, 9 A.M. to 5 P.M.; occasional evening hours; Friday and
    summer hours vary
Mamie Webb Hixon

Georgia

Atlanta 30303
Georgia State University
404-651-2906
Writing Center
Monday through Thursday, 8:30 A.M. to 5 P.M.; Friday, 8 A.M. to 3 P.M.; evening
    hours vary
Patricia Graves

Illinois

Charleston 61920
Eastern Illinois University
217-581-5929
Grammar Hotline
Monday through Friday, 10 A.M. to 3 P.M.; summer hours vary
Jeanne Simpson

Des Plaines 60016
Oakton Community College
The Write Line
24-hour answering machine; calls returned Monday through Friday, 9 A.M. to 3 P.M.
Richard Francis Tracz

Normal 61761
Illinois State University
309-438-2345
Grammar Hotline
Monday through Friday, 8 A.M. to 4:30 P.M.
Janice Neuleib and Maurice Scharton

Oglesby 61348
Illinois Valley Community College
815-224-2720
Grammarline
Monday through Friday, 8 A.M. to 2 P.M.
Robert Howard and Robert Mueller

River Grove 60171
Triton College
312-456-0300, ext. 254
Grammarphone
Monday through Thursday, 8:30 A.M. to 9 P.M.; Friday, 8:30 A.M. to 4 P.M.;
    Saturday, 10 A.M. to 1 P.M.
Hillard Hebda

Indiana

Indianapolis 46202
Indiana University—Purdue University at Indianapolis, University Writing Center
317-274-3000
IUPUI Writing Hotline
Monday through Thursday, 9 A.M. to 4 P.M.
Barbara Cambridge

Muncie 47306
Ball State University
317-285-8387
Grammar Crisis Line
Monday through Thursday, 8 A.M. to 8 P.M.; Friday, 8 A.M. to 5 P.M., September
    through May; Monday through Friday, 11 A.M. to 2 P.M., May through August
Jane Haynes

West Lafayette 47907
Purdue University
317-494-3723
Grammar Hotline
Monday through Friday, 9:30 A.M. to 4 P.M., when a writing instructor is available; closed during May, August, and mid-December to mid-January
Muriel Harris

Kansas

Emporia 66801
Emporia State University
316-343-1200, ext. 380
Writer's Hotline
Monday through Thursday, noon to 5 P.M.; Thursday night, 7 P.M. to 9 P.M.; summer hours vary
Robert Goltra

Louisiana

Lafayette 70504
University of Southwestern Louisiana
318-231-5224
Grammar Hotline
Monday through Thursday, 8 A.M. to 4 P.M.; Friday 8 A.M. to 1 P.M.
Dr. Joseph Andriano

Maryland

Baltimore 21228
University of Maryland, Baltimore County
301-455-2585
Writer's Hotline
Monday through Friday, 10 A.M. to noon, September through May
Barbara Cooper

Frostburg 21532
Frostburg State University
301-689-4327
Grammarphone™
Monday through Friday, 10 A.M. to noon (funded by the Maryland Committee for the Humanities, Frostburg State University Foundation, C&P Telephone Company)
Glynn Baugher

Massachusetts

Boston 02115
Northeastern University
617-437-2512
Grammar Hotline
Monday through Friday, 8:30 A.M. to 4:30 P.M.
Stuart Peterfreund

Lynn 01901
North Shore Community College
617-593-7284
Grammar Hotline
Monday through Friday, 8:30 A.M. to 4 P.M.
Marilyn Dorfman

Michigan

Flint 48503
C.S. Mott Community College
313-762-0229
Grammar Hotline
Monday through Thursday, 8:30 A.M. to 3:30 P.M.; Friday, 8:30 A.M. to 12:30 P.M.;
    Tuesday and Wednesday evenings, 5:30 P.M. to 8:30 P.M.; summer hours vary
Leatha Terwilliger

Kalamazoo 49003
Western Michigan University
616-383-8122
Writer's Hotline
Monday through Friday, 9 A.M. to 4 P.M.; summer hours vary
Eileen Evans

Lansing 48901
Lansing Community College
517-483-1040
Writer's Hotline
Monday through Friday, 9 A.M. to 4 P.M.
Dr. George Bramer

Missouri

Joplin 64801
Missouri Southern State College
417-624-0171
Grammar Hotline
Monday through Friday, 9 A.M. to 4 P.M.
Dale W. Simpson

Kansas City 64110-2499
University of Missouri at Kansas City
816-276-2244
Writer's Hotline
Monday through Friday, 9 A.M. to 4 P.M.
Judy McCormick and David Foster

New York

Jamaica 11451
York College of the City University of New York
718-739-7483
Rewrite
Monday through Friday, 1 P.M. to 4 P.M.
Joan Baum and Alan Cooper

North Carolina

Fayetteville 28301
Methodist College
919-488-7110
Grammar Hotline
Monday through Friday, 8 A.M. to 5 P.M.
Robert Christian, Sue Kimball, and James Ward

Ohio

Akron 44325
University of Akron
216-375-7114
Grammar Hotline
Monday through Thursday, 9 A.M. to 4 P.M.; Friday, 9 A.M. to noon
Dr. Jean Johnston

Cincinnati 45236
Raymond Walters College
513-745-5731
Dial-A-Grammar
Tapes requests—returns calls (long-distance calls returned collect)
Dr. Phyllis A. Sherwood

Cincinnati 45221
University College, University of Cincinnati
513-475-2493
Writer's Remedies
Monday through Friday, 9 A.M. to 10 A.M. and 1 P.M. to 2 P.M.
Jay A. Yarmove

Cincinnati 45223
Cincinnati Technical College
513-569-1736 or 569-1737
Writing Center Hotline
Monday through Thursday, 8 A.M. to 8 P.M.; Friday, 8 A.M. to 4 P.M.; Saturday, 9
    A.M. to 1 P.M.
Cathy Rahmes and John Battistone

Cleveland 44122-6195
Cuyahoga Community College
216-987-2050
Grammar Hotline
Monday through Friday, 1 P.M. to 3 P.M.; Sunday through Thursday, 7 P.M. to 10
    P.M.; 24-hour answering machine
Margaret Taylor

Delaware 43015
Ohio Wesleyan University
614-369-4431, ext. 301
Writing Resource Center
Monday through Friday, 9 A.M. to noon and 1 P.M. to 4 P.M., September through
    May
Dr. Ulle Lewes and Jean Hopper

Oklahoma

Bethany 73008
Southern Nazarene University
405-491-6328
Grammar Hotline
Monday through Friday, 9 A.M. to 4 P.M.; June, July, and August call 405-354-1739
Jim Wilcox

Chickasha 73018
405-224-8622
Monday through Friday, 9 A.M. to 5 P.M.; Saturday, 9 A.M. to noon
Virginia Lee Underwood
Mrs. Underwood, a retired teacher and editor, offers this service from her home
    telephone. She is willing to return long-distance calls collect.

Pennsylvania

Allentown 18104
Cedar Crest College
215-437-4471
Academic Support Center, Writing Center Hotline
Monday through Friday, 10 A.M. to 3 P.M., September through May
Karen Coleman

Glen Mills 19342
Burger Associates
215-399-1130
Monday through Friday, 8 A.M. to 5 P.M.
Robert Burger

Lincoln 19352
Lincoln University
215-932-8300, ext. 460
Grammar Hotline
Monday through Friday, 9 A.M. to 5 P.M., September through May; summer hours
    vary
Dr. Annabelle Linneman

Pittsburgh 15104
Coalition for Adult Literacy
412-344-9759
Grammar Hotline
Monday, Wednesday, and Friday, 8 A.M. to 9:30 A.M.; recorder takes messages at
    other times
Mary Newton Bruder

South Carolina

Charleston 29409
The Citadel Writing Center
803-792-3194
Grammar Hotline
Monday through Friday, 8 A.M. to 4 P.M.; Sunday through Thursday, 6 P.M. to 10
    P.M.
Angela W. Williams

Columbia 29208
University of South Carolina
803-777-7020
Writer's Hotline
Monday through Friday, 8:30 A.M. to 5 P.M.
Bonnie Devet

Spartanburg 29301
Converse College
803-596-9613
Grammar Hotline
Monday through Friday, 10 A.M. to noon
Dr. Karen Carmean

Texas

Amarillo 79178
Amarillo College
806-374-4726
Grammarphone
Monday through Thursday, 8 A.M. to 9 P.M.; Friday, 8 A.M. to 3 P.M.; Sunday, 2
    P.M. to 6 P.M.
Patricia Maddox and Carl Fowler

Houston 77002
University of Houston Downtown
713-221-8670
University of Houston Downtown Grammar Hotline
Monday through Thursday, 9 A.M. to 4 P.M.; Friday, 9 A.M. to 1 P.M.
Linda Coblentz

San Antonio 78284
San Antonio College
512-733-2503
Learning Line
Monday through Thursday, 8 A.M. to 9:45 P.M.; Friday, 8 A.M. to 4 P.M.
Leon Ricketts and Irma Luna

Virginia

Virginia Beach 23456
Tidewater Community College
804-427-7170
Grammar Hotline
Monday through Thursday, 10 A.M. to noon; afternoon hours vary; Friday, 10 A.M.
    to noon; reduced hours during the summer
Donna Reiss Friedman

Wisconsin

Green Bay 54307-9042
Northeast Wisconsin Technical Institute
414-498-5427
Grammar Hotline
Monday through Thursday, 8:30 A.M. to 8 P.M.; Friday, 8 A.M. to 4 P.M.
Rose Marie Mastricola and Joanne Rathburn

Platteville 53818
University of Wisconsin—Platteville
608-342-1615
Monday through Thursday, 9 A.M. to 4 P.M.; Friday, 9 A.M. to noon
Nancy Daniels

Canada

Edmonton, Alberta T5J2P2
Grant MacEwan Community College
403-450-4666
Grammar Hotline
Monday through Friday, 10 A.M. to noon and 12:30 P.M. to 2:30 P.M.
Karl Homann

Fredericton, New Brunswick E3B5A3
University of New Brunswick
506-453-4666 (university officer) or 459-3631 (residence)
Grammar Hotline
Variable hours
A. M. Kinloch

Bibliography

This books can do—nor this alone: they give
New views to life, and teach us how to live;
They soothe the grieved, the stubborn they chastise;
Fools they admonish, and confirm the wise.
Their aid they yield to all: they never shun
The man of sorrow, nor the wretch undone;
Unlike the hard, the selfish, and the proud,
They fly not sullen from the suppliant crowd;
Nor tell to various people various things,
But show to subjects, what they show to kings.

George Crabbe
from "The Library"

The books and publications listed in the annotated bibilography are separated into two categories: those dealing specifically with letter writing, and those that concern grammar and usage.

Under each listing, a brief description is given of the entry. Asterisks indicate books I consider to be especially helpful additions to any professional's reference shelf.

Letter Writing

' Buckley, Earle A. *Let's Write Business Letters* Vol. I, Nos. 1–24 (1961–1963).
Each of Mr. Buckley's newsletters gives practical advice to letter writers. He does not pretend to be an expert grammarian or scholar. He is a businessman who has produced a no-nonsense approach to writing more effective letters.
Although they are out of print, Buckley's newsletters can be found in the files of many businesses.

Geffner, Andrea B. *How to Write Better Business Letters.* Woodbury, New York: Barron's Educational Series, 1982.
Seventy-five model letters are at the heart of Ms. Geffner's book. She also offers some instruction in formatting and writing style. The book is brief, inexpensive, and a good starting point for professionals who are at a total loss when it comes to letter writing.

The Merriam-Webster Handbook of Effective Business Correspondence. New York: Wallaby, 1979.
Merriam-Webster's handbook is the best reference on general business letter

writing I have seen. Every secretary should have a copy nearby ready for reference. The handbook allows for quick reference on myriad points and problems.

Paxson, William C. *The Business Writing Handbook*. New York: Bantam Books, 1981.
> Paxson's book is a good reference that puts the fundamentals of writing into simple language and explanations. He covers most types of writing that professionals would be called on to produce, including memos, letters, reports, and proposals.

*Poe, Roy W. *The McGraw-Hill Handbook of Business Letters (2nd Ed.)*. New York: McGraw-Hill, 1988
> Mr. Poe's book is full of useful model business letters. While his text is short on grammar tips, word usage, and writing instruction, it is among the best model letter books around.

*Seglin, Jeffrey L. *Bank Letter Writing Handbook: A Guide to Planning and Writing Effective Letters*. Rolling Meadows, Il: Bankers Publishing Company/Bank Administration Institute, 1987.
> More than 275 model letters for bankers are included in this book. It also features helpful guides to grammar and writing.

Shurter, Robert L. *Effective Letters in Business*. New York: McGraw-Hill, 1954.
> Shurter's is one of the better general books on business letter writing. His style is clear and he addresses most issues of letter writing, from language to format. The first five chapters of *Effective Letters in Business* include sensible and helpful tips for the letter writer.

U.S. Postal Zip Code Directory. Canton, MA: Arrow Publishing Company, Inc. 1020 Turnpike Street 02021, 1974.
> An inexpensive, useful addition to any secretary's bookshelf.

Venolia, Jan. *Better Letters: A Handbook of Business & Personal Correspondence*. Woodland Hills, CA: Periwinkle Press, 1981.
> Although I don't think the organization of Venolia's book is as helpful as it could be, this is one of the better references on general letter writing around. *Better Letters* is not as exhaustive as Merriam-Webster's Handbook, but it does explain all of the essential elements that go into good letter writing.

Werz, Edward W. *Letters That Sell*. Chicago, IL: Contemporary Books, 1987.
> *Letters That Sell* features 90 model sales letters. The book is lean on anything else, but the sales letters that are included might help the sales professional flailing about for correspondence ideas.

Grammar and Usage

*Bernstein, Theodore M. *The Careful Writer: A Modern Guide to English Usage*. New York: Atheneum, 1977. One of the best books on usage around. Set up in a dictionary format, Bernstein's book explains and clarifies language usage. *The Careful Writer* is more exhaustive than Strunk and White and is a good reference book for all writers to have on their shelves.

The Chicago Manual of Style, Thirteenth Edition. Chicago: The University of Chicago Press, 1982.
> An excellent reference on punctuation, spelling, abbreviations, footnotes, bibliographies, and more. *The Chicago Manual* is the bible of the publishing industry, but it can also be useful for anyone who writes.

*Corbett, Edward P. J. *The Little English Handbook*. New York: John Wiley & Sons, 1973.
> One of the best of the shorter handbooks on grammar and style available. Corbett's book is arranged in a helpful format that makes it a valuable reference for all writers.

Flesch, Rudolf, and A. H. Lass. *A New Guide to Better Writing*. New York: Fawcett Popular Library, 1949.
> A good, inexpensive book on writing clearly and effectively.

Grammar Hotline Directory. Virginia Beach, VA: Tidewater Community College, published annually.
> Tidewater Community College publishes an annual update to the listings in the grammar hotline directory featured in Appendix IV. For a free copy of this update, send a stamped, self-addressed envelope to *Grammar Hotline Directory*, Writing Center, Tidewater Community College, 1700 College Crescent, Virginia Beach, VA 23456.

Fowler, H. W. *A Dictionary of Modern English Usage, Second Edition*. New York: Oxford University Press, 1965.
> Fowler's book on usage is a classic. The style and content, however, make it more useful for editors and professional writers. Bernstein's *The Careful Writer* and Strunk and White's *The Elements of Style* are more practical for the professional's use.

Miller, Casey, and Kate Swift. *The Handbook of Nonsexist Writing*. New York: Barnes and Noble Books, 1980.
> For any writer concerned with sexism in language, Miller and Swift's book is a helpful reference. Although some of their suggestions are, out of necessity, unorthodox, the book is one of the best on this topic available.

Opdycke, John B. *Harper's English Grammar*. New York: Popular Library, 1965.
> Although I find Warriner's and Corbett's books more helpful, Opdycke's is a good reference for anyone who is having problems with grammar. Corbett and Warriner are set up in a more useful format. Opdycke is more formal in his approach, going step-by-step through the parts of speech and the parts of sentences. *Harper's English Grammar* is available in an inexpensive paperback edition.

*Sabin, William A. *The Gregg Reference Manual, Sixth Edition*. New York: McGraw-Hill, 1985.
> Sabin's book is a wonderful reference book for anyone who writes. The book is conveniently organized and covers everything from punctuation, grammar, and usage to dictation, letters, and bibliography formats. The softcover edition is inexpensive and is invaluable on the bookshelves of secretaries and executives.

*Strunk, William, Jr., and E.B. White. *The Elements of Style, Third Edition.* New York: Macmillan, 1979.
   Strunk and White is a good reference on usage and writing. It may not be as exhaustive as Bernstein's *The Careful Writer*, but it can be a saving grace when you are having problems with your writing.

*Warriner, John E., and Francis Griffith. *English Grammar and Composition, Revised Edition.* New York: Harcourt, Brace & World, 1965.
   Warriner's is probably the handiest reference book on grammar around. Although it is a textbook, a copy can usually be found at a used bookstore. If you can find a copy, Warriner's should be on your reference shelf.

Zinsser, William. *On Writing Well.* New York: Harper & Row, 1976.
   Although Zinsser's book is not helpful as a reference, it is useful, enjoyable reading for anyone interested in writing better.

Zinsser, William. *Writing with a Word Processor.* New York: Harper & Row, 1983.
   For those of you who have a phobia about using a word processor, read this book. It is surprisingly nontechnical. Zinsser's whimsical look at the world of word processing is informative and entertaining. It's a quick read and wonderfully puts the mystique of word processors in perspective.